THE GULAG IN EAST GERMANY

THE GULAG IN EAST GERMANY

Soviet Special Camps, 1945–1950

Ulrich Merten

\<teneo\> //press

AMHERST, NEW YORK

Requests for permission should be directed to
permissions@teneopress.com, or mailed to:
Teneo Press
100 Corporate Parkway, Suite 128
Amherst, New York 14226, USA.

ISBN: 978-1-93484-432-8

Library of Congress Control Number: 2018934155

Wherever men and women are persecuted because of their race, religion, or political views, that place must — at that moment — become the center of the universe.
— Elie Wiesel

TABLE OF CONTENTS

LIST OF FIGURES

LIST OF ILLUSTRATIONS

Illustration 8. Colonel General Ivan Serov; he survived the Stalinist and subsequent purges and became head of the KGB (successor to the NKVD) as well of as the GRU (Military Intelligence). Page 103.

Illustration 9. Felix Dzerzhinsky, founder of the Soviet secret police, *Cheka.* Page 110.

Illustration 10. A Soviet prison train. In such cattle cars, the prisoners were taken to the *Spezlager* or to the Gulag Camps in the Soviet Union. Page 141.

Illustration 11. Kurt Schumacher, Head of the Social Democratic Party of Germany. Page 145.

Illustration 12. Prisoner being led away by a Soviet guard, Sachsenhausen Camp. Page 152.

Illustration 13. Interior of a women's Gulag barracks. Page 177.

Illustration 14. The cemetery at Fünfeichen Special Camp #9, containing mass graves of prisoners. Page 186.

Illustration 15. An illegally taken photograph of Special Camp #1, Sachsenhausen in 1949. Page 197.

Illustration 16. Soviet tanks in Berlin, June 17, 1953. Page 219.

Illustration 17. Mine waste in Ronneburg, Thüringen. Page 242.

Please refer to http://www.thegulagineastgermany.com, for all illustrations cited in this book.

LIST OF MAPS

Please refer to http://www.thegulagineastgermany.com, for all maps cited in this book.

FOREWORD

STALINISM EXPORTED ABROAD

Ulrich Merten's new study, *The Gulag in East Germany: Soviet Special Camps, 1945–1950*, gives a much-deserved "voice" to thousands upon thousands of German victims of Stalinism exported abroad.[1] The *Spezlager* (special camps), as they were called, came under the direct control of the Soviet central camp administration in the eastern occupation zone of Germany, which in October 1949 adopted its formal designation as the German Democratic Republic (more commonly known as Communist East Germany). The Red Army's hold over most of Eastern Europe in 1944–1945 permitted Soviet dictator Joseph Stalin and his NKVD (the Soviet secret security services under Lavrentiy Beria) to project their political power beyond the USSR's traditional borders and thereby construct a socialist society that mirrored their own. In other words, to the Soviet victors belonged the spoils of the Great Patriotic War.

Merten's publication appears at a most opportune moment, close to the one hundredth anniversary of the 1917 Bolshevik Revolution in Russia. This tragic and violent event continues to reverberate across the globe, as brutal regimes have claimed either inspiration from it or have modeled themselves after it. Consequently, amid great proclamations to attain a more just society, Communist regimes worldwide have needlessly killed or murdered an estimated ninety to one hundred million persons to date. Merten intends here to detail just one chapter in the longer "Black Book of Communism," explaining how and why the Gulag tried to reshape East Germany in Stalin's image after Nazism's defeat in the Second World War.[2]

Drawing upon older as well as more recent English- and German-language scholarship on the topic, Merten not only seeks to inform the American general public about the Soviet concentration camps in East Germany, a serious matter which remains virtually unknown or forgotten outside of Germany itself, but also to expose at the same time the Soviet Union's clear violation of human rights in this and other instances.[3] More than seventy years later, it is high time to remove the Soviet version of the nefarious "night and fog" of the state-sponsored stealth terror waged against East German citizens. Especially effective and powerful are the eyewitness reports and personal narratives contained in Merten's compilation, putting an all too human face on East Germany's forgotten Gulag.

According to the German government today, 95,000 persons either died in the Soviet special camps or perished while in transit to them during the immediate postwar years. Though also constructing new facilities, the NKVD used a handful of former Nazi concentration camps such as Buchenwald and Sachsenhausen for the detainment of political prisoners. In reference to these camps, however, the Soviet and East German history books later only mentioned the Nazi-era victims, above all emphasizing the brave resistance of Communist anti-fascists at the expense of other victim groups, including Jews.[4]

In 1945, the defeated German people found themselves caught between liberation and occupation, posing a dilemma for both Allied and German leaders after the war. The victors desired to impose their political will on the vanquished, but they also sought to establish a democratic structure in place of Nazism, though the Soviet notion of "liberation" soon varied considerably from those of the other occupation zones. Meanwhile, the German side, embracing myriad perspectives across the political spectrum, wished to represent what they regarded as Germany's best interests, though they also were prepared to collaborate with the Allied authorities. Caught in a sensitive position, German leaders had to act as intermediaries between the occupation powers and the general populace. This uneasy political role applied to the emerging Christian Democrats, Liberals, and Social Democrats (SPD) in the western sectors (American, British, and French) as much as it did for the rising Socialist Unity Party (SED) in the eastern zone (Soviet).

It is true that the American military occupation used the former Nazi concentration camp at Dachau as a detention center, but in view of diverse national priorities and political cultures, the postwar denazification process (1945-1948) differed in all four Allied occupation zones in Germany. In particular, the administrative contrasts stood out most between the eastern and western zones. On the whole, the western Allied sectors, especially in the American, regarded denazification as a question of individual guilt and as a rehabilitation (re-education) program. For the Soviets and their soon-to-be established puppet-regime, denazification was treated mostly as one part of building a Communist political monopoly in their zone. The Soviets and their protégés also employed torture and executions on prisoners, leading to mortality rates in the special camps that were much higher than those in the western sectors.

The Soviet concentration camps ensnared a wide segment of the East German population early on, including civilians who were not necessarily significant Nazi Party members, youths (male and female), and real or perceived class and political enemies of all stripes. This elaborate state system of confinement considered it even more important to prevent any consideration of political resistance rather than combating actual popular resistance to the new political order. State terror unleashed on a few outspoken individuals and political adversaries could therefore serve as a prophylactic measure against potential opposition by frightening the masses into permanent submission.

Kurt Schumacher once remarked that "Communists are only red-painted Nazis." Schumacher rose to prominence as the first postwar SPD leader in West Germany (officially the Federal Republic of Germany). He had survived the Nazi concentration camps but also remained an ardent opponent of German Communists, past and present. His striking observation brings to mind comparisons of the East German police state (symbolized by the *Stasi*) with Hitler's Third Reich (embodied by the *Gestapo*), as well as the continuities of German history's longstanding authoritarian traditions. In 1933, after the Nazis' legal seizure of power, many ordinary Germans assumed that Hitler's new cabinet would only last a few short weeks or months, just another manifestation of the increasingly authoritarian and dysfunctional Weimar republic's ever-revolving door of weak coalition governments. In their view, the Nazis would lock up their German Communist (KPD) opposition, but in due time, if political fortunes allowed the KPD to gain brief control, they would likely turn the tables on the Nazis and do much the same.

For forty years, East Germany under the SED's political stranglehold, led by Walter Ulbricht and Erich Honecker respectively, emerged as probably the most effective and notorious police state in the Soviet Bloc, perhaps rivaled only by that of Nicolae Ceauşescu's Romania. The ruthless foundations of this one-party system took a firm hold during the crucial formative period of state-building between 1945 and 1950, thanks in good measure to the fear and repression instilled on the general populace by the Soviet special camps.

In retrospect, the East German Gulag's terrible effectiveness in establishing and maintaining Communist power in so short a time also contained within it the seeds of the police state's own demise. The exporting of Stalinism abroad raises a critical issue in Merten's overarching analysis, namely that the brutal and repressive treatment of a significant portion of the country's population soon put the embryonic

German Democratic Republic and its ruling SED in a precarious moral and political position vis-à-vis its own citizens.

Indeed, as Merten observes, an East German mass uprising, which cut across class and social lines, erupted in June 1953, despite several years of state intimidation and terror. Though crushed under Soviet tanks, this popular revolt already revealed the first cracks in the seemingly imposing and grand edifice of Soviet power. It occurred shortly after Stalin's death, but it also came as an alarming shock to Ulbricht and his SED so early in their rule. It preceded by nearly three years Soviet leader Nikita Khrushchev's blistering condemnation of Stalin's crimes in his February 1956 "Secret Speech" at the Twentieth Party Congress held in Moscow. Following the "Secret Speech," other powerful expressions of popular discontent broke out in Communist Hungary and Poland in 1956, though they, too, could not overturn the system. Again, a mass uprising exploded in Communist Czechoslovakia during the so-called Prague Spring of 1968, signaling perhaps the last time that the younger generation thought it possible to reform socialism with a "human face." It, too, failed in the face of Soviet tanks, but the political sclerosis of the Communist bureaucratic police states only accelerated after that point. The total collapse of Soviet domination in Eastern Europe arrived on the heels of Czechoslovakia's remarkably peaceful Velvet Revolution of 1989, once it was evident that reformed-minded but beleaguered Soviet leader Mikhail Gorbachev was willing to let the political dominos fall where they may. By 1991, the contagion of political freedom and democratic revolution had spread to the once mighty Soviet Union itself, when it disintegrated as well. Matters had come full circle, as the first threads of the Soviet Empire's unraveling had arisen in East Germany, which had so closely emulated the Russian model. When the Berlin Wall fell on the fateful night of November 8-9, 1989, the SED died with a sudden whimper, exposed for what it was now without its Soviet big brother to support it. To its credit, East Berlin, lacking the confidence or political will at this point to save itself, refused to fire upon its own euphoric citizens, who had gathered together to breach the Brandenburg Gate and Checkpoint Charlie and embrace their western compatriots.

Merten's portrayal of the divergent fates between Western Allied and Soviet detention camps in postwar occupied Germany strikes a powerful chord for this writer. The impact of Allied policy after the Second World War reached far and wide, even affecting the status of prisoners of war and the treatment of real or perceived political enemies half a world away. I reside and work in an unremarkably small, remote southern plains community in northwestern Oklahoma, which once played host to one of the United States' major German prisoner of war (POW) camps during the Second World War. From July 1943 to November 1945, Camp Alva at its peak held about 4,850 German POWs. Most inmates there came from the ranks of Field Marshal Erwin Rommel's famed *Afrika Korps*, soon followed by numerous hardcore SS members. The camp's tough reputation earned it the special, if not notorious, moniker of *Nazilager* (Nazi camp). It was common knowledge at the time in the American camp system that "troublemakers" from nearby prisoner and transit camps would face transport to Alva as a proper punishment.

The Geneva Convention of 1929, however, required the humane treatment of detained enemy prisoners in Camp Alva and elsewhere. Camp facilities had to provide POWs with the same amount and quality of food as their own soldiers, even including access to canteens. Accommodations for recreation also were provided to prisoners, such as sports, music, the arts, and reading materials. Religious expression was permitted to them as well. The Geneva Convention, moreover, allowed the captors to utilize POWs as laborers, training them in agriculture or other work in useful industries and trades. For their services, German POWs earned rations similar to American soldiers, their small salaries going toward the purchase of food and supplies. Medical care was also made available to them. In short, United States authorities envisioned a more humane regard for enemy prisoners as a means of better disposing them toward democratic traditions following the war. At the time, many local Oklahomans, still only recovering from the abyss of the Great Depression with the infamous Dust Bowl's epicenter situated just west of Alva, sometimes thought with bitterness that the POWs were treated too well or better than they deserved.[5]

Indeed, many German prisoners later recalled their overall fair and decent treatment under the Americans during wartime incarceration, whether in the European theater or stateside. As a result, in the 1970s and 1980s, a number of grateful former German POWs and their families traversed the Atlantic to visit the camps, including the former site, or what remained of it, here in Alva, and reminisce about the past. With a second chance at life, most of these men, returning to their devastated homes after 1945, participated, along with assistance from the Marshall Plan and other aid programs, in the rapid construction of a liberal democratic and prosperous West (later united) Germany. More tolerant American, British, and French policies toward German civilians and military personnel ultimately paid economic and political dividends for the western alliance in the emerging Cold War and beyond. So vastly different was the Federal Republic of Germany's postwar fate with that of the cold "night and fog" of Stalin's shadow, which shrouded Communist East Germany.

Dr. Eric J. Schmaltz

Northwestern Oklahoma State University

Alva, Oklahoma

Summer-Fall 2017

Notes

[1] In previous works, Ulrich Merten has performed a great service in providing a sympathetic yet forceful "voice" for other victims of the Second World War or Soviet Communism almost forgotten today: *Forgotten Voices: The Expulsion of the Germans from Eastern Europe after World War II* (New Brunswick, New Jersey: Transaction Publishers, 2012);

and *Voices from the Gulag: The Oppression of the German Minority in the Soviet Union* (Lincoln, Nebraska: American Historical Society of Germans from Russia, 2015).

[2] Stéphane Courtois, ed., et al., *The Black Book of Communism: Crimes, Terror, Repression*, trans. Jonathan Murphy and Mark Kramer (Cambridge, Massachusetts, and London: Harvard University Press, 1999 [1997]). See also the Victims of Communism Memorial Foundation (Washington, D.C.) Website: http://victimsofcommunism.org/ (accessed Nov. 12, 2017).

[3] For additional insights, see Anton Weiss-Wendt, *The Soviet Union and the Gutting of the UN Genocide Convention*, Critical Human Rights Series (Madison: University of Wisconsin Press, 2017).

[4] Jeffrey Herf, *Divided Memory: The Nazi Past in the Two Germanys* (Cambridge, Massachusetts, and London: Harvard University Press, 1997).

[5] One of the most detailed and up-to-date academic treatments of Camp Alva in Oklahoma is the forthcoming article by Kyle Starkey, "Mapping the History of the *Nazilager*," *Civitas: The Journal of Citizenship Studies* (Northwestern Oklahoma State University Institute of Citizenship Studies), Vol. VI (2017).

ACKNOWLEDGEMENTS

I must first acknowledge the untiring work of my wife, Carole, for her editorial assistance in writing this book. Her critique helped me immeasurably in writing it. It is also important to recognize the great assistance of Dr. Eric J. Schmaltz, Professor of History, Northwestern Oklahoma State University, author of the Preface of this book. His wide knowledge of Soviet history aided in my research for the material in this work.

Special mention should also be made of Dr. Rita Steinhardt Botwinick, who ably assisted me with her experience gained in the publishing of her many books on German history and the Holocaust. Appreciation is also expressed to Dr. Robert Meininger, Professor Emeritus of Nebraska Wesleyan University, Lincoln, Nebraska for his very helpful peer- review of my book. I wish to thank also Dr. Volker R. Anding, former German Ambassador in Uruguay and German Consul General in Miami for his comments on my manuscript. His thoughts and comments are appreciated.

Last, but certainly not least, my son, Philip C. Merten unfailingly guided me through the cyber world as well as building the book's website, www.thegulagineastgermany.com, the location of all its maps and illustrations.

ABBREVIATIONS

ACC	Allied Control Council
AMG	American Military Government in Germany
BDM	*Bund Deutscher Mädchen*–Nazi Girls' Organization
CIC	US Army Counter Intelligence Corps
CDU	Christian Democratic Union of Germany
DVdI	German Interior Administration (Soviet Zone of Occupation)
EAC	European Advisory Commission
FDGB	Free German Federation of Unions (Communist)
FDJ	Free German Youth (Communist)
Gestapo	*Geheime Staatspolizei* (Nazi Secret Police)
GDR	German Democratic Republic
HJ	*Hitler Jugend*–Nazi Boys' Organization
IVAN	Name given to all Russians by the German Army and Civilians during WWII
K5	East German Secret Political Police
KgU	*Kampfgruppe gegen Unmenschlichkeit* – Anti-communist German Organization
KPD	Communist Party of Germany
LDP	Liberal Democratic Party of Germany

LDPD	Liberal Democratic Party of Germany (Soviet Zone)
MdI	Ministry of the Interior (GDR)
MfS	Stasi Ministry of State Security (GDR)
MGB	Ministry of State Security (USSR)
MVD	Ministry of Internal Affairs (USSR)
NSDAP	*Nationalsozialistische Deutsche Arbeiterpartei* – Nazi Party
NKFD	National Committee for Free Germany
NKGB	People's Commissariat of State Security
NKVD	People's Commissariat of Internal Affairs
POW	Prisoners of War
RAD	*Reichsarbeitsdienst* – Compulsory Work Programs for Young Adults
RSFSR	Russian Soviet Federative Socialist Republic –Soviet Russia
SA	*Sturmabteilung* – Nazi Para-military Organization
SAG	Soviet Stock Company in the Soviet Zone of Occupation
SBZ	Soviet Zone of Occupation
SD	*Sicherheitsdienst* – The security Services of Nazi Germany, a Division of the SS
SED	Socialist Unity Party
SHAEF	Supreme Headquarters of Allied Expeditionary Forces
SMERSH	Death to Spies (Soviet Military Counterintelligence)
SMTSoviet	Military Tribunals
SPD	Social Democratic Party of Germany
SS	*Schutzstaffel*--Nazi Party Security and Military Organization
SSD/Stasi	State Security Service of the GDR Ministry of State Security,
SVAG	Soviet Military Administration in Germany
VEB	People's (state) Owned Factory
Volksturm	German Para-military Force created from the civilian population at the end of the war
VOPO	*Volkspolizei* (GDR police)
Waffen	Militarized Forces of the SSSS

THE GULAG IN
EAST GERMANY

INTRODUCTION

GERMANS FIND MASS GRAVES AT AN EX-SOVIET CONCENTRATION CAMP

The New York Times reported on September 23, 1992, that investigators digging at the site of a Soviet prison in the former German Democratic Republic had uncovered a mass grave said to contain the bodies of 12,500 prisoners. The camp, Sachsenhausen, near Oranienburg, is north of Berlin, in the state of Brandenburg. It was one of the most important Nazi concentration camps, as well as one of the first established in 1933.

After liberation in 1945, the Soviet secret police, NKVD, kept the camp open from 1945 to 1950. It incarcerated some minor Nazis there but the majority of the prisoners were simply opponents of the Soviet regime. Most were sent there without trial and some were just picked up from the streets in order to fill NKVD arrest quotas. A chain of these *Spezlager*—the Russian name for the concentration camps—existed under the GULAG central camp administration in the Soviet zone of occupation in East Germany. A number took over established Nazi concentration camps such as Buchenwald or Bautzen. Details about these sites of Soviet terror were not known in the West until the collapse of the Communist Government of East Germany in 1990, although they were rumored to exist.* The Brandenburg authorities expected discoveries of more mass graves at the locations of other Soviet camps.

The excavation around Sachsenhausen uncovered 50 group graves, each about 25 feet long and 13 feet wide. Within them, bodies were stacked in heaps of at least 15 feet. Pathologists have determined that most of the victims died of starvation, exposure or communicable diseases. Some showed evidence of having been beaten.

The German Government now estimates that more than 95,000 people died in the Soviet camps or in transport to them. During their more than 40 years of rule in East Germany, the Soviets built memorials at places like Sachsenhausen and Buchenwald dedicated to the victims of Nazism. They made no mention of their post-war use as Soviet prison camps. A memorial will now be erected to the Soviet victims at the Sachsenhausen camp by the Brandenburg state government.[1]

The history of Soviet special camps is generally little known here in the United States and only in German publications has the subject received adequate and extensive coverage. The purpose of the history of the GULAG system in East Germany is not only to make some of this comprehensive German work public, but, in the process, to give exposure to this Soviet violation of human rights in post-war Eastern Germany.

When examining the subject of the Soviet camps, one must consider the original political objectives of the Allies for Germany. Although the Big Three all agreed that there should be a democratic Germany with rule of law, only the Western Allies pursued this aim. The Soviet Union's objective was simply to impose its political and social system, making their occupation zone in East Germany a Soviet satellite state. Thus, the denazification process in each was very different. In the case of the Western military governments, it meant opening several temporary internment camps to imprison leading Nazis, both civilian and military, until they were tried. In the case of the Soviet Union, special camps were opened under NKVD supervision, not to house the leading Nazis, but instead to jail and isolate all opponents of the regime for an indeterminate period of time. As a result, they could not be considered a part of the Soviet denazification program.

In order to fully understand the Soviet camp system in their zone of occupation, one has to realize that the *Spezlager* were not the only GULAG administered camps in Germany. The uranium mines in the Erzgebirge, in the south-eastern provinces of Thüringen and Sachsen were the sites of a number of NKVD mining camps employing forced labor. Stalin gave greatest priority to this mining project in his competition with the United States to produce nuclear weapons. (See addendum Forced Labor in the Soviet Uranium Mines of Eastern Germany.)

Lastly, it is both noteworthy and ironic that despite the fierce repression of the opposition in East Germany, particularly of members of the non-Marxist labor parties, as well as Christian Democrats and Liberal Democrats, East Germany, in the summer of 1953, was the site of the first mass people's uprising in a Soviet satellite state. Although the revolt was led by workers, they were shortly joined by the middle classes. It was a popular uprising. This is the real story behind the history of the *Spezlager* in the Soviet zone of occupation.

NOTES

* The first book on this subject to be published in the German Federal Republic was Gerhard Finn's book, *Die Politischen Häftlinge der Sovjetzone*, published in 1959 by the *Kampfgruppe gegen Unmenschlichkeit,* an anti-communist, activist organization headquartered in West Berlin. It did not receive a good reception by academics in West Germany, as they were still very concerned with the crimes committed by the Nazi regime. The feeling was that such a book was only seeking revenge by right wing ideologues.

[1] Stephen Kinser, "Germany Find Mass Graves at an Ex-Soviet Camp" *The New York Times*, September 24, 1992.

CHAPTER 1

OVERVIEW OF THE SPECIAL CAMPS

This war is not as in the past. Whoever occupies a territory also imposes on it his own social system. Everyone imposes his own social system as far as his army can reach.

From Stalin's conversation with Tito as recorded by Milovan Djilas, in "Conversations with Stalin," Harcourt, Brace & World, New York, 1962.

SPECIAL CAMPS IN THE SOVIET ZONE OF OCCUPATION

At the close of World War II, the Soviets in their zone of occupation established prisons in several former Nazi concentration camps, such as Sachsenhausen and Buchenwald, among others, ostensibly to hold Nazi war criminals, as part of the Soviet denazification process. In reality, however, most prisoners were merely opponents of the Soviet communist system.

As distinct from the prisoners in the Western Allied internment camps, the special camps, or *Spezlager,* did not contain any important Nazis, but only minor party workers who had not committed any criminal offenses. SS and SA leaders and high party officials were usually sent back to the Soviet Union for interrogation and incarceration in the Gulag or for execution. The overriding purpose of the camps was to neutralize all opposition to the Soviet system and, in the process, destroy traditional German *bourgeois* society. Only after the fall of the German Democratic Republic did the truth emerge. The prisoners came from diverse backgrounds but they all were considered by the NKVD (People's Commissariat for Internal Affairs—the Soviet secret police) to be opponents of the Soviet Union and of its occupation of Germany.

For example, among the 60,000 prisoners held in the Sachsenhausen camp in the five year period, 6,000 were former German *Wehrmacht* officers released from Western war prisoner camps. Others were Nazis, but the majority were individuals denounced as anti-communist by the Soviet occupying authorities, or were those tried by military courts after having confessed, often under torture, to anti-Soviet activities. One artifact at the Sachsenhausen museum is a diary of a *Wehrmacht* officer, who threw it out of a train window while being deported to Siberia. It relates a story of cold and hunger and the arbitrary cruelty of the prison guards at the Sachsenhausen camp. "We need to see Sachsenhausen under the Soviets as an integral part of the Gulag system" stated Dr. Gunter Morsch, a historian and director of the Foundation of Memorials in Land (province) Brandenburg.[1]

As a part of the denazification process, all Western Allied Military Governments had short-term civilian internment camps for holding those important Nazis under immediate arrest warrant until they were sent for trial. The Soviets, however, arrested and sent to the special camps all real and imagined enemies of the Soviet occupation. According to Soviet statistics, the NKVD sent approximately 123,000 Germans to these camps from 1945 to 1950. Of those fit to work, a small number, about 10%, were deported as forced labor to the GULAG camps in the Soviet Union. Few were ever tried by a Soviet military court. About 43,000 died or were killed in the camps, with the major causes of death being starvation, disease, tuberculosis, and dysentery, or torture and execution.[2] German statistics, however, were about double those from Soviet sources. According to the German calculations, 240,000 passed through these camps, with a death toll of 95,643, which was a mortality rate of 40%.[3] (see figure 1 for detailed figures per camp). German official sources established these numbers after the collapse of the GDR, (German Democratic Republic-the East German government) from East German files and from mass graves found at the sites of the special camps. For example, at the Bautzen camp, officials discovered 16,000 graves.[4]

Figure 1. Number of Inmates and Dead in the Special Camps.

Camp	Number interned	Number dead
Bautzen	30,000	16,700(12,000)*
Buchenwald	30,600	13,200 (13,000)
Hohenschönhausen	12,000	3,500 (3,000)
Jamlitz	14,200	5,200 (5,000)
Ketschendorf	19,850	7,200 (6,000)
Landsberg	9,800	3,800 (2,500)
Mühlberg	21,750	8,800 (7,000)
Neubrandenburg (Meck.)	17,200	6,700 (6,500)
Sachsenhausen	60,000	26,143 (20,000)
Weesow	13,750	1,400 (1,500)
Torgau	11,050	3,000 (2,000)
Total	240,000	95,643 (78,500)

Source Sopade informationsdienst, Denkschriften 55, "Die Straflager und Zuchthauser der Sowjetzone: Gesundheitszustand und Lebensbedingungen politischen Gefangenen," HIA, Grabe, box I; "Supplement to 'Germany: Weekly Background Notes No. 109.'" September 25, 1949, NA, RG 260, box 75, pp. 5-6; "Penal Camps and Prisons in the Soviet Zone," NA, RG 84, TSGC, box 3.
*Figures in parenthesis are from Karl Wilhelm Fricke, Politik und Justiz in der DDR: Zur Geschichte der politischen Verfolgung 1945-1968 (Cologne: Verlag Wissenschaft und Politik, 1979), pp. 73-79, and are similar to those in the pamphlet, Memorial Library to Honor the Victims of Stalinism, "Sowjetische Internierungslager in der *SBZlDDR 1945-1950.*

Source: Frederick Taylor, *Exorcising Hitler, The Occupation and Denazification of Germany,* (New York, 2011), 323, 324.

The Soviet Military Administration in Germany (SVAG) ordered state security, the NKVD, to establish the special camps to eliminate anyone threatening the Sovietization of Eastern Germany. Especially targeted were those Social Democrats opposed to the new communist unity party, the SED, *Sozialistische Einheitspartei Deutschlands,* founded April, 1946, by the Soviets and their German communist allies along with collaborating socialists. The NKVD also interned those members of the *bourgeois* parties, the Christian Democrats, and the Free Democrats, all of whom refused to cooperate with the occupation authorities. They permitted these two parties to function legally in order to appear to the West as a "democratic" state, but, in reality, they were totally controlled by the Soviets. In short, any person considered a dissident, class enemy, uncooperative professional, or recalcitrant landowners—even peasants— went to the special camps.[5]

Of special concern to the Soviet authorities were the young people whom they considered completely brainwashed by their membership in the Hitler Youth or BDM (*Bund Deutscher Mädchen,* the Nazi youth group for girls), and a potential threat to the occupying power. They considered them all recruits for the Werewolf, a Nazi German guerilla organization (a creation of Goebbels' imagination) and fifth columnists. (See end note below.) There was little serious activity of the Werewolf in the Russian zone of occupation, but nevertheless the NKVD undertook mass arrests of young men who, after interrogation, were sent to the special camps. In classic *Nacht und Nebel* actions, (night and fog-arrest of prisoners in the early hours of the morning), they were accused of Werewolf activities and arbitrarily incarcerated without trial.[6]

The legal basis for arresting any opposition was order #00315 of the Soviet Military Administration of April 18, 1945. It permitted the immediate internment, without prior investigation, of "spies, saboteurs, terrorists, and activists of the Nazi party." This was the same type of order as for the administrative deportations to the Gulag camps, used extensively by the Soviet security services where the victim had absolutely no legal recourse. The Red Army also established military tribunals, which did not permit any witnesses for the accused or defense lawyers.

Convictions were often made under the Soviet criminal code, Article 58, (RSFSR Penal Code) for counter-revolutionary activities, which was the operative law to send Soviet citizens to the Gulag. Not all Germans sent to the camps, however, were convicted by these courts; only those charged with offenses against the Soviet occupation authorities were. A large number of them were just arbitrarily arrested administratively and jailed without any legal action whatsoever. Charges and sentences frequently did not have German translations, so the accused had no knowledge of the reasons for their arrest or terms of their imprisonment. The NKVD also used torture as a method to extract confessions, just like the practice in the USSR.[7]

Aside from the former Nazi German concentration camps of Buchenwald, Land (province), Thüringen, or Sachsenhausen, Land Brandenburg and the Gestapo penitentiary of Bautzen, Land Sachsen, additional camps were opened at Hohenschönhausen in Berlin, Jamlitz, Land Brandenburg, Ketschendorf, Land Brandenburg, Landsberg, Land Sachsen-Anhalt. Mühlberg, Land Sachsen, Weesow, Land Brandenburg ,Torgau, Land Sachsen-Anhalt, Fünfeichen, Neu Brandenburg, Land Brandenburg, Frankfurt/Oder, Land Brandenburg, and Strelitz penitentiary, Land Brandenburg. (See Map#1 of the special camps).[8]

The NKVD's Main Camp Administration (GULAG) controlled them all from Moscow. All of the camp commanders were senior Soviet military officers and the camps were laid out to GULAG camp specifications just as in Siberia or Central Asia. The camps, however, were not slave labor camps attached to factories or collective farms. On the contrary, prisoners were not allowed to work. Strictly speaking they were not death camps such as the Nazi annihilation camps in Poland, but the death rate nevertheless was very high due to malnourishment and disease. A former prisoner of the Gulag in the Soviet Union said, "*In Siberia, the food was better and more regular.*" There were no medicines or doctors, and communicable diseases spread rapidly. Prisoners were not murdered but, in effect, died of neglect.[9]

(Refer to http://www.thegulagineastgermany.com for Map #1. Location of the Special Camps in the Soviet Zone of Occupation. Source: *Speziallager in der* SBZ, *Gedenkstätte* Buchenwald *und der Landescentrale für politische Bildung,* Thüringen, Berlin, 1999)

In an effort to neutralize all opponents or suspected opponents of Soviet rule, during the first three years of the camps' existence, prisoners were neither allowed to send or receive mail, nor did they have access to any news from the outside. There were no newspapers, magazines, or any other types of communication from the world outside of the camps. In many cases, in fact a near majority of cases, the families of the prisoners did not have any knowledge of where they were. Only in 1948 did the Soviet Military Administration permit prisoners to advise their families of where they were being held. In the same year the Soviets also increased the food ration in order to reduce the death rate.[10]

The NKVD wave of arrest of dissidents was so overwhelming that by spring 1946 the special camps became overcrowded, so much so that the Soviet Military Government's special order #201 of August, 1947 calling for the arrest and jailing of some Nazi functionaries could only be partially carried out. In March/ April 1948, SED party leaders, Wilhelm Pieck and Otto Grotewohl complained to Moscow that the disappearances, violence, and deaths in the camps were destroying the confidence of the East German people in the SED and in the Soviet occupying power. Even Soviet military authorities in the occupation zone complained to their supervisors in Moscow, going so far as to send a letter to the Central Committee of the Communist Party in December, 1948, complaining about the excesses of NKVD actions which had led to anti-Soviet propaganda in the West and hate for the Soviet Union by East Germans.[11]

By 1948 and early 1949, nevertheless, the military government began releasing minor Nazis, realizing that there was little benefit in continuing the denazification programs. Both the programs and the denazification commissions were formally disbanded in the spring of 1948. On March

18, 1948, to honor the 100th anniversary of the 1848 revolution, German prisoners, mostly nominal Nazis, serving terms of less than one year were amnestied, as well as those serving sentences for minor crimes. Also amnestied were many young people accused of Werewolf activities. As of March 1948, the number of prisoners released totaled 35,000[12] and by that summer, this figure increased to 46,000.[13] The SED leaders Pieck and Grotewhol, took credit for these releases because of their "intervention" with Comrade Stalin.

Thereafter, conditions in the camps improved, probably in preparation for further releases. Starvation level rations were lifted, and medicines and hospital services became available for the inmates. The death toll decreased rapidly. By the fall of 1948, sufficient prisoners had been released or deported to the Soviet Union so that eight camps could be closed, leaving only Buchenwald, Sachsenhausen, and Bautzen.[14]

The NKVD closed these last three camps in January and February 1950 at the request of Wilhelm Pieck, the president of the GDR, in a previous visit to Moscow. He considered their continuation to be incompatible, even detrimental, to the founding of the new East German communist state, the GDR, (German Democratic Republic), which occurred in October 1949. Hundreds of inmates were deported to the Soviet Union, particularly the burial commandos, so that the secret locations of the mass graves near the camp sites would not be revealed. A greater number, however, were turned over to the control of the GDR's Ministry of Internal Affairs, including 3,400 who were sent for show trials, at the Saxon city of Waldheim. The trials, which often lasted only a few minutes, took place behind closed doors. The judges refused to admit evidence for the accused. The sentences were based on the original arrest protocols, which often involved torture. By June 1950, over 3,000 had been condemned to various additional prison sentences. This process was an ominous foretaste for the people of the GDR of how the judicial system would be used in the future to suppress dissent.

Those who were released rarely spoke of their ordeal, at least until the collapse of the GDR. They and their families were afraid of the Soviet and later of East German security services. The use of violence served the NKVD and then the East German Stasi well. To quote Anne Appelbaum in her book, *Iron Curtain,* "*The use of selective violence and the creation of camps for potential enemies of the regime were also part of a broader Soviet policy. The Red Army and the NKVD knew that in societies as uncertain and unstable as those of postwar Eastern Europe, mass arrest could backfire. But arrests carefully targeted at outspoken people could have a wider echo: if you arrest one such person, ten more will be frightened.*"[15]

NOTE: WEREWOLF

With Germany facing defeat, the leaders of the Nazi Party increasingly began to consider a post-defeat resistance movement, patterned after the Polish Home Army or the French *Maquis.* Like the *Volksturm,* (German home army), it was to be a mass uprising of the German people that supposedly would drive back the Allies. Combined with Hitler's presumed secret weapons of mass destruction, the inevitable (for the Nazis) split between the Western Allies and the Soviet Union would lead to ultimate German victory.

In September 1944, Himmler organized the Werewolf and placed it in the HSSPF (*Höhere SS und Polizeiführer*), his own personal office; it would report directly to him, thereby avoiding the intervention of the *Wehrmacht* and RSHA (Reich Main Security Administration). A senior SS officer was named to lead it, *SS Obergruppenführer* Hans-Adolf Prützmann, a General Inspector of Special Resistance, and a veteran of the SS killing squads in Eastern Europe. This appointment ensured that the Werewolf organization would be effectively run by an expert in guerrilla warfare. On the other hand, as it was independent of the RSHA, head Ernst Kaltenbrunner and chief of intelligence, Walter Schellenberg, they did everything they could to undermine the new organization, in the best traditions of the NAZI bureaucracy's in-fighting.

In every region of unoccupied Germany, the SS established a Commander of Special Resistance, with members made up of Hitler Youth, BDM, (*Bund Deutscher Mädchen*), SA (storm troopers), and local police leaders. On both the western and eastern borders of the Reich, arms and food supply dumps were created. The theory was that Werewolf teams would be overrun by the Allied armies, sit out the occupation, and then begin their resistance work. They would be armed with light infantry weapons and, most critically, with explosives.

As a result of the total collapse of Germany, the war exhaustion of the populace, fear of the Allied armies (particularly of the Russians), and a profound feeling of betrayal by the Nazi government, resistance was practically nil, and then only in the first few months of the occupation. For example, one unit made up of *Wehrmacht* fanatics and willing civilians was sent behind Soviet lines in early November 1944, for the purpose of reporting on troop movements and blowing up bridges. They were captured by the Red Army in a few days without having accomplished any of their tasks.

The most spectacular operation of the Werewolf was the assassination of the Lord Mayor of Aachen, Franz Oppenhoff, on March 25, 1945, because he was cooperating with the US Army, by a commando team led by an SS Lieutenant. Their attack was successful and several members of the team were able to survive the operation and subsequently disappeared into the population; others, however, were killed trying to escape. Although there were no military consequences to this assassination, it did create significant fears in the Allies of the potential dangers in occupying Germany. This affected their subsequent occupation plans, particularly in the Soviet zone. [16]

NOTES

1. Desmond Butler, *The New York Times*, December 17, 2001.
2. Norman M. Naimark, *The Russians in Germany, A History of the Soviet Zone of Occupation, 1945–1949* (Cambridge, Massachusetts, 1995) ,76, 377.
3. Giles Macdonogh, *After the Reich: The Brutal History of the Allied Occupation* (New York, 2007), 214, 215.
4. Frederick Taylor, *Exorcising Hitler, The Occupation and Denazification of Germany* (New York, 2011), 323.
5. Macdonogh, *After the Reich*, 214, 215.
6. Anne Applebaum, *Iron Curtain;1944–1956* (New York: 2012), 104–105.
7. Naimark, *The Russians in Germany*, 378.
8. Applebaum, *Iron Curtain;1944–1956*, 107–108.
9. Ibid., 108.
10. Naimark , *The Russians in Germany*, 393–394.
11. Macdonogh, *After the Reich*, 355.
12. Naimark, *The Russians in Germany*, 394–395.
13. Ibid., 395.
14. Gary Bruce, *Resistance with the People: Repression and Resistance in Eastern German 1945-1955*, (Lanham, Maryland, 2003), 126.
15. Applebaum, *Iron Curtain, 1944–1956*, 109.
16. Taylor, *Exorcising Hitler, The Occupation and Denazification of Germany*, 22.

CHAPTER 2

WESTERN ALLIED INTERNMENT CAMPS AND THE DENAZIFICATION OF GERMANY

The Allied Forces serving under my Command have now entered Germany. We come as conquerors, but not as oppressors. In the area of Germany occupied by the forces under my command, we shall obliterate Nazism and German militarism. We shall overthrow the Nazi rule, dissolve the Nazi Party and abolish the cruel, oppressive and discriminatory laws and institutions which the Party has created. We shall eradicate that German militarism which has so often disrupted the peace of the world. Military and Party leaders, the Gestapo and others suspected of crimes and atrocities, will be tried, and, if guilty, punished as they deserve.

General Dwight D. Eisenhower's proclamation to the German people –Autumn 1944

Allied Objectives for the Denazification of Germany

At the Yalta Conference in February 1945 of The Big Three, Roosevelt, Churchill and Stalin, it was agreed that the basic objectives of the Allied occupation of Germany would be to remove Nazi influence from German society, including the destruction of Nazi institutions, the annulment of Nazi laws, the punishment of war criminals and the removal of active Nazis from all public and private positions of responsibility.[1]

Even before the decisions of the Yalta Conference, the three major powers began planning for Germany's postwar future. In January 1944, The European Advisory Council was formed. One of its first proposals gave Poland large portions of Eastern Germany in compensation for pre-war Polish eastern territories absorbed by the Soviet Union under the 1939 Molotov-Ribbentrop Pact. The Council also determined that the Nazi government would be abolished and the Reich would be divided into military occupation zones, governed separately, even though final zone borders had not, at that time, been established. Berlin would be ruled jointly by the four occupying powers.[2]

In September 1944, The European Advisory Council drafted an agreement for the surrender and occupation of Germany which was formally published on June 5, 1945, as the "Declaration Regarding the Defeat of Germany and the Assumption of Supreme Authority by the Allied Powers." It became the key operating document for the status of a conquered Germany stating, "There is no central government or authority in Germany capable of accepting responsibility for the maintenance of order, the administration of the country, and compliance with the requirements of the victorious powers." Furthermore, "The Governments of the United States of America, the Union of Soviet Socialist Republics, the United Kingdom and the Provisional Government of the French Republic hereby assume supreme authority with respect to Germany, including all powers possessed by the German Government, the High Command and any state, municipal or local government or authority. The assumption, for the purposes stated above, of the said authority and powers do not affect the annexation of Germany."[3] (See note #1 below.)

In April 1945, Churchill and Truman proposed to Stalin the creation of a Control Council of all occupying forces to administer Germany in a coordinated manner, as established in The European Advisory Council agreements. After considerable stalling by Stalin, the Control Council was formally established by the four powers in a Berlin meeting on June 5, 1945, with General Eisenhower representing the United States, General Bernard Montgomery the United Kingdom, Marshal Georgi K. Zhukov the Soviet Union, and General Jean de Lattre de Tassigny France. In a subsequent meeting in August 1945, the Nazi Arrest and Denazification Sub-Committee drafted two directives: CC Directive #24 approved by the four powers on January 12, 1946 and Directive #38 approved October 12, 1946. The former covered criteria for defining active Nazis and conditions for their removal from positions of authority. The second one established procedures for the detention of individuals in the arrest and dismissal categories outlined in the first one, Directive #24.

CC Directive #24 defined 99 compulsory removal categories. These included war criminals, recipients of Nazi honors, various categories of civil servants and business leaders, high officers of the *Wehrmacht* General Staff, and all leaders of the Nazi party and its affiliates. Much of the content of this directive was taken from the United States Joint Chiefs of Staff Directive JC1067 of April 1945, whose purpose was to give the US Army of Occupation the war aims and parameters of United States policy for a defeated and occupied Germany. (See details below.)

CC Directive #38 implemented the provisions of the previous directive, a key law in the denazification of Germany. Its purpose was to purge Nazis from positions of importance, to process them legally and punish them if found guilty. Guilt could be determined by military courts or by German tribunals. It included primarily membership in various organizations judged criminal by the International Military Tribunal (The Nürenberg Trials court) and made public in October 1946. These were the Leadership Corps of the Nazi Party, the Gestapo, and the SD (*Sicherheitsdienst*) and the SS. Any member was considered subject to criminal prosecution. These individuals all fell under Category One (Major Offenders) and would be automatically dismissed from their positions and arrested.

Category Two (Offenders) included Nazi party activists, militarists, and war profiteers. They could also be jailed for various periods, barred from practicing a profession and from holding management positions, and be subject to property loss. Category Three (Lesser Offenders) applied to those who could claim mitigating reasons for their participation in the Nazi party; Category Four (Followers) consisted of nominal party members. Punishment for the last two categories could involve job demotion, reduction of pension benefits, temporary loss of income from investments, and prohibition of the right to participate in political or civic activities.[4] CC38 was the last significant element in the legal denazification structure crafted for all Allied occupation zones. (See Note #2 below for the details of CC Directive #38.)

On August 1st, 1945, Truman, Atlee, and Stalin signed the Potsdam Agreement stating that "The German people have begun to atone for the terrible crimes committed under the leadership of those, whom, in the hour of their success, they openly approved and blindly obeyed." The victors did not wish to "destroy and enslave" the German people but to "help them" prepare for the eventual reconstruction of their lives on a peaceful and democratic basis." (See Note #3 below for the relevant text of the Potsdam Agreement.) Allied polices, "so far as is practicable," toward the Germans would be uniform. The political objectives, as stated, would be demilitarization, denazification, democratization, decentralization, and decartelization. During the occupation, "Germany shall be treated as a single economic unit." Each occupying power would take reparations from its own zones. In addition, the Soviet Union would take 15% of industrial equipment that was "unnecessary for the German peace economy" in exchange for food, coal, and other goods. The Soviet Union would also receive an additional 10%, with no form of compensation required. The Council of Foreign Ministers was to draft a peace treaty, "to be accepted by the government of Germany when a government adequate for that purpose is established."[5]

(Refer to http://www.thegulagineastgermany.com for Map #2 German Zones of Occupation, May 1945. Wikimedia Commons)

UNITED STATES INTERNMENT CAMPS AND THE DENAZIFICATION PROCESS

In order to clarify the war aims of the United States and provide guidance to the US military occupation of Germany, the Joint Chiefs of Staff in Washington issued JCS 1067 in April 1945. It stated:

a) *It should be brought home to the Germans that Germany's ruthless warfare and the fanatical Nazi resistance have destroyed the German economy and made chaos and suffering inevitable; and that the Germans cannot escape responsibility for what they have brought upon themselves.*

b) *Germany will not be occupied for the purpose of liberation but as a defeated enemy nation. Your aim is not oppression but to occupy Germany for the purpose of realizing certain important Allied objectives. In the conduct of your occupation and administration, you should be just but firm and aloof. You will strongly discourage fraternization with the German officials and population.*

c) *The principal Allied objective to prevent Germany from ever again becoming a threat. Essential steps in the accomplishment of this objective are the elimination of Nazism and militarism in all their forms, the immediate apprehension of war criminals for punishment, the industrial disarmament and demilitarization of Germany, with continuing control over Germany's capacity to make war, and the preparation for an eventual reconstruction of German political life on a democratic basis.*

d) *Other Allied objectives are to enforce the program of reparations and restitution, to provide relief for the benefit of countries devastated by Nazi aggression, and to ensure that prisoners of war and displaced persons of the United Nations are cared for and repatriated."* [6]

Regarding the denazification process, JCS 1067, Clause 6, stipulated the following:

"All members of the Nazi Party who have been more than nominal participants in its activities, all active supporters of Nazism or militarism and all other persons hostile to Allied purposes will be removed and excluded from public office and from positions of importance in quasi-public and private enterprises ....[Such] persons are to be treated as more than nominal participants in Party activities and as active supporters of Nazism or militarism when they have 1.) held office or been otherwise active at any level from local to national in the party and its subordinate organizations or in organizations that further militaristic doctrines, 2.) authorized or participated affirmatively in any Nazi crimes, racial persecutions, or discriminations, 3.) been avowed believers in Nazism or racial or militaristic creeds, or 4.) voluntarily given substantial moral or material support or political assistance of any kind to the Nazi Party or Nazi officials and leaders." JCS 1067 also stated that such persons must be removed "*despite administrative necessity, convenience, or expediency*".[7]

Despite its harsh tone, this document for the future treatment of Germany represented a victory for Roosevelt's War Department, and its head, Henry J. Stimson, over the efforts of Treasury Secretary Henry Morgenthau who wanted to break up Germany into many smaller states, dismantle its industry, and make it, in effect, an agricultural state. (See Note #4 below for details of the Morgenthau Plan.) In spite of initial support for Morgenthau's plan, when the war was nearing its end, neither Roosevelt nor Churchill agreed with it and both supported the ideas of Henry Stimson. Stimson's plan was to revive German industry and eventually integrate it into the Western European economy. Stimson believed that Nazi dictatorship resulted from the actions of its leaders and that individual and organizational prosecution would be the best way to purge Germany of the Nazi system. The Nürenberg trials of the Nazi leaders were an integral part of this strategy, but there were also many other trials of important Nazis (see Note #5 below for information relating to the subsequent Nürenberg trials).[8]

The American Military Government, like other Allied military governments, faced a formidable task in the denazification of their respective zones of occupation. How were members of the Nazi party to be dealt with? About 10% of the population belonged to the Party, totaling some 8,000,000 members. In addition, about 17,000,000 members were in affiliated Party organizations, such as the German Labor Front, the National Socialist Welfare Organizations, and leagues of students, lawyers, and doctors. How were the truly guilty to be distinguished from the conformists, careerists, and Nazi bureaucrats? Then there were all the industrialists, landowners, and many others who had benefited materially from the Nazi regime but who were often not members of the party. Fortunately, the complete membership files, located in a paper mill outside of Munich, fell into the hands of the US Army, thanks to an anti-Nazi German who did not destroy them as ordered.[9]

On July 5th, 1945, the American Military Government issued an all encompassing set of denazification regulations listing 136 mandatory removal categories, based on "guilt by virtue of office." Those who had joined the Party after May 1, 1937, however, were spared this action. The AMG made this exception because after that date, all government employees were required to join the Nazi party or lose their jobs. By August 20th, 150,000 Nazis had already been removed from public offices. In addition, the number of automatic arrest detainees had jumped from 1,000 in March 1945 to 80,000 in July and was increasing daily—so much so that detention camps housing them became overcrowded. Thus, by December 1945, there were over 100,000 high ranking Nazi detainees in the camps. The US Military's automatic arrest categories were extensive, and at least initially in 1945, on a per capita basis, the AMG had arrested a higher percentage of the population than any other occupying power, even the Soviets.[10]

Nevertheless, the American Military Government did have a certain amount of discretion for avoiding the removal and incarceration of leading Nazis. Career military officers, large landowners, the aristocracy, and other leading professionals or industrialists could be retained in their positions, if there were no replacements readily available, but these decisions were subject to scrutiny.[11] In time, the pursuit of Nazis in the immediate arrest categories became increasingly difficult, aside from the problem of the overflowing internment camps, because so many of them were required for running the key installations in their occupation zones. More and more professional Germans returned to their old jobs despite their Nazi pasts; examples were those in the court system or employed by the national railway.

Housing of detainees became a serious problem and the obvious solution at the time was to reopen some of the Nazi concentration camps, once the liberated prisoners had been repatriated to their countries of origin. The main civilian internment camp in the U.S. Zone of Occupation was Dachau, the former concentration camp located outside of Munich. In early July 1945, it became US Counterintelligence Corps, "War Crimes Enclosure No.1." Others followed, including one at Nürenberg-Langwasser on the parade grounds of the Nazi Party rallies, the *Reichparteitagsgelände.*[12]

(Refer to http://www.thegulagineastgermany.com for Illustration #1. View of the Dachau Concentration Camp, after the liberation. Germany, April 29, 1945.— *US Holocaust Memorial Museum)*

(Refer to http://www.thegulagineastgermany.com for Illustration #2. View of prisoners' barracks soon after the liberation, at the Dachau Concentration Camp. Dachau, Germany, May 3, 1945. – Wikipedia Commons)

(Refer to http://www.thegulagineastgermany.com for Map #3. Plan of Dachau Concentration Camp: *KZ-Gedenkstätte Dachau; Stiftung Bayrische Gedenkstätte)*

Aside from holding prominent Nazis until they could be tried, the camps were intended to imprison potential saboteurs, thus arresting and isolating possible German resistance members. Incarceration was often based on mere suspicion of being a Nazi terrorist. Such prisoners would then be tried by a military court and sentenced. Because no German resistance appeared, however, the second purpose for the creation of these camps was soon dropped and they were used exclusively, in the Western Allied zones of occupation, for the detention of important Nazis pending trial, in accordance with mandatory removal and detention orders.[13]

The Dachau internment camp housed Nazis subject to immediate arrest from July 1945 until the summer of 1948. During that time, the U.S. Army interned up to 30,000 officials from Nazi Party organizations and officers of the German army in the main camp and in the former SS compound. Parts of the former concentration camp were used for different purposes. For example, the largest area, previously housing concentration camp prisoners became the compound, enclosed by barbed wire, for former concentration camp guards and members of the SS and *Waffen* SS (The latter was the militarized branch of the SS, and, as such, received the most able men and best weapons. It was an elite unit, made up of the ideologically committed, used in battlefield emergencies. It had a deplorable record of war crimes.) A fenced-in, high security area called War Crimes Enclosure was reserved for Nazis who had committed the worst crimes,[14] such as the *Waffen* SS soldiers who were accused of killing American POWs at Malmedy, Belgium, during the Battle of the Bulge. An American Military Tribunal was established at Dachau on November 15, 1945, and 42 members of the Dachau Concentration Camp staff were charged with participating in war crimes. The Commandant, Martin Gottfried Weiss, and 39 others were put on trial in the first proceedings and were all convicted. Twenty-eight of the staff, including the Commandant, were eventually hanged.

There was evidence of some prisoner abuse in these camps which seems to have been quickly corrected. Ambassador Robert Murphy, political advisor to General Eisenhower, reported in a visit to a camp for minor Nazis, "*I was startled to see that our prisoners were almost as weak and emaciated as those I had observed in Nazi camps. The youthful commandant calmly told me that he deliberately kept the inmates on a starvation diet, explaining, "These Nazis are getting a taste of their own medicine."* Murphy told this to the American military governor, Lieutenant General Lucius D. Clay, who then had the officer transferred. Murphy added, "*On another occasion we were informed that a Nazi torture camp, equipped with devices to extract confessions, was still operating under American auspices.*"[15]

Initially, as late as September 1945, General Clay opposed easing mandatory arrest categories, despite crowded conditions, but by the following month, he noted that more than 94,000 prisoners were being held incommunicado in the internment camps without trial. He then recommended that they be permitted to communicate with their families and that their legal processes be expedited. Also in October, the USFET (United States Forces European Theater) ordered that prisoners, even those arrested by the CIC (US Army Counter Intelligence Corps), be notified of the reasons for their arrest within 24 hours. (Aside from running the internment camps, the CIC had wide discretion in arresting "security suspects").[16] At the beginning of the occupation, this often led to abuse such as arresting individuals without hearings, simply because they had held high office in the Nazi regime. Sometimes, people were anonymously denounced and sent to the camps without knowing the reason for their arrest and imprisonment.[17]

By December of that year, General Clay was concerned about the increasing number of prisoners in the internment camps and the slow legal review of their cases. The American military government advised Washington that 80% of the internees were members of organizations under indictment by the International Military Tribunal in Nürenberg and that the resolution of their cases was difficult until this trial was over in October 1946. Clay therefore recommended limiting mandatory arrests to active members of the indicted organizations, dangerous security suspects, and individuals who participated in war crimes. In February 1946, an order was issued permitting the release of general staff officers and high officials of the *Lander* governments, after review of their cases. Reasons given for the releases were over-crowded conditions in the camps, winter with its attendant food shortages, and the slow legal process.[18]

Due to the escalating criticism about the deficiencies of the legal system in processing prisoners, increasingly more were released from the internment camps. By October 1946, 68,000 had been released and the number of internees reduced to 49,000 when the camps were turned over to German authorities in January 1947. After the International Military Tribunal at Nürenberg decided that the SA (*Sturmabteilung*-Brown Shirts) was not a criminal organization, the number of prisoners was further reduced to 27,000[19]; and there were only 3,500 prisoners by June 1948.[20]

Physical and psychological conditions in the camps slowly improved, but even after they were taken over by German administration, it was reported that some individuals still did not know the reasons for their arrest. When the German local courts began to process these prisoners in 1947, they determined that about 80% should be classified as "Followers"; furthermore, if the prisoners had had hearings before their arrests, one-half would not have been interned. As it was, those who were eventually sentenced by the German courts usually received light sentences with imposed prison time rarely greater than their time already served.[21]

PERSONAL HISTORY OF MAJOR GERT NAUMANN, OF THE LUFTWAFFE, A MEMBER OF THE GERMAN AIR FORCE GENERAL STAFF INTERNED IN DACHAU FROM OCTOBER 1945 TO FEBRUARY 1946

The following excerpts from Naumann's diary illustrate camp life at Dachau. A captain in a Luftwaffe reconnaissance squadron, he was promoted to Major and then posted to the Air Force section of the

German Army High Command in Berlin. He was in a military hospital at the time of the fall of Berlin, in April 1945, and later evacuated by plane to an Air Force hospital in Bavaria. On the way, the aircraft was shot down; he survived the crash, but was severely wounded. Released from hospital in late summer of 1945, he was arrested by US forces as a member of the German General Staff. He was in the immediate arrest category as stipulated by Control Council Directive #38-Major offenders. The International Nürenberg Military Tribunal later removed the German Army High Command from the previous designation as a criminal organization but he was not released. Rather, he was then transferred to a holding camp at Aibling, Bavaria, and that fall sent to the former Dachau Concentration Camp.

At Dachau, Naumann relates, the first thing prisoners saw was a huge crucifix on Roll Call Square, in front of the crematorium. This was erected after the war by former Polish prisoners in memory of their comrades who died there. On a tree hung a sign saying "To the Crematorium." American soldiers came and went from a small wooden building on the right. Guards then led the first ten prisoners into the barracks. On coming out, shortly thereafter, some appeared to be slightly wounded. Naumann was in the third group. Photos of concentration camp victims were hung on the walls. The prisoners had to stand close to the photos and a guard came behind each prisoner, hitting him on the neck or head so that he was bashed against the wall. They were then led out. No one said a word.

After this incident, he stated that the American soldiers behaved "correctly and almost politely" while searching their belongings. At this point, his diary was taken from him (it was returned to him in January 1946), but he managed to keep some other personal items. The prisoners were taken to the barracks, to the Special Camp, which mainly housed the *Waffen* SS. Naumann found the Dachau camp quite comfortable compared to his previous holding camp. Dachau's barracks were well built and clean, its paths dry and covered with gravel and sanitary facilities had washrooms with large sinks and flush toilets with seats. The barracks were crowded but tolerable, especially after former *Waffen* SS prisoners were removed. The food was much better and more plentiful than at the Aibling camp. Annoying to him, however, were the constant searches by US Army personnel for contraband goods. He proudly stated that the prisoners had set up a toilet cleaning work schedule even before the Americans asked them to do it.

A cultural program, like that at Aibling, was led by former teachers and professors. Subjects were mostly German history and culture but English lessons were also offered. There was even a lecture series from a professor who was a Dante expert. Naumann reported that these lectures were important as they helped the inmates immensely in forgetting their condition as prisoners. The inmates even formed a men's choir and a small orchestra, both of which were very successful.

From time to time, the inmates were led to hot showers—a real luxury. Naumann also had a job heating water for the inmates of a strictly fenced off camp for war criminals, which belonged to the Dachau Special Camp. It held SS Concentration Camp guards and other SS charged with war crimes. He reported that they looked like real criminal types.

His two greatest sources of dissatisfaction with life at Dachau were boredom and lack of privacy. Unlike the other prisoners, general staff officers were not allowed to work. Lectures and concerts helped, but basically there was nothing to do. He wrote continuously in his diary. There was also a library which he evidently used. German newspapers from Munich and the US Army paper *Stars and Stripes* were received occasionally and passed from hand to hand. Lack of privacy in a prison camp overflowing with senior German officers was normal in the system, often leading to petty quarrels. Naumann's only time alone came during his daily walks outside the barracks; however, these were restricted by prison regulations to three hours, and it was difficult to avoid meeting others in the prison yards.

In order to break the monotony, the high ranking military prisoners also regularly celebrated Christmas, New Years, and each other's birthdays.

The US Army gave each prisoner four packets of tobacco and 200 grams of coffee for Christmas in 1945, an obviously welcome luxury.

The most difficult experience of his early time in Dachau was the steadily decreasing food rations due to the approaching winter, though some prisoners did receive food packages from home. (It should be noted that most Germans were hungry that first winter after the war.)

Naumann's litany: *The American camp administration ordered today another ration cutback. Soup in the evening and occasional chocolate are deleted....* Still, Naumann considered the food rations better here than those in the Aibling camp. *We have in the morning a half liter of soup thickened with flour, for lunch one liter of bean soup, 1/4 rye bread, 30 grams fat or 1/10 of a can of meat and 1/2 liter coffee substitute. Another cut of food rations today. ...* Again Naumann complains. *We received today a further cut in food allowance. Accordingly, we have only a thin soup three times daily, 18 grams of margarine, and five slices of bread. If only there were not this continuously nagging hunger feeling!... Our food rations daily are now only two liters of thin soup "enriched" with some individual sauerkraut threads or a few white beans or unpeeled potato pieces, five slices of bread, and two tiny portions of greasy margarine each the size of a sugar cube....The food ration was again reduced some: instead of margarine or cheese we have daily a teaspoon of jam.*

Another great concern of the internees was lack of news from their families, as correspondence was strictly limited. (However, General Clay rescinded this in late in 1945). Naumann tells us of one incident that winter in which the prisoners cut down some fence posts without permission to heat their barracks. He implied that as punishment, US Army soldiers dumped a whole jeep load of letters and packages from home and burned them in front of the assembled prisoners. They were outraged by this meanness.

The inmates of the internment camps were permitted access to the German and foreign press. Naumann reported their very angry reaction to the reports of abuses and even crimes suffered by German refugees expelled from their homes in Eastern Germany and from Eastern Europe in general. They felt the Allies pursued a policy of revenge against Germans in Eastern Europe and insisted that the German Army never treated civilians in areas occupied by them in this inhuman fashion. They were also dismayed by the untruthful press reports of the comfortable life they were supposedly living in the internment camps. Of special interest to them were the newspaper reports of the Western Allies' increasing friction with the Soviets. The inmates' reaction was that finally the Allies understood the real danger of the Soviet Union, thus, in a way, justifying to themselves their attack on Russia.

Transferred from Dachau in February 1946, Naumann confided to his diary that he was comfortable in the camp and, in a way, sorry to leave it, especially as he had no idea where he was being transferred. He wrote in his diary what he had learned in this internment camp:

I learned a great deal in this camp, Dachau: practical things of daily life, but also deeper insights, which make one more mature. I think of the many hours of close fellowship with the other prisoners who shared the same fate as I....I have developed much inner strength to help me deal with all the miseries here,. so that I am not bothered at all by ever so many human failings of inadequacy or inferiority. It is not my fault that I'm here. My conscience is clear...Others have power over me and I cannot influence how they use it. Of course, I suffer from the unreasonableness and hatefulness of those spirits who need to take out their moods on us, their prisoners and it makes me powerless...

It appears from the tone of Neumann's diary entries that he, like so many former German army officers, had a great sense of self pity because they felt that the Allies were treating them as common criminals. They justified their wartime behavior as fighting for the "Fatherland" without acknowledging the horrors committed by the Nazi regime. Their excuse was that they knew nothing about them. The justification for their actions was always that they did their duty and were proud of having served their country in a time of great need. They considered themselves prisoners of war and could not understand why they continued to be held in an internment camp when the Geneva Convention stated that prisoners of war were to be released as soon as a war was over. The German officers did not take into account, or did not want to take into account, that the mass killing of civilians or prisoners of war, especially in the East, was not a duty of soldiers but a war crime.

Naumann was finally released on August 9, 1947, from the Ludwigsburg internment camp in Württemberg. In the last months of his confinement he did begin to have serious doubts about the Nazi military and civilian leadership. *My experiences come back to me, become alive again, and take me by the throat: this insanity, these illusions, these dilatants, the entire military leadership, a fiasco at the highest levels; and our continued belief and acceptance of these illusions, even two years after the end of the war, is difficult to understand.*

Source: Gert Naeumann, Besiegt und "Befreit." *Ein Tagebuch Hinter Stacheldraht in Deutschland, 1945-1947,* Druffel Verlag, Leoni am Starnberger See, Bavaria 1984.

(Refer to http://www.thegulagineastgermany.com for Illustration #3. Gert Naumann In the Uniform of a Luftwaffe Captain. Source: Besiegt und "Befreit." by Gert Naumann)

BRITISH INTERNMENT CAMPS AND THE DENAZIFICATION PROCESS

The British denazification process was neither as thorough nor as harsh as that of the US Zone. It placed much more emphasis on political re-education, that is, winning over the German populace to a democratic way of life and the rule of law.[22] The British Government did not favor a broad purge of former Nazis in order not to further destabilize an already war weakened economy. The policy was to dismiss all senior officials from administrative posts, but to reinstate them if, after investigation, they were found to be only "nominal" Nazis.[23]

Although at the war's end, the British Government did not accept all of the US Military's JC1067 directions, they did publish an interim directive which had some of the same principals. It did not, however, define the category of Nazis that had to be excluded from government offices or removed from private companies. It did mention that "Germans who are permitted to remain in or are appointed to official posts should understand that they hold office only so long as good behavior is observed."[24] In terms of initial arrests, however, the British were primarily interested in finding Germans who had committed war crimes against British POWs or against Allied airmen. The British Military Government hanged more than 200 of these war criminals.[25]

To implement the Potsdam Agreement of August 1945, the British Government decreed a *Directive on the Arrest and Removal of Nazis from Office* in September 1945. The categories of former Nazis subject to immediate removal and arrest were fewer than those found in the July 5th denazification regulations of the American Military Government. A new category was introduced, called compulsory investigation, which effectively reduced the number of arrests. Persons under mandatory investigation and removal could be retained in office for one month, pending investigation results. For example, senior civil servants who had previously been in the automatic removal and arrest categories were reassigned to a compulsory investigation status. Even after the issuance in 1946 of CC Directives 24, and 38, this British Government policy continued.[26]

At the end of the war, the British established several internment camps and within several months 66,000 important Nazis had been detained, awaiting trial. Due to the Government's arrest and removal decree, this figure increased to 68,500 by the end of 1945, and to 71,000 in May 1946.[27] By July 1946, 42,000 had already been processed and released. In addition, young people, specifically those born after 1919, were freed. In 1947, the British also released most junior officers of organizations classified as criminal by the Nürenberg Military Tribunal, and subsequently, in

November 1947, all SS officers and NCOs were set free on parole. By that time, only 500 prisoners remained; they were ones considered too dangerous to release and were confined to prisons.[28]

To house all these prisoners, the British set up a number of internment camps; among the most important were Neuengamme, a former Nazi concentration camp near Hamburg, and Esterwegen, also a former concentration camp but in Ostfriesland near Holland. In the summer of 1945, the British military government interned in these camps 16,000 important Nazi party officials, including Hitler Youth commanders, regional party group leaders, and 16,000 SS officers and men. (This number fell to 3,000–4,000 internees one year later.) In these early months, the camps were crowded and unsanitary. Moreover, food was inadequate, dropping in some cases to only 900 calories per day—a condition, however, that was widespread in the early years of post-war Germany. Nevertheless, many of the senior Nazi party leaders were allowed to receive food packages from their former associates, a service obviously not available to the average German inmate.[29]

Increased criticism of these failings led to a House of Commons investigation committee, which concluded that they enhanced neither the prestige of the British Military Government nor the British way of life. The British Military also condemned these conditions commenting that prolonged detentions without trial were "not compatible with the professed restoration of the rule of law and the abolition of Gestapo methods."[30] Of further embarrassment to the Government, a British intelligence service interrogation center at Bad Nenndorf near Hannover practiced torture against former Nazis prisoners and later against communist infiltrators. As a result of news reports exposing this center, it was closed in July 1947 and the commander was placed on trial, but later acquitted.[31] Nevertheless, the accelerated freeing of the detainees can be ascribed, in part, to this internal criticism of the government's detention programs. By the end of 1947 and beginning of 1948, the Neuengamme camp closed after the greater part of the high Nazi party and SS leaders there were absolved and released by local German courts.[32]

The Personal History of Jürgen Girgensohn, Corporal in the *Waffen* SS and Prisoner in the British Fallingbostel Internment Camp, on the Lüneburger Heath, in the State of Lower Saxony, as Related to a Conference of British Internment Camp Commanders in February 1947.

Apart from holding important Nazis and war criminals, a further function of the camps was the political re-education of young prisoners, especially those born after 1919. One of these was a young *Waffen* SS soldier, Jürgen Girgensohn.

Girgensohn voluntarily took a democracy orientation course in the prison camp. He was a corporal in the *Waffen* SS and an active combat soldier. He stated that he did not know anything about the crimes of the SS or the persecution of Jews. As a result of his education in Nazi Germany, he was a faithful and dedicated follower of Adolf Hitler.

"I was a National Socialist from the beginning, from my entry, in 1934, into the Jungvolk (a junior group of the Hitler Youth) until the end of the war, and even after. Always important for me were the National Socialist principles." After the war, he remained for one year in a prisoner of war camp in Italy. He then went to a British prisoner of war camp in Münster, Germany and from there to the Sandbostel internment camp. *"At the end of the war and months thereafter, my world collapsed. I was not able to deal with this catastrophe. Then I tried to overcome this feeling by always being active, through comradeship with my friends, by singing the old Nazi songs, which were prohibited, and by a defiant attitude. This defiance really only disappeared due to my experience with many SS officers in the Sandbostel camp. I saw them running around, attempting to convince others that they did not do anything during the war and how they bent over scrounging*

cigarette butts thrown away by the guards. I could not believe this at all of my superiors, when the war was over."

After three months, the young SS prisoners of lower rank, Girgensohn among them, were transferred to the Fallingbostel internment camp. *"The camp was much cleaner and appeared better cared for than the Sandbostel camp. We were housed in barracks with several different groups of prisoners."* In this youth camp, the British authorities offered voluntary courses and lectures which were led by a Jewish captain. *"He was a man who, when he gathered us, said he was a German who escaped from Germany in 1933. He then offered his service to the English and, of course, he participated in the war. He said that this camp, and the group we belonged to, were especially established to help us younger prisoners, who were not subject to a legal process, understand the past and to see what actually happened at this time... For this purpose, courses were arranged in literature, philosophy and history, which we could attend, if we wished. To facilitate this study, a library was created where we could borrow books, again, only if we wished, and he was our teacher. I remember very clearly his lectures on recent history. He helped open my eyes to many things, and I received a different view of what happened. In any event, the singing of Nazi songs ended in this camp whereas previously we were believers and thought that everything that had happened was a terrible tragedy. I think what was most important for me was to learn what was done in the name of the German people in the years between 1933 and 1945. We learned this, not through propaganda served to us by the victors, but through documents and reports, including German reports, which initially were difficult for us to understand. We then studied these documents in our lectures together with this Englishman, and with his help, though not by propaganda means, we received an insight into these events which we then slowly began to understand. That had the effect of curing us (of our previous beliefs), at least myself, and frankly, in hindsight, I was very pleased that I was not released immediately."*

This youth group was released in the winter of 1946–1947. Many years later, Jürgen Girgensohn joined the Social Democratic Party and became Minister of Education and Culture in the State Government of Nordrhein-Westfalen.[33]

(Refer to http://www.thegulagineastgermany.com for Illustration #4. Jürgen Girgensohn as a *Waffen* SS Non-commissioned Officer. Source: Heinz Wember, Umerziehung im Lager)

(Refer to http://www.thegulagineastgermany.com for Illustration #5. View of Neuengamme Concentration Camp near Hamburg, Germany, in Wartime. — *Mahn und Gedenkstätte Neuengamme)*

(Refer to http://www.thegulagineastgermany.com for Illustration #6. Barracks in Esterwegen;. Esterwegen Concentration Camp during the war, located in Ostfriesland, near the Dutch Border, today a Memorial Site. Photo: JewishGen Organization)

   The British Military Government also held war crimes trials in its occupation zone. The first, in September 1945, was for the camp commander and 45 of the staff of the Bergen-Belsen Concentration Camp near Hamburg. It was one of the largest concentration camps in Nazi Germany, holding some 60,000 prisoners at the end of the war and with more than 50,000 deaths recorded during its period of operation. Eleven people received the death sentence, including the camp commander. Further war crimes trials conducted by the British included those of the camp commander, guards, and staff of the Stutthof Concentration Camp near Danzig (Gdansk) Poland. Concentration camp commanders and many of the staff received the death sentence; others were given prison time.[34] In March 1946,the British military government held a war crimes trial of the camp commander and fourteen other officers, including the deputy commander, guards and doctors of the Neuengamme Concentration Camp near Hamburg. Eleven were condemned to death by hanging for crimes committed against personnel of the Allied nations.[35]

FRENCH INTERNMENT CAMPS AND THE DENAZIFICATION PROCESS

In the French zone of occupation, the south-western Germans states bordering France, denazification was called *epuration*, a cleansing, reflecting a more personal and individual approach to the endeavor, rather than a massive, all encompassing process of investigation and arrest of former Nazis as in the American, and to a lesser degree, in the British zones of occupation. *Comités d'Epuration*, investigation committees, were created, just as in neighboring Alsace (see endnote #6 for details of the French denazification process in Alsace—whose population is majority ethnic German—to investigate and eventually try Nazis). Because of this individually focused treatment, the French military authorities were sometimes accused, particularly by communists, of being soft on Nazis.[36]

At the end of the war, the overwhelming French objective in occupying Germany was to ensure that it would never attack France again. They wanted to annex the Saar, to divide Germany into many independent mini-states, and to internationalize the Ruhr and Rheinland into autonomous regions. Under no circumstance was there to be a centralized state in Germany, with Berlin as its capital.[37] They encouraged separatism in their zone of occupation with the objective that it would eventually become a region dominated by France. Because both the United States and Great Britain strongly opposed the French objectives of dividing Germany, the French government eventually acceded to Allied demands and joined their zone of occupation with that of the other two Western Allies in the spring of 1949, and then supported the creation of the German Federal Republic on May 23, 1949.[38]

Security was their primary and immediate concern because of France's long border with Germany and, of course, of the history of the many German invasions. In terms of the denazification process, this initially meant a French policy that, instead of arresting leading Nazis, assigned them to positions of lesser importance, under strict supervision, to prevent them from harming the French occupation. The French Military

Government was willing to employ former Nazis in order to win over local civilian leaders to pro-French sympathies, and form, sometime in the future, a separatist protectorate allied to France.[39] As part of this effort to create support for French culture and society, the occupiers aimed to eventually instill in the Germans their republican and secular ideals.[40]

In the early days of their occupation, French efforts to arrest important Nazis appeared rather haphazard, arbitrary, and inconsistent. The automatic removal and arrest categories of CC Directives 24 and 38 were only partially followed. The French Security Services admitted in 1946 that in some areas only minor Nazis and followers were arrested. At the same time, 1,200 prisoners were released following an additional screening process. In another case, in the Rheinland, the French officials ordered the release, subject to prior investigation, of pre-1933 Nazi party members, SA, and SS members, and officers of the Hitler Youth, and National Labor Service as well as members of the German Army General Staff, Gestapo, and SD members. Irreplaceable German technical experts and bureaucrats could be retained in their positions on a month to month basis but their supervisors were responsible for their good conduct.[41] Basically, membership in the Nazi party or its affiliated organizations was not considered a reason for internment and trial in the French zone of occupation.[42] French officers were very much aware of the ways which recent purges in their own country had gotten out of control, at least briefly. Also, many army officers were still loyal Vichyites and tended to display an aversion to any kind of blanket charges against former Nazis, particularly for political behavior based more on their local actions than on their ideology.[43]

The French Military Government on September 19, 1945, issued a more functional and consistent approach to denazification in their Directive CABIC 722. It followed much more closely similar directives in the American and British zones. This may have resulted, in part, from the change in French military governors from General de Lattre to General Marie-Pierre Koenig in August 1945.The French were proponents of *auto-Epuration*—self cleansing with emphasis on acceptance of individual guilt—and the participation of German courts in the denazification trials, the first occupied zone to do so. The new directive included automatic removal categories including those holding senior rank in the Nazi party prior to 1933, as well as in various Nazi affiliated organizations, subject however to prior court review. They were also permitted to continue in their jobs while their cases were being heard. When the Control Council issued Directives 24 and 38, the Military Government ignored those provisions which were not in accord with their own regulations.[44]

By the spring of 1947, the French administration had investigated the Nazi pasts of more than 500,000 individuals. About 133,000 of them were considered merely nominal Nazis, and only 18,000 were charged and penalized. Penalties were not severe—chiefly fines or job losses—and often just temporary. In fact, in July 1948, General Koenig cancelled all small and moderate fines, those for less than 15,000 marks. Finally, only 13 Germans were classified as major offenders.[45]

Major offenders were held for trial in retention camps in or near the towns of Lahr, Freiburg, and Bühl . The French military government conducted these trials including the prosecutions, as distinct from turning over most denazification cases to German courts. For this purpose, three French magistrates were assigned to each internment camp. There was no process for automatic arrest in the French denazificatin system, like that which existed with the other Western Allies. French prosecution was usually based on denunciations, most often by other Germans. In those cases, as in the entire denazification process, the trials relied more heavily on personal testimony rather than on documentation demonstrating past membership in the Nazi party or in other Nazi criminal organizations.[46] By the end of 1945, the French military government had interned 12,500 major offenders in these camps and there were additional arrests in 1946. But by May 1947, 13,000 prisoners were released, leaving 8,500 internees. In September, 1947 the French turned the camps over to the local German authorities.[47]

In summary, the French denazification program was considered the least harsh of the four Allied powers including that of the Soviet Union.[48] Like what had happened in the other occupation zones, nominal Nazis often received disproportionately harsher sentences than leading Nazis did. Additionally, French prosecutors relied more on personal denunciations in their trials, just as in the Alsace, which often led to village conflicts, business and community rivalries, and even personal feuds. On the other hand, the French implementation of denazification appears to have found a balance between excessive severity and over-leniency, As Perry Bidiscombe stated in his book, *The Denazificatin of Germany: A History 1945-1950*, "The very nature of the French approach, because of its humanism and recognition of the individual, set the tone for a policy that would eventually take shape as Franco-German reconciliation."[49]

THE DIFFERENCES BETWEEN WESTERN ALLIED INTERNMENT CAMPS AND SOVIET SPECIAL CAMPS

Probably the most important difference between the two internment systems was who was arrested and then interned and the reason why. The military governments of the Western Allies sent leading Nazis and members of organizations judged criminal by the Nürenberg Military Court to their internment camps pending court trial or administrative review, whereas in the Soviet *Spezlager* the majority of the prisoners were opponents or suspected opponents of the Soviet regime. The Soviets arrested some nominal Nazis but high Nazi officials and particularly those of the *Waffen* SS and security services were sent to the Soviet Union, condemned, and incarcerated in the GULAG. A number of them were also executed. In the Soviet camps some prisoners had already been tried by military courts for anti-Soviet activities with the majority arrested administratively, without any trial, all for the purpose of making them harmless by removing them from society.[50]

The original, fundamental Allied motive for the denazification of Germany was the reconstruction of German political life on a democratic basis. To this end, the Nazi party and all affiliated organizations had to be eliminated and their leaders purged from positions of importance. To achieve this, the Allied Control Council by its Directives #24 and #38 established the category of Major Offenders who were subject to automatic arrest and imprisonment. These directives were supplemented by implementation regulations of each Western Allied military government. Thus, the majority of the inmates in the Western internment camps were members of the SS, the *Waffen* SS, and other Nazi security services, as well as important members of the Nazi hierarchy, with their arrests based on the Nürenberg military trials criteria of Nazi criminal organizations.[51] Of importance was the Western allies' differentiation between security operations and the denazification process. The overwhelming number of prisoners were there because of the denazification program awaiting court trial. Security operations, on the other hand, ended almost immediately after the war, once the Western military governments realized that there was no armed German resistance.

The Soviet objective for a post-war German state was fundamentally different from that of the Western Allies, despite the Yalta and Potsdam agreements. The Russians intended to establish a Soviet totalitarian state under the leadership and control of the Communist Party. To achieve this end, they were not particularly interested in who was or was not a Nazi. Their political control mechanism permitted them to employ, without fear, whomever they considered useful or important in the administration of their zone of occupation and the advancement of their objectives. The Soviet attitude assumed that their military administration was unlikely to be influenced by Nazis ideologically, so they were used when needed.[52]

Their real concern was political opposition, particularly from the left wing political parties, of those Germans who wanted a pluralistic state and who refused to follow the directives of the Soviet military government, the Soviet Communist Party, and their German allies. These individuals became the principal occupants of the special camps. For the Soviets, the establishment of the camps was strictly a security operation to safeguard their zone of occupation. There were few military court trials and then only in the most egregious cases of anti-Soviet activity, with the majority arrested and imprisoned without trial. An important component of Soviet security operations were the widespread raids against young Germans suspected of belonging to the Werewolf. These raids were particularly prevalent in the early months of the occupation.

Another crucial difference with the Western camps was the prisoner survival rate. In the Soviet special camps, the mortality rate was about 40% because malnutrition and poor sanitary conditions led to tuberculosis, dysentery, and dystrophy. (See figure 1, Chapter 1.) In other words, a total neglect of the living conditions of the prisoners was prevalent. In early 1947, Soviet camp commanders deemed only 5% of the prisoners fit to work, when they were requested to send labor to the Soviet Union.[53] In the Western internment camps, the death rate was the same as in the overall German civilian population. Although food was often scarce in Western Germany, especially in the first winter after the war, the rations received by the internees resembled those received by the German population through the rationing system. In general, the health and psychological state of prisoners in the Western internment camps far surpassed that of the Soviet special camps.[54]

In the Western camps, for example, prisoners could send and receive mail and food packages. Many had libraries and inmates were permitted to stage musical events, plays, lectures and occasionally even film presentations. In the principal British internment camp of Neuengamme, near Hamburg, a report stated the following:

> "Except for the SS concentration camp guards and personnel, who were in a separate part of the camp, the inmates could determine their own daily activities, for which they even received material to pursue their hobbies..... Starting in December 1945, those who wished could finish their education at the high school level and receive a degree, conducted by the Hamburg Secondary School Administration..... In February 1946 courses were increased to include advanced trade, commerce, farming including gardening, and electronics.... The

> *School Administration also offered foreign language courses of which English was the most popular.*[65]

The two sets of camps also differed fundamentally in length of incarceration; prisoners spent far less time in the Western internment camps. For example, by the summer of 1946 more than 1/2 of the internees had been released from the Western Allied camps; in the Soviet camps, however, the first releases, the majority nominal Nazis, only occurred in 1948 with serious cases released just in 1950. Nevertheless, this did not end the imprisonment for many, with a large number tried and sentenced by the Waldheim courts of the East German Ministry of Justice.

In the Soviet special camps, the prisoners were not forced to work as they were in the Gulag camps in the Soviet Union. On the contrary, work was prohibited. The Soviets totally isolated the inmates. They were permitted no contact with the outside world until the release of some of them in 1948. In the internment camps of the Western Allies, the inmates often had to work at tasks such as clearing rubble in the cities and towns, but by end 1945, they could send and accept mail, receive visitors, and even leave the camps on a temporary pass. When the internment camps in the Allied zones were turned over to the German provinces in 1947, prison conditions became even more benign and certainly much less disciplined.[56] (See the personal narratives of Major Gert Neumann on conditions at Dachau internment camp and Jürgen Girgensohn, a former member of the *Waffen* SS and a prisoner in the British Fallingbostel internment camp.)

American forces arrested and incarcerated more Germans than the other Western Allies, but their incarceration period was the shortest. The British camps, followed by the French, kept prisoners somewhat longer but arrests and internments affected only limited groups of individuals. The Soviet special camp system had the longest period of incarceration and by far the most prisoners. The total number arrested was greater than the total for all the Western camps combined. Further, the Western arrest process differentiated clearly between security measures and the denazification process; those arrested for security reasons were quickly released and the others shortly thereafter, following their denazification trials. For the Soviets, the arrest and imprisonment process, without trial, was strictly a security operation to isolate all elements who were suspected of being spies or opponents of the Soviet state.[57]

SOME CONCLUSIONS ON THE DENAZIFICATION PROCESS OF THE WESTERN ALLIES

It is not the purpose of this work to analyze and critically examine the denazification program of the American, British, and French military governments, but only to present their involvement in the creation and operation of their internment camps in order to show how they differed from the Soviet special camps. A few words nonetheless should be said about the success or lack of success of the denazification program in the West.

It seems that most historians agree that the denazification program failed. It was overextended and too much was attempted, resulting in a vast purge of minor Nazis, while many important party members, including those of the SS, escaped punishment or even censure. The "small fry" were punished but the "big fish" escaped. Most senior levels of German society, however, especially public administration, with some exceptions, were purged of Nazis and a number were imprisoned for a time. A fairly large number of the worst murderers of the Nazi system were tried, condemned and hanged or received long prison sentences by the military courts of the Western Allies (see note #5 below on the subsequent Nürenberg military trials). The great mass of the nominal Nazis and their non-party supporters, however, came through the process quite well.[58]

Yet today, the Federal Republic is one of the leading liberal democracies in the world. Granted that many factors contributed to this state: the Marshall Plan and the economic recovery after the war which made

Germany a leading industrial power again; the Cold War which made Germany a bulwark against Soviet expansion; its key participation in the successful creation of the European Common Market and later the European Union and so forth. But the basic objective of the denazification program, the creation of a moral and political compass for a new democratic Germany through education and the institution of a state of law has been achieved. In the light of this achievement, the denazification program could be called a success.

NOTE #1: DECLARATION REGARDING THE DEFEAT OF GERMANY AND THE ASSUMPTION OF SUPREME AUTHORITY BY ALLIED POWERS; JUNE 5, 1945

Declaration Regarding the Defeat of Germany and the Assumption of Supreme Authority with Respect to Germany by the Governments of the United States of America, the Union of Soviet Socialist Republics, the United Kingdom and the Provisional Government of the French Republic.

The German armed forces on land, at sea, and in the air have been completely defeated and have surrendered unconditionally; Germany, which bears responsibility for the war, is no longer capable of resisting the will of the victorious Powers. The unconditional surrender of Germany has thereby been effected, and Germany has become subject to such requirements as may now or hereafter be imposed upon her.

There is no central Government or authority in Germany capable of accepting responsibility for the maintenance of order, the administration of the country, and compliance with the requirements of the victorious Powers.

It is in these circumstances necessary, without prejudice to any subsequent decisions that may be taken respecting Germany, to make provision for the cessation of any further hostilities on the part of the German armed forces, for the maintenance of order in Germany, and for the administration of the country, and to announce the immediate requirements with which Germany must comply.

The Representatives of the Supreme Commands of the United States of America, the Union of Soviet Socialist Republics, the United Kingdom, and the French Republic, hereinafter called the Allied Representatives, acting by authority of their respective Governments and in the interests of the United Nations, accordingly make the following Declaration:

The Governments of the United States of America, the Union of Soviet Socialist Republics and the United Kingdom, and the Provisional Government of the French Republic hereby assume supreme authority with respect to Germany, including all the powers possessed by the German Government, the High Command, and any state, municipal, or local government or authority. The assumption, for the purposes stated above, of the said authority and powers does not affect the annexation of Germany.

The Governments of the United States of America, the Union of Soviet Socialist Republics and the United Kingdom, and the Provisional Government of the French Republic will hereafter determine the boundaries of Germany or any part thereof and the status of Germany or of any area at present being part of German territory.

In virtue of the supreme authority and powers thus assumed by the four Governments, the Allied Representatives announce the following requirements arising from the complete defeat and unconditional surrender of Germany with which Germany must comply:

ARTICLE 1

Germany, and all German military, naval, and air authorities and all forces under German control shall immediately cease hostilities in all theatres of war against the forces of the United Nations on land, at sea and in the air.

ARTICLE 2

(a) All armed forces of Germany or under German control, wherever they may be situated, including land, air, anti-aircraft and naval forces, the S.S., S.A. and Gestapo, and all other forces of auxiliary organizations equipped with weapons, shall be completely disarmed, handing over their weapons and equipment to local Allied Commanders or to officers designated by the Allied Representatives.

(b) The personnel of the formations and units of all the forces referred to in paragraph (a) above shall, at the discretion of the Commander-in-Chief of the Armed Forces of the Allied State concerned, be declared to be prisoners of war, pending further decisions, and shall be subject to such conditions and directions as may be prescribed by the respective Allied Representatives.

(c) All forces referred to in paragraph (a) above, wherever they may be, will remain in their present positions pending instructions from the Allied Representatives.

(d) Evacuation by the said forces of all territories outside the frontiers of Germany as they existed on the 31st December, 1937, will proceed according to instructions to be given by the Allied Representatives.

(e) Detachments of civil police to be armed with small arms only, for the maintenance of order and for guard duties, will be designated by the Allied Representatives.

ARTICLE 3

(a) All aircraft of any kind or nationality in Germany or German-occupied or controlled territories or waters, military, naval or civil, other than aircraft in the service of the Allies, will remain on the ground, on the water or aboard ships pending further instructions.

(b) All German or German-controlled aircraft in or over territories or waters not occupied or controlled by Germany will proceed to Germany or to such other place or places as may be specified by the Allied Representatives.

ARTICLE 4

(a) All German or German-controlled naval vessels, surface and submarine, auxiliary naval craft, and merchant and other shipping, wherever such vessels may be at the time of this Declaration, and all other merchant ships of whatever nationality in German ports, will remain in or proceed immediately to ports and bases as specified by the Allied Representatives. The crews of such vessels will remain on board pending further instructions.

(b) All ships and vessels of the United Nations, whether or not title has been transferred as the result of prize court or other proceedings, which are at the disposal of Germany or under German control at the time of this Declaration, will proceed at the dates and to the ports or bases specified by the Allied Representatives.

ARTICLE 5

(a) All or any of the following articles in the possession of the German armed forces or under German control or at German disposal will be held intact and in good condition at the disposal of the Allied Representatives, for such purposes and at such times and places as they may prescribe:

   i. all arms, ammunition, explosives, military equipment, stores and supplies and other implements of war of all kinds and all other war materials;

ii. all naval vessels of all classes, both surface and submarine, auxiliary naval craft and all merchant shipping, whether afloat, under repair or construction, built or building;

iii. all aircraft of all kinds, aviation and anti-aircraft equipment and devices;

iv. all transportation and communications facilities and equipment, by land, water or air;

v. all military installations and establishments, including airfields, seaplane bases, ports and naval bases, storage depots, permanent and temporary land and coast fortifications, fortresses and other fortified areas, together with plans and drawings of all such fortifications, installations and establishments;

vi. all factories, plants, shops, research institutions, laboratories, testing stations, technical data, patents, plans, drawings and inventions, designed or intended to produce or to facilitate the production or use of the articles, materials, and facilities referred to in sub-paragraphs (i), (ii), (iii), (iv) and (v) above or otherwise to further the conduct of war.

(b) At the demand of the Allied Representatives the following will be furnished:

i. the labour, services and plant required for the maintenance or operation of any of the six categories mentioned in paragraph (a) above; and

ii. (ii) any information or records that may be required by the Allied Representatives in connection with the same.

(c) At the demand of the Allied Representatives all facilities will be provided for the movement of Allied troops and agencies, their equipment and supplies, on the railways, roads and other land communications or by sea, river or air. All means of transportation will be maintained in good order and repair, and the labour, services and plant necessary, therefore, will be furnished.

ARTICLE 6

(a) The German authorities will release to the Allied Representatives, in accordance with the procedure to be laid down by them, all prisoners of war at present in their power, belonging to the forces of the United Nations, and will furnish full lists of these persons, indicating the places of their detention in Germany or territory occupied by Germany. Pending the release of such prisoners of war, the German authorities and people will protect them in their persons and property and provide them with adequate food, clothing, shelter, medical attention and money in accordance with their rank or official position.

(b) The German authorities and people will in like manner provide for and release all other nationals of the United Nations who are confined, interned or otherwise under restraint, and all other persons who may be confined, interned or otherwise under restraint for political reasons or as a result of any Nazi action, law or regulation which discriminates on the ground of race, colour, creed or political belief.

(c) The German authorities will, at the demand of the Allied Representatives, hand over control of places of detention to such officers as may be designated for the purpose by the Allied Representatives.

ARTICLE 7

The German authorities concerned will furnish to the Allied Representatives:

(a) full information regarding the forces referred to in Article 2 (a), and, in particular, will furnish forthwith all information which the Allied Representatives may require concerning the numbers, locations and dispositions of such forces, whether located inside or outside Germany;

(b) complete and detailed information concerning mines, minefields and other obstacles to movement by land, sea or air, and the safety lanes in connection therewith. All such safety lanes will be kept open and clearly marked; all mines, minefields and other dangerous obstacles will as far as possible be rendered safe, and all aids to navigation will be reinstated. Unarmed German military and civilian personnel with the necessary equipment will be made available and utilized for the above purposes and for the removal of mines, minefields and other obstacles as directed by the Allied Representatives.

ARTICLE 8

There shall be no destruction, removal, concealment, transfer or scuttling of, or damage to, any military, naval, air, shipping, port, industrial and other like property and facilities and all records and archives, wherever they may be situated, except as may be directed by the Allied Representatives.

ARTICLE 9

Pending the institution of control by the Allied Representatives over all means of communication, all radio and telecommunication installations and other forms of wire or wireless communications, whether ashore or afloat, under German control, will cease transmission except as directed by the Allied Representatives.

ARTICLE 10

The forces, ships, aircraft, military equipment, and other property in Germany or in German control or service or at German disposal, of any other country at war with any of the Allies, will be subject to the provisions of this Declaration and of any proclamations, orders, ordinances or instructions issued there under.

ARTICLE 11

(a) The principal Nazi leaders as specified by the Allied Representatives, and all persons from time to time named or designated by rank, office or employment by the Allied Representatives as being suspected of having committed, ordered or abetted war crimes or analogous offences, will be apprehended and surrendered to the Allied Representatives.

(b) The same will apply in the case of any national of any of the United Nations who is alleged to have committed an offence against his national law, and who may at any time be named or designated by rank, office or employment by the Allied Representatives.

(c) The German authorities and people will comply with any instructions given by the Allied Representatives for the apprehension and surrender of such persons.

ARTICLE 12

The Allied Representatives will station forces and civil agencies in any or all parts of Germany as they may determine.

ARTICLE 13

(a) In the exercise of the supreme authority with respect to Germany assumed by the Governments of the United States of America, the Union of Soviet Socialist Republics and the United Kingdom, and the Provisional Government of the French Republic, the four Allied Governments will take such steps, including the complete disarmament and demilitarization of Germany, as they deem requisite for future peace and security.

(b) The Allied Representatives will impose on Germany additional political, administrative, economic, financial, military and other requirements arising from the complete defeat of Germany. The Allied Representatives, or persons or agencies duly designated to act on their authority, will issue proclamations, orders, ordinances and instructions for the purpose of laying down such additional requirements, and of giving effect to the other provisions of this Declaration. All German authorities and the German people shall carry out unconditionally the requirements of the Allied Representatives, and shall fully comply with all such proclamations, orders, ordinances and instructions.

ARTICLE 14

This Declaration enters into force and effect at the date and hour set forth below. In the event of failure on the part of the German authorities or people promptly and completely to fulfill their obligations hereby or hereafter imposed, the Allied Representatives will take whatever action may be deemed by them to be appropriate under the circumstances.

ARTICLE 15

This Declaration is drawn up in the English, Russian, French and German languages. The English, Russian and French are the only authentic texts.

BERLIN, GERMANY, June 5, 1945.

Signed at 1800 hours, Berlin time, by Dwight D. Eisenhower, General of the Army USA; Georgi K. Zhukov, Marshal of the Soviet Union; B. L. Montgomery, Field Marshal, Great Britain; Jean de Lattre de Tassisny, General d'Armee, French Provisional Government.

NOTE #2 ALLIED CONTROL COUNCIL DIRECTIVE #38

PART II

ARTICLE 1

GROUPS OF PERSONS RESPONSIBLE

In order to make a just determination of responsibility and to provide for imposition (except in the case of 5 below) of sanctions, the following groupings of persons shall be made:

1. Major offenders;
2. Offenders (activists, militarists, and profiteers);
3. Lesser offenders (probationers);
4. Followers;
5. Persons exonerated. (Those included in the above categories who can prove themselves not guilty before a tribunal.)

ARTICLE 2

MAJOR OFFENDERS

Major Offenders are:

1. Anyone who, out of political motives, committed crimes against victims or opponents of national socialism;
2. Anyone who, in Germany or in the occupied areas, treated foreign civilians or prisoners of war contrary to International Law;
3. Anyone who is responsible for outrages, pillaging, deportations, or other acts of brutality, even if committed in fighting against resistance movements;

4. Anyone who was active in a leading position in the NSDAP, one of its formations or affiliated organizations, or in any other national socialistic or militaristic organization;

5. Anyone who, in the government of the Reich, the *Länder*, or in the administration of formerly occupied areas, held a leading position which could have been held only by a leading national socialist or a leading supporter of the national socialistic tyranny;

6. Anyone who gave major political, economic, propagandist or ·other support to the national socialistic tyranny, or who, by reason of his relations with the national socialistic tyranny, received very substantial profits for himself or others;

7. Anyone who was actively engaged for the national socialistic tyranny in the Gestapo, the SD, the SS, or the *Geheime, Feld- or Grenz Polizei*; .

8. Anyone who, in any form whatever, participated in killings, tortures, or other cruelties in a concentration camp, a labor camp, or a medical institution or asylum;

9. Anyone who, for personal profit or advantage, actively collaborated with the Gestapo, SD, SS or similar organizations by denouncing or otherwise aiding in the persecution of opponents of the national socialistic tyranny;

10. Any member of the High Command of the German Armed Forces so specified.

ARTICLE 3

OFFENDERS

(A) Activists

I. An activist is:

1. Anyone who, by way of his position or activity, substantially advanced the national socialistic tyranny;

2. Anyone who exploited his position, his influence or his connections to impose force and utter threats, to act with brutality and to carry out oppressions or otherwise unjust measures;

3. Anyone who manifested himself as an avowed adherent of the national socialistic tyranny, more particularly of its racial creeds.

II. Activists are, in particular, the following persons, insofar as they are not major offenders:

1. 1.Anyone who substantially contributed to the establishment, consolidation or maintenance of the national socialistic tyranny, by word or deed, especially publicly through speeches or writings or through voluntary donations out of his own or another's property or through using his personal reputation or his position of power in political, economic or cultural life;

2. Anyone who, through national socialistic teachings or education, poisoned the spirit and soul of the youth;

3. Anyone who, in order to strengthen the national socialistic tyranny, undermined family and marital life disregarding recognized moral principles;

4. Anyone who in the service of national socialism unlawfully interfered in the administration of justice or abused politically his office as judge or public prosecutor;

5. Anyone who in the service of national socialism agitated with incitement or violence against churches, religious communities or ideological associations;

6. Anyone who in the service of national socialism ridiculed, damaged or destroyed values of art or science;

7. Anyone who took a leading or active part in destroying trade unions, suppressing labor, and misappropriating trade union property;

8. Anyone who, as a provocateur, agent or informer, caused or attempted to cause, institution of a proceeding to the detriment of others because of their race, religion or political opposition

to national socialism or because of violation of national socialist rules;

9. Anyone who exploited his position or power under the national socialistic tyranny to commit offences, in particular, extortions, embezzlements and frauds;

10. Anyone who by word or deed took an attitude of hatred towards opponents of the NSDAP in Germany or abroad, towards prisoners of war, the population of formerly occupied territories, foreign civilian workers, prisoners or like persons;

11. Anyone who favored transfer to service at the front because of opposition to national socialism.

III. An activist shall also be anyone who, after 8 May 1945, has endangered or is likely to endanger the peace of the German people or of the world, through advocating national socialism or militarism or inventing or disseminating malicious rumors.

(B) Militarists

I. A Militarist is:

1. Anyone who has sought to bring the life of the German people into line with a policy of militaristic force;

2. Anyone who advocated or is responsible for the domination of foreign peoples, their exploitation or displacement, or

3. Anyone who, for these purposes, promoted armament.

II. Militarists are in particular the following persons, insofar as they are not major offenders:

1. Anyone who, by word or deed, established or disseminated militaristic doctrines or programs or was active in any organization (except the *Wehrmacht*) serving the advancement of militaristic ideas;

2. Anyone who before 1935 organized or participated in the organization of the systematic training of youth for war;

3. Anyone who, exercising the power of command, is responsible for the wanton devastation, after the invasion of Germany, of cities and country places;

4. Anyone without regard to his rank who as a member of the Armed Forces (*Wehrmacht*), the Reich Labor Service (*Reichsarbeitsdienst*), the Organization Todt (OT), or Transport Group Speer, abused his official authority to obtain personal advantages or brutality to mistreat subordinates;

5. Anyone whose past training and activities in the General Staff Corps or otherwise has in the opinion of Zone Commanders contributed towards the promotion of militarism and who the Zone Commanders consider likely to endanger Allied purposes.

(C) Profiteers

A profiteer is:

Anyone who, by use of his political position or connections, gained personal or economic advantages for himself or others from the national socialistic tyranny, the rearmament, or the war.

II. Profiteers are in particular the following persons, insofar as they are not major offenders:

1. Anyone who, solely on account of his membership in the NSDAP, obtained an office or a position or was preferentially promoted therein;

2. Anyone who received substantial donations from the NSDAP or its formations or affiliated organizations;

3. Anyone who obtained or strove for advantages for himself or others at the expense of those who were persecuted on political, religious or racial grounds, directly or indirectly, especially in connection with appropriations, forced sales, or similar transactions;

4. Anyone who made disproportionately high profits in armament or war transactions;

5. Anyone who unjustly enriched himself in connection with the administration of formerly occupied territories.

ARTICLE 4

Lesser Offenders (Probationers)

I. A lesser offender is

1. Anyone including former members of the Armed Forces who otherwise belongs to the groups of offenders but because of special circumstances seems worthy of a milder judgment and can be expected according to his character to fulfill his duties as a citizen of a peaceful democratic state after he has proved himself in a period of probation;

2. Anyone who otherwise belongs to the group of followers but because of his conduct and in view of his character will first have to prove himself.

II. A lesser offender is more particularly:

1. Anyone who, born after the first day of January 1919, does not belong to the group of major offenders, but seems to be an offender, without however having manifested despicable or brutal conduct and who can be- expected in view of his character to prove himself:

2. Anyone, not a major offender, who seems to be an offender but withdrew from national socialism and its methods, unqualifiedly and manifestly, at an early time.

ARTICLE 5

Followers

A follower is:

Anyone who was not more than a nominal participant in, or a supporter of, the national socialistic tyranny.

II. Subject to this standard, a follower is more particularly:

1. Anyone who as a member of the NSDAP or of one of its formations, except the HJ and BDM, did no more than pay membership fees, participate in meetings where attendance was obligatory, or carry out unimportant or purely routine duties such as were directed for all members;

2. Anyone, not a major offender, an offender, or a lesser offender, who was a candidate for membership in the NSDAP but had not yet been finally accepted as a member;

3. Anyone being a former member of the Armed Forces who, in the opinion of the Zone Commander, is liable by his qualification to endanger Allied purposes.

ARTICLE 6

Exonerated Persons

An exonerated person is:

Anyone who, in spite of his formal membership or candidacy or any other outward indication, not only showed a passive attitude but also actively resisted the national socialistic tyranny to the extent of his powers and thereby suffered disadvantages.

NOTE #3: POTSDAM AGREEMENT OF AUGUST 1, 1945

II. THE PRINCIPLES TO GOVERN THE TREATMENT OF GERMANY IN THE INITIAL CONTROL PERIOD

A. POLITICAL PRINCIPLES

1. In accordance with the Agreement on Control Machinery in Germany, supreme authority in Germany is exercised, on instructions from their respective Governments, by the Commanders-in-Chief of the armed forces of the United States of America, the Unitedingdom, the Union of Soviet Socialist Republics, and the French Republic, each in his own zone of occupation, and also jointly, in matters affecting Germany as a whole, in their capacity as members of the Control Council.

2. So far as is practicable, there shall be uniformity of treatment of the German population throughout Germany.

3. The purposes of the occupation of Germany by which the Control Council shall beuided are:

> (i) The complete disarmament and demilitarization of Germany and the elimination or control of all German industry that could be used for military production. To these ends:

> (a) All German land, naval and air forces, the SS., SA., SD., and Gestapo, with all their organizations, staffs and institutions, including the General Staff, the Officers' Corps, Reserve Corps, military schools, war veterans' organizations and all other military and semi-military organizations, together with all clubs and associations which serve to keep alive the military tradition in Germany, shall be completely and finally abolished in such manner as permanently to prevent the revival or reorganization of German militarism and Nazism;

(b) All arms, ammunition and implements of war and all specialized facilities for their production shall be held at the disposal of the Allies or destroyed. The maintenance and production of all aircraft and all arms. ammunition and implements of war shall be prevented.

(ii) To convince the German people that they have suffered a total military defeat and that they cannot escape responsibility for what they have brought upon themselves, since their own ruthless warfare and the fanatical Nazi resistance have destroyed German economy and made chaos and suffering inevitable.

(iii) To destroy the National Socialist Party and its affiliated and supervised organizations, to dissolve all Nazi institutions, to ensure that they are not revived in any form, and to prevent all Nazi and militarist activity or propaganda.

(iv) To prepare for the eventual reconstruction of German political life on a democratic basis and for eventual peaceful cooperation in international life by Germany.

4. All Nazi laws which provided the basis of the Hitler regime or established discriminations on grounds of race, creed, or political opinion shall be abolished. No such discriminations, whether legal, administrative or otherwise, shall be tolerated.

5. War criminals and those who have participated in planning or carrying out Nazi enterprises involving or resulting in atrocities or war crimes shall be arrested and brought to judgment. Nazi leaders, influential Nazi supporters and high officials of Nazi organizations and institutions and any other persons dangerous to the occupation or its objectives shall be arrested and interned.

6. All members of the Nazi Party who have been more than nominal participants in its activities and all other persons hostile to Allied purposes shall be removed from public and semi-public office, and from positions of responsibility in important private undertakings. Such persons shall

be replaced by persons who, by their political and moral qualities, are deemed capable of assisting in developing genuine democratic institutions in Germany.

7. German education shall be so controlled as completely to eliminate Nazi and militarist doctrines and to make possible the successful development of democratic ideas.

8. The judicial system will be reorganized in accordance with the principles of democracy, of justice under law, and of equal rights for all citizens without distinction of race, nationality or religion.

9. The administration in Germany should be directed towards the decentralization of the political structure and the development of local responsibility. To this end:

> (i) local self-government shall be restored throughout Germany on democratic principles and in particular through elective councils as rapidly as is consistent with military security and the purposes of military occupation;

> (ii) all democratic political parties with rights of assembly and of public discussion shall be allowed and encouraged throughout Germany;

> (iii) representative and elective principles shall be introduced into regional, provincial and state (*Land*) administration as rapidly as may be justified by the successful application of these principles in local self-government;

> (iv) for the time being, no central German Government shall be established. Notwithstanding this, however, certain essential central German administrative departments, headed by State Secretaries, shall be established, particularly in the fields of finance, transport, communications, foreign trade and industry. Such departments will act under the direction of the Control Council.

10. Subject to the necessity for maintaining military security, freedom of speech, press and religion shall be permitted, and religious institutions

shall be respected. Subject likewise to the maintenance of military security, the formation of free trade unions shall be permitted.

B. ECONOMIC PRINCIPLES.

11. In order to eliminate Germany's war potential, the production of arms, ammunition and implements of war as well as all types of aircraft and sea-going ships shall be prohibited and prevented. Production of metals, chemicals, machinery and other items that are directly necessary to a war economy shall be rigidly controlled and restricted to Germany's approved post-war peacetime needs to meet the objectives stated in Paragraph 15. Productive capacity not needed for permitted production shall be removed in accordance with the reparations plan recommended by the Allied Commission on Reparations and approved by the Governments concerned or if not removed shall be destroyed.

12. At the earliest practicable date, the German economy shall be decentralized for the purpose of eliminating the present excessive concentration of economic power as exemplified in particular by cartels, syndicates, trusts and other monopolistic arrangements.

13. In organizing the German Economy, primary emphasis shall be given to the development of agriculture and peaceful domestic industries.

14. During the period of occupation Germany shall be treated as a single economic unit. To this end common policies shall be established in regard to:

    (a) mining and industrial production and its allocation;

    (b) agriculture, forestry and fishing;

    (c) wages, prices and rationing;

    (d) import and export programs for Germany as a whole;

(e) currency and banking, central taxation and customs;

(f) reparation and removal of industrial war potential;

(g) transportation and communications.

In applying these policies account shall be taken, where appropriate, of varying local conditions.

15. Allied controls shall be imposed upon the German economy but only to the extent necessary:

(a) to carry out programs of industrial disarmament, demilitarization, of reparations, and of approved exports and imports.

(b) to assure the production and maintenance of goods and services required to meet the needs of the occupying forces and displaced persons in Germany and essential to maintain in Germany average living standards not exceeding the average of the standards of living of European countries. (European countries means all European countries excluding the United Kingdom and the U. S. S. R.).

(c) to ensure in the manner determined by the Control Council the equitable distribution of essential commodities between the several zones so as to produce a balanced economy throughout Germany and reduce the need for imports.

(d) to control German industry and all economic and financial international transactions including exports and imports, with the aim of preventing Germany from developing a war potential and of achieving the other objectives named herein.

(e) to control all German public or private scientific bodies research and experimental institutions, laboratories, *et cetera* connected with economic activities.

16. In the imposition and maintenance of economic controls established by the Control Council, German administrative machinery shall be

created and the German authorities shall be required to the fullest extent practicable to proclaim and assume administration of such controls. Thus it should be brought home to the German people that the responsibility for the administration of such controls and any break-down in these controls will rest with themselves. Any German controls which may run counter to the objectives of occupation will be prohibited.

17. Measures shall be promptly taken:

(a) to effect essential repair of transport;

(b) to enlarge coal production;

(c) to maximize agricultural output; and

(d) to erect emergency repair of housing and essential utilities.

18. Appropriate steps shall be taken by the Control Council to exercise control and the power of disposition over German-owned external assets not already under the control of United Nations which have taken part in the war against Germany.

19. Payment of Reparations should leave enough resources to enable the German people to subsist without external assistance. In working out the economic balance of Germany the necessary means must be provided to pay for imports approved by the Control Council in Germany. The proceeds of exports from current production and stocks shall be available in the first place for payment for such imports.

The above clause will not apply to the equipment and products referred to in paragraphs 4 (a) and 4 (b) of the Reparations Agreement.

III. REPARATIONS FROM GERMANY.

1. Reparation claims of the U. S. S. R. shall be met by removals from the zone of Germany occupied by the U. S. S. R., and from appropriate German external assets.

2. The U. S. S. R. undertakes to settle the reparation claims of Poland from its own share of reparations.

3. The reparation claims of the United States, the United Kingdom and other countries entitled to reparations shall be met from the Western Zones and from appropriate German external assets.

4. In addition to the reparations to be taken by the U. S. S. R. from its own zone of occupation, the U. S. S. R. shall receive additionally from the Western Zones:

> (a) 15 per cent of such usable and complete industrial capital equipment, in the first place from the metallurgical, chemical and machine manufacturing industries as is unnecessary for the German peace economy and should be removed from the Western Zones of Germany, in exchange for an equivalent value of food, coal, potash, zinc, timber, clay products, petroleum products, and such other commodities as may be agreed upon.

> (b) 10 per cent of such industrial capital equipment as is unnecessary for the German peace economy and should be removed from the Western Zones, to be transferred to the Soviet Government on reparations account without payment or exchange of any kind in return.

Removals of equipment as provided in (a) and (b) above shall be made simultaneously.

5. The amount of equipment to be removed from the Western Zones on account of reparations must be determined within six months from now at the latest.

6. Removals of industrial capital equipment shall begin as soon as possible and shall be completed within two years from the determination specified in paragraph 5. The delivery of products covered by 4 (a) above shall begin as soon as possible and shall be made by the U. S. S. R. in agreed installments within five years of the date hereof. The determination of the amount and character of the industrial capital equipment unnecessary

for the German peace economy and therefore available for reparation shall be made by the Control Council under policies fixed by the Allied Commission on Reparations, with the participation of France, subject to the final approval of the Zone Commander in the Zone from which the equipment is to be removed.

7. Prior to the fixing of the total amount of equipment subject to removal, advance deliveries shall be made in respect to such equipment as will be determined to be eligible for delivery in accordance with the procedure set forth in the last sentence of paragraph 6.

8. The Soviet Government renounces all claims in respect of reparations to shares of German enterprises which are located in the Western Zones of Germany as well as to German foreign assets in all countries except those specified in paragraph 9 below.

9. The Governments of the U. K. and U. S. A. renounce all claims in respect of eparations to shares of German enterprises which are located in the Eastern Zone of occupation in Germany, as well as to German foreign assets in Bulgaria, Finland, Hungary, Rumania and Eastern Austria.

10. The Soviet Government makes no claims to gold captured by the Allied troops in Germany.

Note #4. The Morgenthau Plan

The Morgenthau Plan

Under the Morgenthau Plan, all German heavy industry would be destroyed. The Ruhr and adjacent areas would be internationalized and never again allowed to become an "*industrial area.*" All Germans in the Ruhr with industrial training or skills would be "*encouraged* "to leave the country forever. German plants and equipment, German labor and other assets would be given to the Soviet Union and other nations that were Germany's victims. There would be no reparations in the form of recurrent payments or goods, which would require the German economy to be rebuilt and ultimately give it a larger share of foreign markets than in the 1930s. The Allied armies' only involvement in the German economy should be to support their own military operations. Feeding, housing and clothing the Germans should be the burden of the German people.

Germany should be permanently dismembered. Under the Morgenthau Plan, East Prussia would be divided between the Soviet Union and Poland. France would receive the Saar and nearby lands. A northern German state would be organized around the old Prussia, Saxony and Thuringia. A southern state would include Bavaria, Wurtemberg and Baden.

All German schools, universities, radio stations and periodicals would be shut down until the Allies restructured them; all German aircraft, military uniforms, bands and parades would be banned. The Allies would draw up a list of "*arch-criminals of the war*," to be "*apprehended as soon as possible*" and "*put to death forthwith by firing squads.*"

According to the Morgenthau Plan, "*The Nazi regime is essentially the culmination of the unchanging German drive toward aggression.*" German society had been "*dominated for at least three generations by powerful forces fashoning the German state and nation into a machine for military conquest and self-aggrandizement.*" German industrial growth had "*immeasurably strengthened the economic base of German militarism without weakening the Prussian feudal ideology or its hold on German society .... What the Nazi regime has done has been to systematically debauch the passive German nation on an unprecedented scale and shape it into an organized and dehumanized military machine*". "*Therefore, German militarism cannot be destroyed by destroying Nazism alone.*"[59]

NOTE #5. SUBSEQUENT NÜRENBERG WAR CRIMESTRIALS (INTERNATIONAL MILITARY TRIBUNAL)

Lieutenant General Lucius D. Clay United States military governor of the US Zone of Occupation, and US delegate to the Allied Control Council had planned in 1947 to schedule only six more trials of German war criminals in Nürenberg, which was in the US Zone of Occupation. Control Council Law No.10, issued December 20, 1945, authorized military governments to try suspected war criminals in their respective zones of occupation. In all, however, there were twelve subsequent war crimes trials before the Nürenberg U.S.Military Courts.

The first trial on December 9,1946 involved 23 Nazi medical doctors accused of conducting medical experiments on prisoners, resulting in sixteen convicted including seven death sentences.

The second on January 2, 1947 charged German Field Marshal Erhard Milch with the murder and cruel treatment of POWs. He was convicted and sentenced to life imprisonment.

The third on March 1947 tried nine members of the Reich Ministry of Justice as well as members of the Nazi People's Courts charged with crimes against humanity; ten were convicted. (The movie, *Judgment at Nuremberg*, was based on this trial.)

In the fourth trial on April 8,1947, Oswald Pohl and two other concentration camp commanders received the death sentence, and the rest prison terms.

The fifth, the Flick trials on April 19,1947 accused leaders of major German industrial concerns of using slave and POW labor and plundering the private property of enemies of the Nazi regime; they were convicted and sentenced to various prison terms; three were acquitted.

The sixth on August, 27, 1947, the IG Farben (the major German chemical company) trials, charged 24 senior managers with looting private property in German occupied territories. Thirteen were found guilty and sentenced to prison.

The seventh trial on July 15, 1947 charged high officers of the *Wehrmacht* with murdering thousands of civilians in Greece, Yugoslavia and Albania, plus acts of destruction in Norway and ordering the murder of surrendering troops. Eight defendants, including Field Marshal List, were found guilty and sentenced to prison; two were acquitted.

In the eighth trial on October 20, 1947, 14 officers of the RUSHA (Reich Race and Resettlement Office) were charged with crimes against humanity, including the murder, deportation, and torture of prisoners on political, religious and racial grounds; 13 defendants were found guilty and received prison time.

The ninth trial on September 29, 1947, tried 24 leading members of the SS *Einsatzgruppen* (SS killing squads). Five death sentences were carried out, nine death sentences were commuted to life in prison; all the rest were also found guilty and imprisoned.

The tenth trial on December 8, 1947 charged the leading German industrialist, Alfred Krupp and 11 of his senior managers with using slave labor in their industries and plundering public and private property. On July 31,1948, Alfred Krupp received a 12-year prison sentence and ten others were sentenced to various years in prison. Krupp was released from prison in 1951 by the U.S. High Commissioner, John J. Mc Cloy.

The eleventh trial on January 6, 1948 involved 21 defendants of several Reich ministries, including the Foreign Office, and senior members of the Nazi Party. Nineteen were found guilty and sentenced to from four to 25 years in prison.

The last trial, from December 30, 1947 to October 28, 1948 was that of the *Wehrmacht* High Command. Fourteen senior *Wehrmacht* officers were tried, spanning the ranks from Field Marshal to Colonel General, including an Admiral. They were charged with having participated in or planned or facilitated the execution of numerous atrocities committed in the countries occupied by the German Army. Nine defendants received prison sentences, running from three years to life. One committed suicide.

With the establishment of the Federal Republic in May 1949, considerable pressure was placed on the U.S. High Commissioner, John J. Mc Cloy (successor to General Clay) to establish a panel to review these sentences particularly as there were then discussions on rearming Germany. This review panel in 1950 reduced the sentences of those *Wehrmacht* officers still in prison at that time, with the last being released in 1953.

There were also trials in late 1945, before U.S. Military Courts, of the commanders and staff of the Dachau and Buchenwald concentration camps. The commanders received the death sentence with prison for the guards.[60]

Of the 185 arrested and tried by the US military courts, 142 defendants were found guilty. Twenty four persons received death sentences of which 11 were subsequently commuted into life imprisonment; 20 were sentenced to life in prison. Ninety-eight received prison sentences of varying lengths. In 1951 a decree signed by U.S. High Commissioner, John J. Mc Cloy, reduced the longer prison terms substantially.

NOTE #6. THE DENAZIFICATION OF ALSACE

As in the purge of Nazis in the rest of France, in the Alsace, which had been incorporated into the *Reich* during the war, there were denunciations of collaboration with the Nazi government by neighbors, as well as by partisans of opposing political parties, (settlements of old accounts). In general, however, as in the French occupation zone of Germany, there was no mass arrest of former Nazis. The denazification process was not harsh because the French Government did not want to alienate a bi-cultural people. Indeed, it wanted to retain their loyalty to the French state. A majority of Alsatians, nonetheless, found the process somewhat less than gentle.

The denazification program was handled through the *Comités d'Epuration* , Cleansing Committees, in which individual cases were heard and those charged were sent to the courts or civil chambers. There were about 50 summary executions compared to 10,822 summary executions of collaborators in the rest of France.[61] Local justice and revenge accounted for some 300 incidents, with no more than 12 deaths among them. (These occurred prior to the establishment of the Cleansing Committees.) About 6,000 to 7,500 accused were interned in camps, but these were only transit camps (Struthof, Schirmeck) until the individuals were sent to their home towns for trial. Those charged included not only important Alsatian Nazis but also French volunteers in the *Waffen* SS (Division Charlemagne); and volunteer laborers in Germany.[62] The former *Gauleiter* (Nazi political governor) of the Alsace, Robert Wagner, was tried and condemned to death. He was executed on August 14, 1945.[63] Many of those French accused were not even from the Alsace.

Some 5,000 to 6,000 professionals, of whom about one-half were state employees, lost their jobs and/or pensions as a result of the purge. It was difficult, if not impossible, at that time to receive redress through the court system or professional organizations. Only beginning 1951/1952 did certain public employees regain their positions or receive their pensions again. The case was similar for private employees. This purge of professionals was generally considered the gravest injustice of the French denazification program.[64]

Punishment given by the courts was generally forced labor or prison time. There were 3,870 guilty verdicts among a population of 1,270,000 which included the Lorraine-Moselle region which had also been incorporated into the *Reich*. *Chambres Civiques*, Civil Chambers, which also functioned as local courts, tried and condemned a higher number than the Courts of Justice, 8,403.[65] In later years, many of the prison sentences were reduced by court processes or cancelled by presidential pardon.[66] At the time, the limited trials and light penalties of individuals in the Nazi security apparatus, SD and Gestapo and their collaborators caused general condemnation. Many of the leading members of those organizations were able to avoid trial altogether, by displaying a new patriotism for France. In many court cases, especially several years after war's end, guilty verdicts produced sentences of only three months. As also occurred in the French zone of occupation in Germany, some important Nazis avoided trial and only nominal party members were generally convicted.[67]

A further difficulty in coming to a just decision in the denazification trials was the case of many young German speaking Alsatians drafted into the *Wehrmacht* and near the end of the war even into the *Waffen* SS; the so-called, *malgre-nous* (in spite of ourselves). The latter included some 14 *Waffen* SS soldiers of Alsatian origin who participated in the massacre at Oradour sur Glane. They were charged in the famous Bordeaux trials in 1953, and were found guilty, but later amnestied by the French parliament as they had been forced to serve in the *Waffen* SS.

NOTES

1. Harold Marcuse, *Legacies of Dachau* (Cambridge, UK, 2001), 67.
2. Frederick Taylor, *Exorcising Hitler; The Occupation and Denazification of Germany*, 4–5.
3. Ibid., 96.
4. Perry Biddiscombe, *The Denazification of Germany: A History 1945–1950*, (Stroud, Gloucestershire, UK, 2007), 38–39, 40.
5. Michael Beschloss, *The Conquerors; Roosevelt, Truman and the Destruction of Hitler's Germany, 1941–1955*, (New York, 2002), 261,268.
6. Taylor, Exorcising *Hitler; The Occupation and Denazification of Germany*, 118.
7. Biddiscombe, *The Denazification of Germany: A History 1945–1950*, 37.
8. Ibid., 31.
9. Taylor, Exorcising *Hitler; The Occupation and Denazification of Germany*, 226, 236, 250.
10. Biddiscombe, *The Denazification of Germany: A History 1945–1950*, 58–59.
11. Ibid., 39.
12. Marcuse, *Legacies of Dachau*, 68–69.
13. Lutz Niethammer, "Alliierte Internierungslager in Deutschland nach 1945, Ein Vergleich und Offene," in *Sowjetische Speziallager in Deutschland 1945 bis 1950 Band I*, eds. Sergej Mironenko, Lutz Niethammer, and Alexander von Plato (Berlin: Akademie Verlag, 1998), 114.
14. Marcuse, *Legacies of Dachau*, 3, 69.
15. Edward N. Peterson, *The American Occupation of Germany :Retreat to Victory*, (Detroit, Michigan, 1978), 145.
16. Ibid.
17. Ibid.
18. Ibid., 146.
19. Taylor, Exorcising *Hitler; The Occupation and Denazification of Germany*, 264.
20. Niethammer, *Alliierte Internierungslager in Deutschland nach 1945, Ein Vergleich und Offene Fragen*, 107.
21. Peterson, *The American Occupation of Germany :Retreat to Victory*, 147.
22. Biddiscombe, *The Denazification of Germany: A History 1945–1950*, 85–86.

23. Taylor, *Exorcising Hitler; The Occupation and Denazification of Germany*, 300.
24. Biddiscombe, *The Denazification of Germany: A History 1945–1950*, 91.
25. Taylor, *Exorcising Hitler; The Occupation and Denazification of Germany*, 295.
26. Biddiscombe, *The Denazification of Germany: A History 1945–1950*, 91.
27. Niethammer, *Alliierte Internierungslager in Deutschland nach 1945, Ein Vergleich und Offene Fragen*, 107.
28. Biddiscombe, *The Denazification of Germany: A History 1945–1950*, 110, 115, 117.
29. Fritz Bringmann & Hartmut Roder, *Neuengamme,Verdrängt-Vergessen-Bewäitigt* (Hamburg, 1987), 34.
30. Biddiscombe, *The Denazification of Germany: A History 1945–1950*, 109, 115.
31. Giles, Macdonogh, *After the Reich: The Brutal History of the Allied Occupation* (New York, 2007), 414–415.
32. Bringmann & Roder, *Neuengamme,Verdrängt-Vergessen-Bewäitigt.* 38.
33. Heiner Wember, *Umerziehung im Lager, Internierung und Bestrafung von Nationalsozialisten in der Britischen Besatzungszone Deutschlands*, (Essen, Germany, Klartext Verlag, 1991), 171–172.
34. Macdonogh, *After the Reich: The Brutal History of the Allied Occupation*, 464.
35. Bringmann & Roder, *Neuengamme,Verdrängt-Vergessen-Bewäitigt*, 29.
36. Constantine FitzGibbon, *Denazification*, (New York, 1959), 103.
37. Biddiscombe, *The Denazification of Germany: A History 1945–1950*, 159.
38. Taylor, *Exorcising Hitler; The Occupation and Denazification of Germany*, 349.
39. Biddiscombe, *The Denazification of Germany: A History 1945–1950*, 159.
40. Taylor, *Exorcising Hitler; The Occupation and Denazification of Germany*, 316.
41. Biddiscombe, *The Denazification of Germany: A History 1945–1950*, 161.
42. Ibid., 172.
43. Ibid., 159.
44. Ibid., 166–167, 168.
45. Ibid., 172.
46. Ibid., 178–179.
47. Niethammer, *Alliierte Internierungslager in Deutschland nach 1945, Ein Vergleich und Offene Fragen*, 107.
48. Biddiscombe, *The Denazification of Germany: A History 1945–1950*, 172.

49. Ibid., 181–182.
50. Niethammer, *Alliierte Internierungslager in Deutschland nach 1945, Ein Vergleich und Offene Fragen* , 99, 102–104.
51. Niethammer, *Alliierte Internierungslager in Deutschland nach 1945, Ein Vergleich und Offene Fragen*, 99.
52. Biddiscombe, *The Denazification of Germany: A History 1945–1950*, 128.
53. Niethammer, *Alliierte Internierungslager in Deutschland nach 1945, Ein Vergleich und Offene Fragen*, 99.
54. Ibid., 104–105.
55. Bringmann & Roder, *Neuengamme,Verdrängt-Vergessen-Bewäitigt*, 37.
56. Ibid., 106–107.
57. Ibid., 114–115.
58. Biddiscombe, *The Denazification of Germany: A History 1945–1950*, 215.
59. Beschloss, *The Conquerors; Roosevelt, Truman and the Destruction of Hitler's Germany, 1941–1955*, 116–117.
60. Macdonogh, *After the Reich: The Brutal History of the Allied Occupation*, 461.
61. Jean-Laurant Vonau, *L'Epuration en Alsace*, (Strasbourg, France, 2005), 168.
62. Ibid., 169.
63. Ibid., 120.
64. Ibid., 171.
65. Ibid., 171–172
66. Ibid., 177.
67. Ibid., 173–174.

CHAPTER 3

DENAZIFICATION IN THE SOVIET ZONE OF OCCUPATION

> Historical experience shows that Hitlers come and go, but the
> German nation and the German state remain.
>> Source: J.V. Stalin's Order of the Day, No. 55, February 23,
>> 1942. (It was given extensive publicity in the Soviet Zone of
>> Occupation right after the war to assure the German people that
>> the intention of the SovietUnion was to preserve the German
>> nation and state.)

SOVIET OBJECTIVES IN THEIR OCCUPATION ZONE

Even though the Soviet Union, as signatory to the Yalta and Potsdam
Agreements, committed itself to a democratic and peaceful Germany,
their interpretation of "democracy" was quite different from that of the
Western Allies. It became rapidly clear to the West that the Soviets
intended to install a communist state, a Soviet satellite such as Poland
or Czechoslovakia, in their zone of occupation. "Anti-fascist" became
the definition of democracy and being "democratic" took on communist
forms. This also meant that from the very beginning of their occupation,

the Soviets took control of all strategic levers of power in their zone. The enemy at that time were the large landholders, capitalists, and *Junkers,* (landed aristocracy), representing the Prussian Military tradition. But this definition of the enemy rapidly shifted to the democratic middle class political parties and the workers' social democratic party. These, in turn, became the principal critics and later the major opponents of the new communist system.

Because the Soviet Union was devastated by the Nazi German army, at the Yalta Conference of Allied Leaders, the Soviets set forth claims for reparations of $10 billion, as well as access to the Ruhr's heavy industry production, coal fields, and German technology. This required dismantling plants for transfer to the Soviet Union as well as shipping all output of those not dismantled to Russia.

Although some reparations from the Western zones of occupation were allocated to the Soviet Union by the Potsdam Agreement, by 1946 they had ceased with the onset of the "cold war;" $22.3 million in reparations were taken from the Western Zones, which is minimal compared to the approximately $10 billion which the Soviets took from their own zone in the period of 1945–1950. According to Soviet records, from 1945–1948, reparations included these: $801.million from East Germany, in the form of factories, production, and raw materials; $566.million from Soviet owned corporations (SAG)—many industries especially heavy industry in East Germany were confiscated and managed by the Soviets as stock companies; $603.4 million from current production; $355.4 million from German owned property outside of Germany; $127.4 million in German transport equipment; and $200 million in German patents.[1]

One further Soviet justification for the dismantling of German industry was to prevent Germany from ever making war against the Soviet Union again. This entailed the demilitarization of the country, the decartelization of industry, and the denazification of public administration; all were aims shared by the Western Allies. The Soviets, however, went beyond the objectives of the West when they insisted that Germany, in their zone of occupation, required a land reform and the expropriation of industry in order to destroy the power of the *Junker* landowners and industrial elite who were responsible, according to the Soviets, for creating the Nazi German regime and making its war machine possible.[2]

The rapid Soviet control of all facets of public life in their zone of occupation was facilitated by these two factors:

The first was when the Red Army initially appeared in Eastern Germany, in early 1945, former members of the KPD (Communist Party of Germany), many recently released from concentration camps, volunteered their services to the Soviets. Many then assumed leadership positions in zonal administration. They were knowledgeable about local conditions, they were disciplined, and above all they were committed to building a Communist system in Germany—the same aims as they had before 1933.[3]

The second was that besides taking political control of their zone of occupation and planning for a future German communist government, the Soviets also relied heavily on German Communists who were in exile in Moscow during the Hitler period. In the summer of 1943, the Soviets established the National Committee for a Free Germany (NKFD) composed of leading German Communist exiles as well as the Union of German Officers, initially created with German army officers who were captured at the battle of Stalingrad. These were to be used in case the Third Reich attempted to make a separate peace with the Soviet Union or if the *Wehrmacht* overthrew Hitler.[4]

Of the two, of greater importance was the Soviet Communist Party's use of German Communists, grouped in the National Committee for a Free Germany, in order to create a German shadow government under the tutelage of Giorgi Dimitrov, General Secretary of the Communist International, Comintern. The most important were Walter Ulbricht, later first secretary of the SED (Socialist Unity Party of Germany); Wilhelm Pieck, first President of the GDR (German Democratic Republic); and Anton Ackermann, member of the SED politburo and briefly Minister of

Foreign Affairs of the GDR. Ulbricht and a group of nine other important German communists landed outside Berlin at the end of April, days before the end of the war, in order to build a new German anti-fascist regime in the Soviet zone. At that time Ulbricht said, *"Es muss demokratisch aussehen, aber wir müssen alles in der Hand haben."* (It must look democratic, but we have to control everything).[5]

His strategy was to permit the existence of individual political parties, including the democratic middle class (CDU–Christian Democratic Party and FDP–Free Democratic Party, liberals) and the workers' party (SPD–Social Democratic Party), but grouped them all together in an "anti-fascist democratic block." This aimed to prevent the parties from operating independently, a move to permit the German communists to seize political control.[6] In the summer of 1945, the KPD (Communist Party of Germany) was re-established, lasting until April 21, 1946, when the Social Democratic Party (SPD) was forced to merge with it, as a result of pressure from SVAG (Soviet Military Administration in Germany), Ulbricht, and the cadre of the KPD, forming the SED (Socialist Unity Party). The SED then held a monopoly of power in East Germany (until the collapse of the GDR in 1989) with the middle class parties functioning as a "democratic" façade. The formation of the SED was essentially an anti-Social Democratic Party maneuver by the German communists to prevent the SPD from increasing its support in the Soviet zone of occupation. (See note #1 for the history of the formation of the SED.)

When the KPD was re-established in the summer of 1945, Ulbricht issued the following manifesto, clearly stating the communist party's objectives at that time. It must be noted, however, that it still followed the principle of an "anti-fascist democratic block" which was discarded by the formation of the SED, about one year later.

> *"Simultaneously, with the destruction of Hitlerism, we must also carry through to completion the tasks of democratizing Germany and of transforming the bourgeois democratic system, which was begun in 1848; and we must completely eradicate the remains of feudalism*

and destroy the tradition of reactionary Prussian militarism, with all its economic and political accretions. We take the view that the method of imposing the Soviet system on Germany would be wrong, since this method does not correspond to present-day conditions of development in Germany. We take the view rather that the overriding interests of the German people in their present-day situation prescribe a different method for Germany, namely the method of establishing a democratic anti-fascist regime, a parliamentary democratic republic with full democratic rights and liberties for the people." [7]

THE DENAZIFICATION PROCESS IN THE SOVIET ZONE OF OCCUPATION

In the Soviet zone, denazification was subordinated to political control and the construction of a Communist system. The Soviets repeatedly stated that they were not interested in those who had been merely members of the Nazi Party, but only those who were active, high ranking Nazis, or if they were guilty of war crimes or had contributed to criminal Nazi policies.[8] Their stated aim was to purge the civil service, commerce and industry, and society in general of Nazis, just as it was in the Western Zones of Occupation.

Despite these aims, in many locations in their zone, the Soviets kept Nazis in place because they needed their administrative and technical knowledge. Some former SS and SA members were even able to find jobs in local police forces. Former Nazis were particularly abundant in the fields of economic administration, justice, and education.[9] One Russian in the SVAG justified this practice by noting that the Soviets would hardly be influenced by Nazi ideology, saying, *"We used the brains of Nazis as much as possible."* [10]

At the beginning of their occupation, the Soviet military government made it a policy to hire many KPD veterans. However, many of these German Communists were reported to be unhappy about the policies established by Ulbricht, giving more emphasis to an efficient and well-functioning administration than to revolutionary politics. One complained of his difficulty dealing with non-communists or even former Nazis who were assigned to important positions by SVAG. Another, who was in SVAG interior administration, complained to the Soviet military head that except for the few Communists in charge, the majority were all former military specialists of the *Wehrmacht*. It also occurred that SVAG employees, previously in the German army, found jobs for their friends who were also formerly in the army or Nazi party which, of course, created a great deal of friction with KPD members.[11]

When the CC Directive #24 was approved on January 12, 1946, requiring that Nazi party members be fired from all public offices, that action created a heavy burden for Soviet military administration. The Soviets did not have a plan to deal with individual Nazis such as the US Army's JCS 1067. SVAG was now forced to develop a formal denazification program. On October 30, 1945, Order #124 confiscated all Nazi held property, government or private, totaling 890 seizures.[12] On December 23, 1945, SVAG issued Order #128 which instructed all state and county provincial officials to assist Allied military tribunals in the prosecution of German war criminals. This marked the launch of the Soviet denazification program during the winter of 1945/1946, and by early 1946, more than 300,000 former Nazis had been released from state and county government offices. Those individuals who were in the "compulsory dismissal" categories in CC Directive #38 had to be dismissed by February 29, 1947.[13]

Furthermore, in December 1946, the Soviets ordered the formation of county-wide denazification commissions, i.e. "Commissions for the implementation of CC Directive #24," *Ausschüsse zur Durchführung des Direktive #24*. Their chief duty was to place charged Nazis into the various categories of CC Directive #38. These were essentially political courts with no defense counsel or prosecutors, though oral as well as written statements from witnesses were permitted. Testimonies from "anti-fascists" held special weight, and "Certificates of Harmlessness," issued by Anti-Fascist Committees in 1946/1947, were especially sought after by "nominal" Nazis. When the denazification commissions judged party members as "nominal," their employment could continue at the discretion of the commission. Anything greater than "nominal" resulted in instant loss of jobs. Such active Nazis could no longer earn a living and had to survive as best as they could. About 70%–80% of hearings resulted in the designation of "nominal" Nazi.[14]

German employees of three essential sectors of the East German economy—coal mining, the national railways, and the post office—were exempted from district commission hearings. They were allowed to develop their own denazification commissions, which allowed them to do a self-vetting process. These three industries were considered by the Soviets too important to the maintenance and rebuilding of the Zonal economy to be subjected to interference by other government bodies.[15]

According to Soviet denazification orders, all Nazis should have been removed from public administration by the end of 1945. But this was not always the case. For example, in the national railways, the SVAG transport administration admitted to the presence of many Nazis in positions of responsibility and it was charged that they were even harboring saboteurs. SVAG officers admitted that they had permitted so many exemptions from the denazification process that these became the rule, and all because they were overwhelmed with the requirements of reconstruction work.[16]

This problem also persisted in factory administration. The SED protested to SVAG about the continuing presence there of former Nazis. Thus, on August 16,1947, Order #201 was issued, establishing procedures for removing remaining former, active Nazis from positions of responsibility in German public administration and industry. But this order was also ignored, particularly by directors of Soviet owned corporations (SAG), because it jeopardized their production norms. Therefore, Marshal Sokolovskii, Soviet Military Governor of the Soviet occupation zone, issued a new directive on October 9,1947, insisting that former Nazis be removed from all Soviet-owned corporations (SAG), and complaining that the directors were doing too little to purge their companies of these subversive elements. The Soviet Ministry of State Security, MGB, then became involved with former Nazis in these state corporations. In the *Sachsenwerke*, a large state industry near Dresden, for example, the MGB ascertained that of 1,800 workers, 201 were former Nazis, of whom 41 held important positions. The Soviet security service blamed the presence of the many Nazis in key jobs to the increase of reported acts of sabotage in state industry. They stated that *"the organs of the MGB in Germany have uncovered the attempts of former Nazis and other hostile elements....to destroy the work of the factories of the Soviet stock companies. MGB organs in Germany will step up their Chekist (secret police) work in the SAGs."* [17]

Despite these admonitions from SVAG, it became clear to the Soviets that, in past years, contradictory instructions and unrealistic deadlines on how to proceed with the denazification process had made the reconstruction process much more complicated, causing serious delays. SVAG, therefore, decided that all remaining former Nazis could continue in their present functions, although none should be retained in leading positions, and former Nazi technical experts could now be hired. Those Nazis, however, who had been fired, as a part of the denazification process, could not be rehired. [18]

At this point, Stalin was fed up with the slow pace and complications resulting from denazification in the Russian zone, especially as he was afraid that Soviet policy was forcing "nominal" Nazis into the hands of the Western Allies. In January 1946, he met with future leaders of the SED, telling them to lighten the pressure on such former party members, as many were "good patriots and well-meaning workers." In fact, he suggested that they could even form their own right wing political party, which he suggested be called National Democratic Party. Despite the fact that it would only be a "front" organization without authority, the reaction of the SED directors was negative, particularly as they had always insisted that the Western denazification process fostered the revival of right-wing German nationalism. As a result, Stalin discarded this idea. [19]

As another example of Soviet leniency toward former Nazis, Moscow turned down Ulbricht's request to start a judicial process against Martin Mutschmann, the former *Gauleiter* (Nazi leader) of Saxony, in order to publicize the horrors of Fascism to doubting Germans. The Soviets argued that Mutschmann was too old and sick to be tried. But the real reason was that the Soviets did not think it would be good politics in the zone to stage Nazi show trials, as it could alienate too many people.[20]

Order #201 also stated that the denazification program had to end by the end of 1947, but it was only officially completed on February 16, 1948 by Order #35.[21] In the process, more than 500,000 ex-Nazis lost their jobs temporarily and could only be employed for menial work; out of a population of 18 million, these were about 2.7%. Between 1945 and 1948, nominal Nazis could always be rehabilitated, especially if they accepted the new political and social systems and if their knowledge was needed for the Soviet zone economy.[22] By the end of this period, 75% of all former Nazi government employees, including those in the provinces, remained in their jobs or returned to them.[23] Overall, the Soviet denazification program could be considered as the least severe of those of the four Allied powers, with perhaps the United States having had the most thorough program. (For the presence of former Nazis in the SED, please see Note #2.)

NOTE #1 THE CREATION OF THE SED, *SOZIALISTISCHE EINHEITSPARTEI DEUTSCHLANDS* (SOCIALIST UNITY PARTY OF GERMANY).

In late 1945, the Soviet Military Administration and the KPD saw, with alarm, the increasing strength of the SPD and the lack of popular support for the KPD. The head of the SPD, Kurt Schumacher, was a strong leader of the German Socialists and an adversary of the KPD in East Germany. The SPD had a larger following among East German workers and their unions than the KPD; for all these reasons, the Soviets and KPD leadership, especially Ulbricht and Pieck, considered it necessary to eliminate the SPD from the political scene. The Socialists had become the most serious domestic threat to Soviet rule in their zone of occupation.[24]

Additionally, as the KPD and Soviets realized that the Communist Party could not win an election by itself, the Soviets and the KPD leadership devised a plan to force a merger of the two parties. They thought this would offer a double benefit: the elimination of the SPD threat in East Germany, as well as the formation of a winning combination for elections in the Soviet zone.

The head of the SPD in the Soviet zone, Otto Grotewohl, and its membership, were opposed to the merger, not only for ideological reasons, but for the obvious fear of losing their identity and freedom of action. Considerable pressure was placed on Grotewohl, including measures to co-opt him by offering him attractive benefits from the Soviet Military Administration, including some even from Marshal Zhukov personally. The communists argued that only through the unity of the working class could a "German road to socialism" be achieved.[25]

SPD leaders and its members suffered great pressures, especially from acts of harassment. Those who publicly opposed this unification were turned over to Soviet military tribunals for alleged crimes against the Soviet occupation authorities and then sentenced to the special camps.[26] The SPD also complained about the unequal treatment their members received from the Soviet Military administration, compared to the favors shown to KPD members. The communists assured them that this would not happen in the merged party.

In a meeting between Marshal Zhukov and Grotewohl in February 1946, the Marshal urged Grotewohl to merge with the Communist Party, promising that the Military Administration would ensure the improvement of conditions in the zone and that the Soviet troop level would even be reduced. Moreover, Zhukov made it clear to Grotewohl that he really had little choice in the matter.[27]

The Soviets and KPD introduced tactics of beginning the mergers first at the local, next at the state, and then ending at the national level with the election of a united leadership. Intimidation and threats were used on the local and state SPD leadership. Recalcitrant SPD members were threatened with loss of administrative jobs and privileges, as well as cuts in their rations.[28] The first SPD/KPD merger was announced in the province of Thüringen on April 6, 1946.[29] Due to their isolation from the SPD in the West, many SPD leaders reluctantly acceded to this merger, arguing that not to do so would eliminate all possibility of influencing political developments in the Soviet zone.

On February 11, 1946, the Central Executive of the SPD in the eastern zone approved the merger. Wilhelm Pieck gave his approval for a referendum of the Berlin SPD members to be held on March 31, to approve this merger, without first consulting the Soviet military authorities. They were furious, and the referendum was never held in the Eastern Sector of Berlin. In the vote in the Western Sectors, the merger was overwhelmingly defeated, and the SPD in the Western Sectors never joined the SED. On April 21, 1946, the two parties, led by their respective leaders, Grotewohl and Pieck, formally signed the merger agreement.[30] Theoretically, there was a parity of power between the two parties, until July 1948 when the Communists dominated, a "party of the new type" based on the scientific principles of Marxism-Leninism."[31] Otto Grotewohl became the first Prime Minister of the German Democratic Republic (GDR) when it was established on October 7, 1949. He then became Chairman of the Council of Ministers, a position which he held until his death in 1964. Real power, however, was always maintained by Walter Ulbricht as General Secretary of the Central Committee of the SED.

Note #2 Nazis in the *Sozialistische Einheitspartei Deutschlands* (Socialist Unity Party of Germany)

In a speech in the town of Halle on January 11, 1946, Wilhem Pieck, one of the founders of the SED, and later President of the German Democratic

Republic, stated that it was time to bring the nominal Nazis, who were not liable for human rights abuses or war crimes into society to help them become responsible members of the state.[32] On June 29, 1946, the leadership of the SED then issued a resolution to this effect. All former Nazi party members who were not guilty of war crimes and who were active workers in the new democratic order should have their citizenship rights returned to them.[33]

In October 1952, the GDR congress, passed a law entitled "The Curtailment of Citizen Rights of Former Officers of the *Wehrmacht* and Former Members and Followers of the Nazi Party," who were still subject to these restrictions. According to this law, they received back their full civil and political rights, provided they had not committed any war crimes.[34]

An academic research document, originally published in 1954, stated that at the beginning of the 1950s, 106,377 former Nazis were members of the SED; in addition, 74,223 were part of the Nazi party cadre; and 149,986 were former members of the Hitler Youth and BDM. Based on a total SED membership at that time of 1,256,002, former Nazi party members alone comprised 8.5% ; counting Nazis formerly in affiliated Nazi organizations, that was 25% of the total membership.[35]

On the other hand, according to GDR statistics from 1953, 13,000 leaders of SED organizations had Nazi backgrounds and over 10,000 were members of the Nazi party or affiliated organizations. As for the general SED membership, 15% were former members of the Nazi party. In1958, the People's Parliament even contained 58 former members of the Nazi party.[36]

NOTES

1. Norman M. Naimark, *The Russians in Germany: A History of the Soviet Zone of Occupation, 1945–1949*, (Cambridge, Massachusetts, 1995), 168–169.
2. Ibid., 10.
3. Frederick Taylor, *Exorcising Hitler: The Occupation and Denazification of Germany*, (New York, 2011), 97.
4. Naimark, *The Russians in Germany: A History of the Soviet Zone of Occupation, 1945–1949*, 10.
5. Uwe Greve, *Lager des Grauens:Sowjetische KZ in der DDR nach 1945*, (Kiel,Germany,1990), 70–71.
6. Naimark, *The Russians in Germany: A History of the Soviet Zone of Occupation, 1945–1949*, 10.
7. Wolfgang Leonhard, *Child of the Revolution*, (Chicago, Illinois, 1958), 414.
8. Constantine FitzGibbon, *Denazification*, (New York,1969), 201.
9. Naimark, *The Russians in Germany: A History of the Soviet Zone of Occupation, 1945–1949*, 406.
10. Perry Biddiscombe, *The Denazification of Germany: A History 1945–1950*, (Stroud, Gloucestershire,UK, 2007), 128.
11. Naimark, *The Russians in Germany: A History of the Soviet Zone of Occupation, 1945–1949*, 44.
12. Biddiscombe, *The Denazification of Germany: A History 1945–1950*, 138.
13. Ibid., 141.
14. Ibid., 151.
15. Ibid., 147.
16. Ibid., 133.
17. Naimark, *The Russians in Germany: A History of the Soviet Zone of Occupation, 1945–1949*, 192–193.
18. Biddiscombe, *The Denazification of Germany: A History 1945–1950*, 134.
19. Ibid., 143.
20. Naimark, *The Russians in Germany: A History of the Soviet Zone of Occupation, 1945–1949*, 287, 288.
21. FitzGibbon, *Denazification*, 202.
22. Taylor, *Exorcising Hitler: The Occupation and Denazification of Germany*, 330.
23. Biddiscombe, *The Denazification of Germany: A History 1945–1950*, 152.

24. Naimark, *The Russians in Germany: A History of the Soviet Zone of Occupation, 1945–1949*, 276.

25. Ibid., 278.

26. Ibid., 279.

27. Ibid., 281.

28. Ibid.

29. Ibid.

30. Ibid., 282–283.

31. Naimark, *The Russians in Germany: A History of the Soviet Zone of Occupation, 1945–1949*, 387.

32. Jürgen Danyel, "Zwischen Repression und Toleranz: Die Politik der SED zur politischen Integration der ehemaligen NSDAP-Mitglieder in der SBZ/DDR," in *Die Sowjetischen Speziallager in der gesellschaftlichen Wahrnehmung, 1945 bis heute*, eds. Petra Haustein, Annette Kaminsky, Volkhard Knigge, and Bodo Rischer (Göttingen, Wallstein:Verlag, 2006), 224.

33. Ibid., 225.

34. Ibid., 227.

35. Ibid., 236 .

36. Ronny Kabus, *In der Gewalt Stalins und der SED,* (Norderstedt, Germany, 2011), 78.

CHAPTER 4

SECURITY ORGANIZATION IN THE SOVIET ZONE OF OCCUPATION

"Let our enemies know that anyone who attempts to raise a hand against the will of our people, against the will of the party of Lenin and Stalin, will be mercilessly crushed and destroyed."
Lavrentiy P. Beria, Member of the Politburo and Soviet Minister of Internal Affairs, Head of the NKVD

NKVD ANTI-TERRORIST ACTIONS BEHIND THE RED ARMY FRONTS AT THE END OF THE WAR

At the beginning of 1945, as the Red Army was rolling through Western Poland and Eastern Germany, the MVD (the Ministry of Internal Affairs) and its operating security organization, the NKVD (People's Commissariat for Internal Affairs) both headed by Lavrentiy P. Beria, were ordered to rid the conquered territories behind each Red Army Front of enemy elements through arrests and executions; to register Germans for the purpose of conscripting German civilians capable of working as forced labor in the Soviet Union and eventually to cleanse these areas of their

German inhabitants. The NKVD had its own troops and received the assignment of protecting the rear areas of the advancing Red Army. The NKVD designated about 35,000 of its men to this task.[1]

(Refer to http://www.thegulagineastgermany.com for Illustration #7. Lavrentiy P. Beria, Head of the Ministry of Internal Affairs, of the MVD, of the NKVD, and Marshal of the Soviet Union. After the death of Stalin in 1953, he became First Deputy Chairman of the Council of Ministers of the Soviet Union and Deputy Premier. On June 26, 1953, he was arrested by his fellow Politburo members and executed on December 23, 1953. Source: Wikimedia Commons)

The NKVD safeguarded the rear areas of the Soviet Army groups from scattered *Wehrmacht* units or other enemies, such as the Polish Home Army or the anti-Soviet Ukrainian nationalists. Above all, it was to prevent the formation of guerilla forces which could attack the rear formations of the Red Army, as had been the case with the Red partisan bands operating behind the *Wehrmacht* front. It was also given the task of preventing the retreat of Soviet soldiers, especially in the early years of the war.[2]

In order to fulfill this mandate, the NKVD issued order #0016 of January 11, 1945, "Regarding Measures to Cleanse the Rear Areas of the Red Army of Enemy Elements." This order empowered NKVD members to arrest and intern people deemed enemies of the Soviet state.

> *NKVD officers empowered to operate behind the Army front, have the obligation, in accordance with the advance of the Red Army in the territory freed of enemy troops, to undertake the necessary Chekist ("energetic revolutionary measures"-see Note #1 on the Cheka) measures to cleanse the area of spies and opponents belonging to the Nazi German secret services, of terrorists, and members of various enemy organizations and groups, bandits and rebels. The following categories must be arrested: leaders and personnel of the police, senior officers of prisons and concentration camps, military commanders, court prosecutors and investigators, members of military courts, civilian leaders of regions and counties, town mayors,*

members of fascist organizations, managers of large companies and administrators, newspaper editors, authors of anti-Soviet publications, commanders, and members of armies who fought against the USSR and members of the Russian Army of Liberation (General Andrey Vlasov, ally of Nazi Germany) as well as any other suspicious persons.

On January 15, 1945, the anti-terrorist drive began. The head of military counter-intelligence, SMERSH, Viktor Abakumov, reported the following:

Six Operations Groups were formed in each military front who undertook the Chekist work. Each group has a leader, two deputies, 20 operations men, and two translators. Each group is subordinated to an NKVD regiment. As a reserve for special operations, an additional operations group from NKVD units was formed. The entire organization of Operations Groups and their personnel were carefully trained and charged with discovering and arresting spies, terrorists, bandits, and revolutionaries as well as members of the Nazi secret service and police, along with adherents of any other fascist-Nazi organizations and all suspicious persons. They were also to locate arms dumps and radio stations left behind by the enemy and confiscate technical material. The Operations Groups were especially instructed to pursue these operations in cities, large towns, railway centers and industries. On January 16, 1945, the Operations Groups with their NKVD troops left for their assigned fronts. Ten trucks were assigned to each Operations Group to transport prisoners and to serve their own needs. A prison has already been established for those arrested in East Prussia.[3]

When the Red Army entered Germany in January 1945, three Soviet security organizations arrived with it.

-SMERSH – Soviet Military Counter-intelligence, under Viktor Abakumov, reported directly to Stalin. Its primary objective was to find traitors in the Red Army as well as enemy spies. The Soviet Navy had a similar organization.

-NKGB –People's Commissariat of State Security was the secret political police and reported to the MGB, Ministry of State Security.

Viktor Abakumov became Minister of State Security in 1946 and
remained so until 1951. After the death of Stalin in 1953, he was
executed for treason on December 19, 1954.

-NKVD-People's Commissariat for Internal Affairs, a part of the
MVD, Ministry of Internal Affairs, headed by L.P. Beria, was
responsible for prisoner of war camps, the Main Camp Administration GULAG, the Soviet Militia, and the NKVD troops.[4]

There was certainly an overlapping of responsibilities and operations,
but Stalin always approved of competition among the various security
organizations.[5]

The NKVD/Operations Groups' anti-terrorist drive turned up very
few Nazi terrorist groups or activity. Most of those arrested were minor
Nazis. The main objective of the operation now became the deportation
of German labor to the Soviet Union under the guise of securing the
hinterland. (Soviet leaders did not wish to have these workers counted
by the Western Allies as German reparations.[6]) Beria, Serov (Colonel
General Ivan Serov was Deputy Commissar of the NKVD), and Abakumov
were nonetheless pleased with the results of the operation in securing
the fronts behind the Red Army in Germany. This situation was quite
different from Poland, Lithuania, the Ukraine, and Byelorussia where anti
Soviet partisan wars arose in the wake of the Red Army's occupation.[7]

The deportation of Germans started already in late 1944, when the
Red Army penetrated the Balkans, even before the Three Power Yalta
Agreements authorized the use of German forced labor. (See End Note #2
for an overview of the deportation of ethnic German civilians to the Soviet
Union from the Balkans.) Arrests included men, women, and sometimes
even children and the elderly who were literally herded together and sent
to transit camps. They were mostly ethnic Germans from Eastern Europe
attempting to escape from the Red Army. The Soviets also deported
Reich Germans from East Prussia, Pomerania, eastern Brandenburg, and
Silesia, all scenes of vicious battles as the war neared its end. The latter

territories were ceded to Poland by the Allies after the war. (See Map #4 for German post-war territorial loss below.)

At the February1945 Yalta meeting, Stalin received the agreement of Roosevelt and Churchill for the Soviet Union's conscription of German workers for reconstruction work as a part of Soviet post-war reparations claims on Germany.

(Refer to http://www.thegulagineastgermany.com. for Map# 4. Postwar German Territorial Loss in the East (Source: Wikimedia Commons). Citation:Map by User Adam Carr, August 2006.http://en.wikipedia.org/wiki/File:Oder-neisse.gif)

Those German civilians arrested behind the fronts of the Red Army were subject to various resolutions of the State Defense Committee of the USSR, for mobilizing all civilians capable of labor for service in the USSR, including the use of interned Germans in Soviet industry. These included all men from the ages of 17 to 50 and women from 18–30.[8] Such mobilization efforts appeared to have been more important than the punishment of Nazis or the Soviet denazification process.[9]

A further directive of the State Defense Committee of February 3, 1945 authorized the NKVD to "Stop Terrorist Attacks and Expand the Mobilization of Germans."

> The NKVD will act. . . by means of a pitiless on site liquidation of individuals who committed terrorist attacks or were involved in acts of opposition.
>
> In the sectors of the army fronts mentioned in these instructions, all German men capable of work or of bearing arms, aged 17 to 50 are to be mobilized. Those Germans who were determined to be members of the German army, including the Volksturm, are to be treated as prisoners of war and sent to NKVD prisoner of war camps. . . . the commanders of the Army Fronts are required, in the name of the Front High Command, to issue the necessary instructions for the mobilization of Germans and together with empowered NKVD officers, ensure that they meet all required measures for the

organization of collection camps, the reporting of the mobilized persons to these collection camps, and their secure transport to the places determined by the NKVD.[10]

In a letter dated April 17, 1945, to Stalin, Beria requested that the categories of individuals subject to arrest and mobilization for work be increased and that German civilians no longer be deported for work in Russia. Stalin approved the edict and it resulted in Order #00315 of April 18, stating who was to be arrested.

An investigation conducted by the NKVD, showed that among those (Germans) arrested, a great number are nominal members of Fascist organizations, (unions, workers organizations, youth organizations). The capture of these individuals was dictated, at that time, by the need for the rapid cleansing of the areas behind the front lines of enemy forces. It is determined that of the prisoners sent to the NKVD camps, only one half are capable of hard labor because the other half consists of old people and those incapable of hard labor. Up to now, only 25,000 persons have been sent to the coal mines, heavy industry, mining peat fields for the electric industry, and construction sites.

I request your agreement to the following NKVD order.
Peoples' Commissar for Internal Affairs, L. Beria

Order #00315

In the future, advance of troops of the Red Army, on the territory liberated from the enemy, and in carrying out Chekist measures to cleanse the territory behind the front of the fighting troops of the Red Army, NKVD officers have the authority to arrest the following enemy categories:

1. Spies, agents, and terrorists of the Nazi German Secret Service.

2. Members of armed groups who could create resistance in the rear of the Red Army.

3. Operators of illegal radio transmitters, arms depots, and printing shops.

4. Active members of the Nazi party.

5. Hitler Youth and BDM leaders down to the community level.

6. Members of the Gestapo and other Nazi security organizations. Leaders of German government administrations down to the community level and editors of newspapers and magazines and authors of anti-Soviet publications.

7. Other dispositions: Individuals who carried out terrorist or rebellious activities are to be liquidated on the spot.

All military officers and non-commissioned officers of the Wehrmacht, Volksturm, SS and SA, and personnel of prisons, concentration camps, military lawyers, and tribunals are to be sent to NKVD prisoner of war camps.

Members of the Russian Army of Liberations are to be sent to NKVD filtration camps (special camps set up to purge members of this military unit. The soldiers were usually sent to the Gulag camps, and the leading officers, including General Vlasov, were hanged).

In the process of cleansing the rear areas behind the fighting troops of the Red Army, German civilians arrested are no longer to be deported to the Soviet Union. Special NKVD permission is required for any German technical specialist to be sent to the USSR.

In order to house the arrested individuals, the NKVD is responsible for establishing camps and prisons. In order to guard these prisoners, the designated NKVD officers are authorized to employ NKVD troops.

The authorized NKVD officers have the responsibility to review the underlying documents of all arrested persons. Invalids, sick and infirm individuals incapable of work, people over 65 years of age, and women are all to be set free, unless they have been arrested under the first point.

All others arrested, if they are in capable physical condition, are to be sent to work in industry. The elderly, invalids, and those incapable of work are to be released to their most recent location of residence."

Peoples' Commissar for Internal Affairs, L. Beria[11]

Concerning the arrest of Nazis, Beria in the same letter to Stalin, of April 17, 1945, criticized the then current practice of arresting Nazis. He wrote, *"A large number of simple members of various Fascist organizations were arreste*d," implying that it was a wasted effort. He named the Nazi labor unions, *Deutsche Arbeitsfront* and *Reichsarbeitsdienst, RAD,* (obligatory government work program for youths) and youth groups, such as HJ and BDM. The arrest of these individuals was required, nevertheless, to bring about the rapid cleansing of enemy elements behind the fronts.[12]

To accommodate those arrested, the NKVD constructed collection camps and prisons from late 1944 to early 1945 behind the fronts of the 1st, 2nd, and 3rd Red Army's Belorussian Front, and behind the 1st and 4th Red Army's Ukrainian Front. (See Note #3 indicating the different locations of the individual camps for German civilians.) These camps had several functions, one of which was to mobilize German civilians for deportation to the Soviet Union for forced labor. The second was to hold arrested German civilians for forced labor in the Soviet/Polish occupied former German areas. The third was to gather prisoners of war from the remnants of the German Army. Deportations reached their climax in March 1945.[13] According to German and Soviet sources, 370,000 German civilians were arrested by the NKVD and placed in transit camps while 280,000 were deported to the Soviet Union for forced labor in the period up to April 17, 1945. Of these, it is estimated that 90,000 died or disappeared.[14]

This policy of arresting and deporting German civilians for forced labor in the Soviet Union ended on April 17, 1945, with the end of the war and the surrender of Germany. Beria then began to liquidate the camps in the East as there was no longer a security threat in the rear of the Red Army units. Another significant reason for ending the deportation of German labor to the Soviet Union was that about one-half of those deported were incapable of work due to their weakened and sick condition.[15] All members of the Nazi para-military and security organizations, SA, SS, *Waffen SS,* and *Volksturm* who were in the transit camps were sent to the prisoner of war camps where they were then destined for labor in the USSR.[16] The elderly, children, and those who were neither capable of work nor of any danger politically were released to the reception camp at Frankfurt an der Oder. Others were sent to the newly established special camps in the Soviet Zone of Occupation.[17] The last of the civilian deportees returned to Germany from the Soviet Union in 1949.[18] This date is disputed by some sources, stating that the last civilian German workers, numbering 4,823, were repatriated only at the end of 1953, in accordance with a resolution of the Presidium of the Central Committee of the Communist Party of November 30, 1953, concerning those Germans convicted by Soviet courts.[19]

The following personal narrative of a German civilian relates his arrest by the NKVD, transport, and life in a Soviet forced labor camp in the Donets Basin, in Southern Ukraine. The eyewitness was a teacher in a professional school, Karl Theodor Maschwitz of Trebniiz in Lower Silesia. He tells what happened to 15 deportees of Trebnitz and environs and their imprisonment in the camps of Alschewsk and Makejewka in the Donets territory.

On 4th February, 1945, the Russian Secret Police requisitioned the office rooms in the monastery at Trebnitz and began their work.

On 5th February all male persons staying in the monastery from 16-60 years of age were locked up, under guard, in the hut for Frenchmen, which was in the monastery, and some of them were continually brought up for cross-examinations. Most of the men were detailed for clearing-up work. On 6th February I was twice cross-examined, with the help of an interpreter, who understood hardly any German; I was then suddenly arrested. Even today I do not understand why. After all that I owned, including the clothing which I had on my back, had been taken away from me; I was shut up in the cellar of the house of Prehn in Breslauer Street, along with the druggist Fila and the wheelwright May of Peterwitz. Here we remained 12 days under the most horrible conditions, without light, in the midst of filth, and overrun by lice; there were Poles and Russians along with us. The number of those from Trebnitz and the neighborhood amounted to 15....

On 15th February I was suddenly brought with a transport to Heinzendorf, but came back again on the 17th to Trebnitz. The food in the cellar at Trebnitz was monotonous, but good and sufficient; the treatment was severe but without excesses.

At 6 o'clock in the morning, on 18th February, we suddenly received double bread rations. At 7 o'clock about 150 prisoners, were brought out of the cellars everywhere, and departed for Oels. Almost without stopping once, we went by way of Bingerau to Oels. This was a distance of 35 kilometers, which I had to do, although I had an artificial leg.

... The same evening we proceeded by train to Krakow,(Poland_) and got there after 3 days, with practically no food on the way. There we were confined in the prison of Monte Lupa, and remained there about 12 days. The food was extremely scanty, and the plague of lice was unbearable. After we had been deloused, and all our hair shorn off, we went with a big transport to the interior of Russia, or a distance of about 2,000 kilometers.

The journey was awful. There were more than 40 men in each wagon; 18 of them were Germans, the rest were Vlasof soldiers, that is to say Turcomans, Tartars, Caucasians, and Russians. The food was very bad, as we Germans were at a disadvantage in almost everything. We received no water to drink, and, therefore, ate snow on the way. The result were catarrhs of the stomach, accompanied by severe diarrhea, and several of us became very ill. These men were hardly able to stand on their legs, after they had been 14 days on the way.

When we reached the end of our journey, and came to Alschewsk near Voroshiloffgrad in the Donets coal district, we were at once put into a camp, where we remained, until the 18th September 1945. A state of chaos reigned when we arrived; only 3 huts, in which about 2,400 men were packed together, 80–100 men in one room. There were no latrines, and no kitchen, before the third day. The snow was about half a meter deep, but was beginning to thaw. After 2 days the Vlasof soldiers were separated from us, and taken away. They numbered about 800. The rest of us were gradually distributed to the other huts. The internees were sent to the town to get steel bedsteads, which had been made by German prisoners of war in the steel-works. The whole town consisted almost entirely of these works. There were about 30 men in one room, so that after 3-6 days the accommodation was fairly comfortable.

The above-mentioned men, who were seriously ill, were brought in a dying condition to a provisional military hospital, and died there the next day. The doctor, who was a Pole from the neighborhood of Rybnik, detested Germans, and left as many as possible to die. The personnel, who were both Germans and Poles, robbed the patients of everything valuable, and the stolen things were sold at the bazaar and at the public Russian black-market. They also stole, as far as they could, the patients' food, and then thought that they had done their duty...

The Russians left all management to the leaders of sections, who were themselves prisoners, and mostly Poles. The corpses of the dead were buried in the camp cemetery, without any ceremony, in mass graves. The mortality was initially very high. By September 1945, 1,100 of the 1,600 occupants of the camp had died.

When the kitchen had been fitted up, the food got better, particularly during the first 14 days. Then corruption gained the upper hand, particularly in the kitchen. The result was that the quality and quantity of the food continually worsened and led to general debility among the inmates of the camp.

After 6 weeks' quarantine the inmates of the camp had to work, if they were capable. For this they received a 200 gram extra allowance of bread.

I managed to keep going until September, by selling my clothes to Russians, and buying bread with the money. The general state of health had become so bad in July, that work was stopped in the town and in the steelworks. Meanwhile some 15 men had gone to a better world. All of them, did so, owing to the same causes: exhaustion, diarrhea, accompanied by dropsy coming from hunger, and resultant weakness of the heart. By 26th. July 1945 there were only 5 of 15 men still living.

On 25th. July the first transport returned home, unfortunately taking only Poles and Upper Silesians. Nevertheless, everyone had new hopes. It was also said, that the rest, about 250 men, were to go immediately afterwards. However, hoping and holding out made fools of almost all of us in this case. The fact that the internal administration of the camp, up to then had consisted almost entirely of Poles, and now passed into the hands of the Germans, led to a deterioration of the food situation because of even more racketeering.

The Russians were indeed quite correct towards us, and sometimes very generous; however, they did nothing to stop the corruption. They too participated in it themselves, particularly three lady doctors, who continually misappropriated the property of the sick and the dead.

On 18th September 1945, the camp (No. 1236) at Alschewsk was suddenly closed, and 150 men transferred to a camp near Makejewka, 200 kilometers to the west, and in the coal-field district of the Donets; among these men were all 4 survivors of Trebnitz. Things here were the same as in most of the camps. There was corruption and racketeering everywhere. The accommodation, however, was much worse. I got weaker and weaker, and terribly thin. Therefore, my artificial limb no longer fitted me, so that the stump got hopelessly sore in November 1945, and I had to go into the hospital on the 20th.

In December 1945, 73 men were sent home unfit for work, and I was among them. The transport ended in Frankfurt on the Oder. I myself was in an ambulance car in the train, and during the 3 weeks' journey 53 men died, and were thrown out of the train. As many people died, there was plenty of food in this car, so that I kept going. Almost all the occupants were sick with diarrhea and died, but I remained lying there because of my leg.

We were all discharged in Frankfurt, except those of us who were not able to walk, and these came into a prisoners' hospital, from which we were to be sent, at the latest after 8 days, to a hospital in Magdeburg or Dessau. As a result of 3 men in my room getting spotted fever, and having to be quarantined, we remained there for another 5 weeks. The food was indescribably bad, and the corruption of the personnel was shocking. After having received new clothes from the Russians for our discharge, the personnel took them away from us, and then gave us rags for our discharge from the hospital. Mortality was high in the hospital solely due to underfeeding. Much of this would have been avoided, if the Russian supervisors had taken action.

I was finally discharged on 5th February 1946 from Frankfurt.[20]

THE CREATION OF THE SOVIET SECURITY STATE IN EAST GERMANY

From the very start of the Soviet occupation of Germany, Colonel General Ivan Serov, Deputy Commissar of the NKVD, under Beria, and deputy commander-in-chief for civilian affairs of the Soviet Military Administration in Germany, headed the construction of a Soviet security state in the Soviet zone of occupation. Serov was responsible only to his NKVD/MVD superiors in Moscow, and he himself was appointed Deputy Minister of Internal Affairs in 1946, while he still served in Germany. He was also said to have had the personal confidence of Stalin.

(Refer to http://www.thegulagineastgermany.com. for Illustration # 8. Colonel General Ivan Serov. He survived the Stalinist and subsequent purges and became head of the KGB (successor to the NKVD) as well as the GRU (Military Intelligence).Wikimedia Commons.)

His authority was virtually unlimited. He was the NKVD officer responsible for the purge of anti-Soviet elements in the annexed Balkan territories and Eastern Poland from late 1939 until June 1941, when Nazi Germany attacked the USSR. He organized the mass deportation of Baltic and Polish people to Siberia as well as the execution of many opponents of the Soviet state.

The mission of the NKVD in East Germany was "the planning, arrest, and investigation of cases against spies and diversionists; the planting of agents for intelligence purposes in the Western Allied zones of occupation; the investigation of agents of the previous intelligence services of Nazi Germany; the processing of émigrés, etc." In all, NKVD tasks in the SBZ (Soviet Zone of Occupation) were basically the same as in the USSR: to protect the Soviet state against real or potential threats. As the NKVD had a countrywide network of informants and was also in charge of the civilian affairs office of the Military Government, it was able to control all branches of life in the Soviet zone of occupation. Serov led the NKVD officers and troops in Eastern Germany on an intense campaign to remove resistance, real or suspected, to the Soviet military government.[21]

Serov also oversaw the uranium mining operation in the Wismut Mines in the *Erzgebirg*e, (ore mountains), in the provinces of Sachsen and Thüringen, near the Czech border, (see addendum) and provided technical experts and atomic scientists for Beria, whom Stalin had placed in charge, in August of 1945, of the Soviet atom bomb project.[22] He also recruited German scientists in advanced weaponry design, aeronautics, and, above all, in rocket sciences for Beria's special projects.[23]

Serov constructed a network of Operational Groups, called *Opergrupy* that had the free run of the Soviet zone. They were present in every Soviet military administrative unit in their zone of occupation, from the local army command posts and *kommandanturas* (local military headquarters) to the Soviet military headquarters for their zone of occupation in Karlshorst, on the outskirts of Berlin. The Operational Groups, as their name implies, were at the heart of all NKVD/MVD security activities in the Soviet Zone.[24] They located and arrested important or active former Nazis as well as supposed Werewolf groups which were suspected of planning terrorist acts against the Soviet occupation. But in a short time, their main focus of action became the arrest of Socialist Party members who fought the enforced fusion of their SPD with the communist party, the KPD, into the SED,. as well as other opponents from democratic political parties.[25] These opponents to Soviet rule also frequently included dissident student groups or non-communist labor union activists, who were all subject to arrest and incarceration.

The Operational Groups generally worked in groups of 4 to 8 officers. Whenever Soviet military political officers suspected any resistance to the occupation, they invariably called on the Operational Groups for assistance. The *Opergrupy* also recruited Germans to act as informers or as *agents provocateurs*, particularly former Nazis, who considered their assistance to the occupation authorities a form of protection from prosecution. The NKVD/MVD Operational Groups concentrated on internal security issues, working openly and in uniform, whereas the NKGB/MGB were undercover operatives involved in spying[26] in their zone or recruiting agents for the Western zones of occupation.

In order to isolate and incapacitate all those arrested by the NKVD, by order of Ivan Serov in April 1945, a system of Special Camps in the Soviet zone was established. Initially, in 1945 and early 1946, those subject to arrest and imprisonment in the Special Camps were in the immediate detention category of Allied Control Council Directive #38, These instructions were amplified by incorporating the main elements of Beria's Order #00315 of April 18th:

1. Spies, agents, and terrorists of the Nazi German Secret Service.
2. Members of armed groups who could create resistance in the rear of the Red Army.
3. Operators of illegal radio transmitters, arms depot, and printing shops.
4. Active members of the Nazi party.
5. Hitler Youth and BDM leaders down to the community level.

6. Members of the Gestapo, and other Nazi security organizations. Leaders of German government administrations down to the community level, editors of newspapers and magazines, and authors of anti-Soviet publications.[27]

The NKVD arbitrary arrests and camp system caused much anxiety in the population. For example, when marching prisoners between camps, NKVD officers would often arrest people off the street to make up for any prisoner who escaped along the way (a practice common in the Soviet Union because NKVD officers were personally responsible for the numbers stated on the transport roster). When the Germans saw these marching prisoner columns, a general panic usually arose.[28]

K5. THE FIFTH DEPARTMENT OF EAST GERMAN CRIMINAL POLICE

In May 1945, at war's end, one of the most important Soviet security tasks was the reorganization of the German police. For the German communists, particularly Walter Ulbricht, sending the police into the streets was a critical first step in restoring order. At the time, there were still many Nazi party members in the police aside from former *Wehrmacht* and even SS and SA members. At that point there was not a general purge of Nazis in the police, though all senior positions were firmly in the hands of the Soviets.[29]

By June 28, 1945, however, Erich Mielke, a German communist leader, agent of the NKVD, and future head of the Stasi, instructed by Serov to build the first East German secret police, ordered that all employees of the East German police who had been members of the Nazi Party or its affiliated organizations, except the Hitler Youth, were to be dismissed from the police. Highly qualified ex-Nazis, however, could continue to work in the police force. For example, those who had demonstrated their anti-fascism by putting their lives on the line for the police in confrontations with anti-Soviet elements, were exempted from Mielke's orders.[30]

The first German secret police in the Soviet zone of occupation was the 5th Department of the East German Criminal Police, K5. It was formed in late summer 1945 by the Soviets. The Soviets stationed special K5 units in the criminal police stations located in the various provinces. No one from the pre-1945 German police was allowed to join this new organization. The Soviets gave K5 the authority to recruit large numbers of new officers from the working class, and in accordance with their class based ideology, automatically rendered them untainted by Nazi or bourgeois ideology.[31]

The K5 then became the East German political security police organization in the Soviet zone. According to its organizational chart of January 8, 1948, it was divided into five sections. The first section was to investigate political crimes, including violation of SVAG decrees and administrative orders; the second would investigate violation of Control Council orders; the third dealt with sabotage of reconstruction in East Germany; the fourth addressed anti-democratic (anti-communist) activity, and the fifth was a technical support group. The last section was responsible for surveillance of suspects, even prominent individuals, data collection, and postal censorship. The first four groups focused on the prevention of political crimes, including assassinations, sabotage, unauthorized public demonstrations, and underground resistance; in other words they went after any pro-fascist or anti-Soviet activities. This included such mundane incidents as tearing down opposition posters or the destruction of opposition literature.[32]

The K5 was the office of East German state security that operated on the Soviet model, namely, carrying out its responsibilities on behalf of a ruling political party, in this case the SED, as well, of course, of the Soviet security apparatus. For example, if the SED had a political enemy whom it wished to place in a compromising position, the K5 would receive an order to construct a case. Despite the growing SED control over the K5, it was very clear that the Soviet authorities, particularly the NKVD/MVD and the MGB, directed the activities of the K5. It was frequently charged with carrying out specific missions ordered by the Soviet Security organs and K5 officers could not undertake any major operation without prior Soviet approval.[33]

In time, the K5 took on some of the forms of the former Gestapo. Some SED heads complained that the security police were receiving a terrible reputation for their brutal methods and people feared it as much as they did the Gestapo. In the course of 1948, the SED attempted to take a more active part in controlling the activities of the K5. The Soviets were reluctant to allow this but agreed to keep the SED leadership informed about important arrests, especially of members of the political opposition.[34]

Ulbricht wanted Moscow to organize K5 units into an East German secret police but his request was denied. At the end of 1948, Ulbricht suggested to Moscow the creation of an East German security organization called, "Main Administration to Protect the Economy and the Democratic Order," but Abakumov, who had then become the head of the MGB, did not trust the German communists and did not want another security service, over which he had no control, to interfere with his work. Stalin, however, over-ruled him, and the Politburo approved the creation of an East German security organization on December 28, 1948.[35]

The Soviets and the SED created the Stasi, *Staatssicherheitsdienst, SSD,* under the Ministry of State Security, to safeguard the East German state making permanent the Sovietization of East Germany, later the GDR (created in October 1949). The Stasi was the result of the fusion of the K5 of the Criminal Police and the intelligence and information department of the East German interior ministry.[36] Stasi continued to dominate the East German security apparatus until the collapse of the GDR in October of 1990.

NOTE #1. *CHEKA*

"The All-Russian Extraordinary Commission for Combating Counter-Revolution and Sabotage" was the first of a succession of state security organizations, founded by decree on December 20, 1917, by Vladimir Lenin. He appointed Felix Dzerzhinsky, a Polish aristocrat turned Bolshevik, as its chairman as well as Commissar for Internal Affairs. Dzerzhinsky had a reputation of complete incorruptibility; he was a communist idealist but also totally fanatic and an inquisitor.

Its purpose was to "liquidate counter-revolution and sabotage, to hand over counter-revolutionaries and saboteurs to the revolutionary tribunals and to apply such measures of repression as confiscation of property, deprivation of ration cards, publication of lists of enemies of the people, etc." The *'Cheka* targeted "class enemies," the bourgeoisie, clerics, and even democratic socialists and anarchists. One of the most famous *Cheka* actions was the suppression of the Kronstadt Rebellion in 1921. Sailors of the Baltic Fleet, specifically on the battleship *Petropavlovsk,* denounced the lack of democracy and the Communist Party's War Communism policy. They passed a resolution calling for full political freedom. Lenin denounced it as a White Army/European plot. In the repression, over 500 sailors were executed. This was particularly noteworthy as sailors from the Kronstadt naval base carried out one of the first Bolshevik uprisings.

By September 1918, Dzerzhinsky had introduced a government policy of Red Terror, as the only way to save the Bolshevik revolution, under which the state security forces shot, arrested, imprisoned, and executed thousands of persons, regardless of whether or not they had actually planned a rebellion against the communist government. Those not shot were deported to Siberian labor camps run by the *Cheka.* For the period of the Bolshevik Civil War, 1917–1920, estimates of *Cheka* executions range from 50,000 to 500,000 though the consensus appears to be in the higher range of these figures. No official, complete figures were ever kept by the Soviets. In May 1921, the Politburo, under Lenin, passed a motion increasing the scope of the *Cheka* in the use of the death penalty.

It was in this revolutionary Civil War period that the Soviet state security methods were created; utter ruthlessness and terror which survived the *Cheka* and its succeeding organizations prevailed.[37]

(Refer to http://www.thegulagineastgermahny.com for Illustration #9. Felix Dzerzhinsky, founder of the Soviet secret police. Source: spartacus-educational.com.)

NOTE #2. AN OVERVIEW OF THE DEPORTATION OF GERMAN CIVILIANS TO THE SOVIET UNION FROM THE BALKANS

The Big Three Yalta Conference approved in February 1945 the use of German forced labor. Both President Roosevelt and Prime Minister Churchill were in agreement. The Soviet Union considered it part of German war reparations. They had first raised this issue at the 1943 Tehran meeting when Stalin said he needed 4 million Germans to repair war damage.

The deportation of German civilians began in late 1944, when the Red Army marched into the Balkans, with forced recruitment from the ethnic German communities living there. (See Map #5 of German communities in the Balkans below.) On December 16, 1944, the State Defense Committee of the USSR issued Decree No. 7151, calling for mobilization of all able-bodied German civilian labor in the territories of Romania, Yugoslavia, Hungary, Bulgaria, and Czechoslovakia. All men from the ages of 17 to 45 and women aged 18 to 30 were to be recruited and interned to be subsequently transported to the USSR.[38]

The operations were executed by NKVD troops supported by regular Red Army soldiers. The schedule of deportations was as follows: December 28, 1944 to January 5, 1945, for ethnic Germans living in Yugoslavia and Hungary (within the operating area of the 3rd Ukrainian Front); January 1–10, 1945, for Hungarian Germans (within the operating area of the 2nd Ukrainian Front); January 10 to February 1, 1945, for ethnic Germans from Romania, including Transylvania; and December 27, 1944, to January 1,

1945, for Sudeten Germans from Czechoslovakia. The deportees were to be sent to collection points and then to railroad stations for transport to their work destinations in the Soviet Union.[39]

The trains were made up of 40–50 cattle cars into each of which 40 to 50 men and women were forced. Sanitary conditions consisted of a hole cut in the middle of the wagon floor. The trip to the labor camps in the Soviet Union lasted from three to six weeks. Due to hunger and cold, the mortality rate on the transports sometimes reached 10%.[40]

The above time schedules were generally adhered to. For example, from December 23rd, 1944, to January 14th 1945, in the operating area of the 3rd Ukrainian Front, in Yugoslavia and part of Hungary, 21,695 ethnic Germans were transported to the USSR, the majority being women, using 17 trains consisting of 786 railway cars.[41]

In the period of January to March 1945, 111,831 ethnic German deportees were sent from East European countries to the Soviet Union for forced labor, although the NKVD objective was to send at least 140,000 workers.[42] This transport consisted of 61,375 men and 50,456 women, with 67,332 coming from Romania, 31,920 from Hungary, and 12,579 from Yugoslavia.[43] Most of the deportees were sent to the Donbas, into the coal mines and nearby industry in Southeastern Ukraine. An additional 11%, approximately, did forced labor in the heavy industry area of the Urals.[44] Working conditions were indescribably bad, sanitation was almost non-existent, and food rations insufficient, leading to widespread sickness. Typhoid epidemics were common with a resulting high death rate.

Because so many workers were sick or incapable of hard labor, the Soviets began their repatriation in the latter part of 1945. By December 1945, 36,039 German deportees had already been sent to East Germany, even though they were citizens and residents of other countries. Their reception camp was in Frankfurt an der Oder, in the Soviet Zone of Occupation. The bulk of German forced laborers were sent back in the years from 1946 to 1948, with the last, large transport occurring in 1949.[45]

It should be noted, however, that the majority of German forced labor in the Soviet Union consisted of German prisoners of war, totaling over 2,000,000. The last war prisoners were released and sent back to Germany in 1956. The other Allied powers, mainly the French and English, also used prisoners of war as forced labor, the former in land mine clearing and the later in agriculture with most having been repatriated to Germany by 1948/1949. German civilian forced labor, however, was never used by the Western Allies.

(Refer to http://www.thegulagineastgermany.com for Map #5: The locations of ethnic German communities in the Balkans (Wikimedia Commons). Citation: Map by Andrei nacu, December 22, 2008.http://en.wikipedia.org/wiki/File:Austria_Hungary_ethnic.svg.)

NOTE #3. LOCATION OF THE INDIVIDUAL DEPORTATION CAMPS FOR GERMAN CIVILIANS

Order of the NKVD of the USSR Nr. 0461-1945 for the establishment of collection camps. Location of the camps and prisons under the control of the authorized officers the NKVD of the USSR for each Military Front.

Cities are all located in Germany unless otherwise indicated.

1. Belorussian Front

Lembertow Camp

Lodz, Poland Camp

Poznan, Poland Camp

Danzig Camp

Krakow, Poland Camp

Schneidemühl Camp

Schwiebus Camp

Landsberg Camp

Fürstenwalde Camp

Werneuchen Camp

2. Belorussian Front

Graudenz Prison

Gollnow Prison

Stargard Prison

3. Belorussian Front

Insterburg Prison

Tapiau Prison

Bartenstein Prison

Konigsberg Prison

Preussisch Eylau Camp

Domtau Camp

Panar Camp

4. Ukrainian Front

Tost Prison/Camp

Oppeln Prison/Camp

Rawitsch Prison/Camp

5. Ukrainian Front

Wadowice, Poland Prison

Bielsko, Poland Prison

Ratibor, Poland Prison

Ruzomberok,Poland Prison

Myslovice, Poland Camp

These locations, for the temporary holding of German civilians prior to their deportation to the USSR, were all in Eastern Germany, east of the *Oder/Neisse* Line before its annexation by Poland or in Western Poland. None were in the Soviet Zone of Occupation in Germany[46] (See Map #4 for the post war German territorial loss in the east).

NOTES

1. Vladimir A. Kozlov, "Die Operationen des NKVD in Deutschland während des Vormarsches der Roten Armee (Januar bis April 1945)," in *Sowjetische Speziallager in Deutschland 1945 bis 1950 Band I*, eds. Sergej Mironenko, Lutz Niethammer, and Alexander von Plato (Berlin: Akademie Verlag, 1998), 133.
2. Nikita Petrov, "Die Apparate des NKVD/MVD und der MGB in Deutschland (1945–1953) Eine Historische Skizze," in *Sowjetische Speziallager in Deutschland 1945 bis 1950 Band I*, eds. Sergej Mironenko, Lutz Niethammer, and Alexander von Plato (Berlin: Akademie Verlag, 1998), 144.
3. Kozlov, *Die Operationen des NKVD in Deutschland während des Vormarsches der Roten Armee (Januar bis April 1945)*, in *Sowjetische Speziallager in Deutschland 1945 bis 1950 Band I*, eds. Sergej Mironenko, Lutz Niethammer, and Alexander von Plato (Berlin: Akademie Verlag, 1998), 134–135.
4. Petrov, "Die Apparate des NKVD/MVD und der MGB in Deutschland (1945-1953) Eine Historische Skizze," in *Sowjetische Speziallager in Deutschland 1945 bis 1950 Band I*, eds. Sergej Mironenko, Lutz Niethammer, and Alexander von Plato (Berlin: Akademie Verlag, 1998), 153.
5. Ibid.
6. Ralf Possekel, ed., "Band 2: Sowjetische Dokumente zur Lagerpolitik in Sowjetische Speziallager," in *Sowjetische Speziallager in Deutschland 1945 bis 1950 Band I*, eds. Sergej Mironenko, Lutz Niethammer, and Alexander von Plato (Berlin: Akademie Verlag, 1998), 36.
7. Kozlov, "Die Operationen des NKVD in Deutschland während des Vormarsches der Roten Armee (Januar bis April 1945)," in *Sowjetische Speziallager in Deutschland 1945 bis 1950 Band I*, eds. Sergej Mironenko, Lutz Niethammer, and Alexander von Plato (Berlin: Akademie Verlag, 1998), 141.
8. Sergej Mironenko, Lutz Niethammer, and Alexander von Plato, eds., *Sowjetische Speziallager in Deutschland 1945 is 1950, Band I*,(Berlin, Germany, 1998), 50.
9. Ibid., 25.
10. Ibid.
11. Ibid., 26–27.
12. Ibid., 60–61.

13. Theodor Schieder, *The Expulsion of the German Population from the Territories East of the Oder-Neisse Line, Vol 1.1 & 1.2* (Bonn, Germany, 1956), 63.
14. Sergej Mironenko, Lutz Niethammer, and Alexander von Plato, eds., *Sowjetische Speziallager in Deutschland 1945 is 1950, Band I*, 24, 52, 53.
15. Kozlov, "Die Operationen des NKVD in Deutschland während des Vormarsches der Roten Armee (Januar bis April 1945)," in *Sowjetische Speziallager in Deutschland 1945 bis 1950 Band I*, eds. Sergej Mironenko, Lutz Niethammer, and Alexander von Plato, 140–141.
16. Jan Lipinsky, "Mobilität zwischen den Lagern," in *Sowjetische Speziallager in Deutschland 1945 bis 1950 Band I*, eds. Sergej Mironenko, Lutz Niethammer, and Alexander von Plato, 226–227.
17. Ibid
18. Schieder, *The Expulsion of the German Population from the Territories East of the Oder-Neisse Line, Vol 1.1 & 1.2*, 67.
19. P.M. Polian, *Against their Will: the History and Geography of Forced Migrations in the USSR* (Budapest, Hungary, 2004), 296.
20. Schieder, *The Expulsion of the German Population from the Territories East of the Oder-Neisse Line, Vol 1.1 & 1.2*, 186–189.
21. Gary Bruce, *Resistance with the People, Repression and Resistance in Eastern Germany, 1945 –1955* (Lanham Maryland, 2003), 48.
22. Norman M.Naimark,*The Russians in Germany; A History of the soviet Zone of Occupation,1945–1949*, (Cambridge, Massachusetts, 1995), 379.
23. Ibid.
24. Ibid.
25. Bruce, *Resistance with the People, Repression and Resistance in Eastern Germany, 1945–1955*, 48.
26. Naimark,*The Russians in Germany; A History of the soviet Zone of Occupation,1945–1949*, 380.
27. Ibid., 376.
28. Bruce, *Resistance with the People, Repression and Resistance in Eastern Germany, 1945–1955*, 48.
29. Naimark,*The Russians in Germany; A History of the soviet Zone of Occupation,1945–1949*, 355.
30. Ibid., 366.
31. Ibid., 360.
32. Naimark, *The Russians in Germany; A History of the soviet Zone of Occupation,1945–1949*, 362.
33. Ibid.

34. Petrov, "Die Apparate des NKVD/MVD und der MGB in Deutschland (1945-1953). Eine Historische Skizze," in *Sowjetische Speziallager in Deutschland 1945 bis 1950 Band I*, eds. Sergej Mironenko, Lutz Niethammer, and Alexander von Plato (Berlin: Akademie Verlag, 1998), 153.
35. Ibid.
36. Naimark, *The Russians in Germany; A History of the soviet Zone of Occupation,1945–1949*, 360.
37. *Retrieved from Internet, spartacus-educational.com*
38. Polian, *Against their Will: the History and Geography of Forced Migrations in the USSR*, 250.
39. Ibid., 253.
40. Schieder, *The Expulsion of the German Population from the Territories East of the Oder-Neisse Line, Vol.1.1 & 1.2*, 66.
41. Polian, *Against their Will: the History and Geography of Forced Migrations in the USSR*, 259.
42. Kozlov, *Die Operationen des NKVD in Deutschland während des Vormarsches der Roten Armee (Januar bis April 1945)*, in *Sowjetische Speziallager in Deutschland 1945 bis 1950 Band I*, eds. Sergej Mironenko, Lutz Niethammer, and Alexander von Plato (Berlin: Akademie Verlag, 1998), 136.
43. Polian, *Against their Will: the History and Geography of Forced Migrations in the USSR*, 266.
44. Ibid., 277.
45. Schieder, *The Expulsion of the German Population from the Territories East of the Oder-Neisse Line, Vol 1.1 & 1.2*, 67.
46. Mironenko, Niethammer, and von Plato, eds., *Sowjetische Speziallager in Deutschland 1945 bis 1950 Band I*, 28.

CHAPTER 5

ESTABLISHMENT OF THE SPECIAL CAMPS

Let me have one night with him and I will have him confessing
he's the King of England
A boast attributed to Lavrentiy P. Beria, Soviet Minister of
Internal Affairs and head of the NKVD

THE ADMINISTRATIVE PROCESS OF SPECIAL CAMPS ESTABLISHMENT

As the war was drawing to a close in May 1945, Soviet security services were sending their systems and personnel to their occupation zone in Germany. Concentration camps were a fundamental part of this system. They immediately began to construct camps, eventually establishing 13 special concentration camps and prisons, called *Spezlager*. Two of them, Sachsenhausen and Buchenwald, were former Nazi concentration camps reopened by the Soviets and one, Bautzen, was a former Gestapo prison. They were under the control of the NKVD/MVD, and later under the direct supervision of the GULAG (Soviet Main Camp Administration of the Ministry of Internal Affairs-MVD). All were organized and laid out according to Soviet design in the same way as the GULAG camps in the Soviet Union, with minimal rations, poor medical services, and overcrowded barracks. Senior camp commanders were Soviet military personnel. Some 240,000 prisoners passed through these camps in the five years of their existence with a death toll of approximately 95,000 or a 40% mortality rate.[1]

Although the Soviets always claimed that only Nazis were held in the special camps, as in Western internment camps, this was not the case. The special camps were not designed as a part of the Soviet denazification process, but rather as a strategy to isolate and detain all enemies of Soviet rule in East Germany.[2]

The Soviet Union justified its arrest and imprisonment of dissident elements as a facet of their "anti fascist" policies. In fact, the entire legitimization of their rule in the Soviet Zone of Occupation rested on their claim to being the only occupying power that effectively purged the Nazi system from the German body politic. For example, young people were frequently accused and persecuted for Werewolf pro-Nazi activities when, in reality, they had simply exhibited anti-Soviet attitudes.[3]

Specifically, The NKVD/MVD had two basic objectives in establishing the special camps: 1. Arrests and incarceration were meant to create a state of fear in order to eliminate any thought of opposition to Soviet occupation authorities and their communist system 2. All actual or potential opponents were to be isolated by lowering their physical health and psychological spirit, thus making them harmless.[4]

According to Soviet propaganda, these camps, *Spezlager,* were a part of the denazification process and used only to hold high ranking Nazis or war criminals. Those prisoners, however, were usually taken back to Moscow, interrogated, and put directly into Soviet POW camps or the GULAG. The majority of the special camp prisoners were not guilty of any crime, in the legal sense. Those arrested were "class enemies," namely, government employees, journalists, judges, lawyers, teachers, scientists, merchants, factory managers, wealthy peasants, and junkers (large landowners), clerics, and doctors, etc., all of whom had or exhibited dubious loyalty to the Soviet State. The Soviets wanted to isolate and destroy the elite in order to avoid any counter-revolutionary activity. There were even opponents of Hitler, involved in the July 20, 1944, anti-Nazi uprising, such as Justus Delbrück and Ulrich Freiherr von Sell who died in the Jamlitz camp; Horst von Einsiedel, a member of the anti-Nazi "Kreisau Circle," died in the Sachsenhausen camp in 1946; and Count Joachim Ernst von Anhalt, who was a prisoner in the Nazi Dachau camp, died in the NKVD camp Buchenwald in 1947. Even KPD party members, of the ultra left opposition (i.e. those who wanted an immediate, communist revolutionary government and opposed the SED) ended up in the special camps.[5]

At the same time, the special camps in East Germany were not GULAG labor camps of the type that the NKVD ran in the Soviet Union. They were not attached to factories, mines, collective farms, or building projects, as Soviet camps normally were, and prisoners did not go out to work. On the contrary, survivors often describe the excruciating boredom of being forbidden to work, forbidden to leave their barracks, forbidden to walk or move. In the Ketschendorf Camp, for example, reports said that inmates begged to work in the kitchens just to have some kind of activity (and, of course, to have access to more food). In Sachsenhausen there were two zones, in only one of which people were allowed to work on tasks in the camp. Prisoners much preferred that one.[6]

Shortly before the end of the war, a Department of Special Camps of the NKVD in Germany was established under the jurisdiction of the Soviet Ministry of Internal Affairs (MVD), in close coordination with the SVAG (Soviet Military Administration in Germany). Order #00315, of April 18, 1945, created the Department of Special Camps of the NKVD of the USSR in Germany. It was placed under the control of the authorized representative of the Soviet Ministry of Internal Affairs in the Soviet Military Administration in Germany and the deputy Minister of Internal

Affairs, Colonel General Ivan A. Serov, a man who then also became the chief officer responsible for the Soviet special camps.[7]

Order #00461, gave concrete instructions for the registration of prisoners. They differentiated between those interned administratively without any conviction or court order by Soviet military courts, and those who were so convicted. For prisoners interned without court order, the instructions were as follows: *"Those persons who were sent to the special camps under order #00315 of the NKVD of April 18, 1945 by a special regulation will be isolated from society. They will not be prosecuted and there will be no court process."*[8]

Enemies of the Soviet occupation were immediately interned. Of special concern were those young people thought to belong to the Nazi Werewolf. In a June 22, 1945, report to General L.P.Beria Minister of Internal Affairs, NKVD chief in Germany, General Ivan Serov reports:

Recently, as a result of actions by the NKVD Operations Groups in Berlin and Provinces, more than 600 members of the underground fascist Party organization, Werewolf, were arrested. Weapons and munitions were confiscated from the Werewolf members and from their hiding places; they took five heavy machine guns, 12 light machine guns, 135 rifles, 320 hand grenades, 68 anti-tank rockets and much ammunition.

From our agents and other sources, it was established that by the orders of the fascist party leaders, Bormann and Goebbels, to all Nazi party leaders at all levels in the nation in February 1945, they were to create new underground organizations called Werewolf.

The Werewolf underground groups were given the task of creating diversions and terror actions in the areas occupied by the units of the Red Army and troops of the Allied armies.

To lead these underground groups, Werewolf, composed of only the most fanatical followers of Hitler and the Nazi party, would be designated. In order to fill the membership in the Werewolf, the Hitler Youth should be used.[9]

The NKVD established specific charges for immediate arrest and transfer to the special camps of those groups listed in Beria's Order #00315, as instructed by Gerneral Serov in April 1945 and his Order #00461. These automatic administrative arrests of the individuals listed therein were principally carried out in the years 1945/1946. Thereafter, many of those sent to the camps were sentenced by Soviet Military Tribunals.[10]

General Serov decided on May 28,1946, that all members of the Nazi para-military and security organizations SA, SS, *Waffen SS*, and *Volksturm* who were in the special camps had to be sent to prisoner of war camps where they were destined for labor in the USSR. Subsequently, all those members who were not capable of work were to be released from the special camps provided that they were not guilty of any war crimes, as per the MVD decree of August 16, 1946.[11]

Also, in May 1946, all security operations in the Soviet Zone of Occupation were turned over to SMERSH, which now was placed in the MGB (Ministry of State Security) under the command of Viktor Abakumov, who became Minister of State Security. The management of the special camps and prisons continued under the NKVD/MVD. Serov returned to Moscow, to the Ministry of Internal Affairs, in April 1947 and in August of 1948, the GULAG administration assumed direct control of the camps.[12]

THE LEGAL PROCESS OF SPECIAL CAMPS ESTABLISHMENT

As stated previously, the basis for arrest in the Soviet Zone of Occupation was decree #00315 of April 18, 1945, of the NKVD in the Soviet Military Administration.. This decree called for the immediate internment, without prior investigation, of "spies, saboteurs, terrorists, and activists of the Nazi party," as well as people maintaining "illegal" print and broadcasting devices, people with weapons, and former members of the German civil administration. The order resembled the regulations put in place in the other Allied occupation zones, where "active" Nazis were also arrested and interrogated. The difference between the Soviet zone and other Allied zones was one of purpose, degree, and practice. The Soviet order made it possible to arrest almost anyone who had held any position of authority, whether or not he or she had been a Nazi. Town mayors, businesspeople, and prosperous farmers all qualified on the grounds that they could not have been so successful unless they had collaborated with the Nazi regime, for them a reasonable assumption.[13]

The Red Army set up military tribunals (SMT) which were courts without defense lawyers or witnesses for the defendants. These Soviet military tribunals operated in East Germany until 1955. They had no relationship to international law or German law. Trials and convictions were normally made on the basis of Article 58 of the RSFR (Russian Socialist Federated Republic) Penal Code of the Soviet Union of February 25, 1927, as well as of a directive of the Presidium of the Supreme Soviet of April 19, 1943, both statutes that were used to arrest and condemn political prisoners in the Soviet Union.[14] The tribunals consisted generally of only a military judge and two legal assistants. The position of an accused was always very weak, for it was left up to the military tribunal itself to determine its own makeup and structure. If a charge was considered to be sufficiently proven, then the inclusion of a Soviet military prosecutor might be dispensed with altogether. In such a case, no defense counsel was permitted, either. The verdicts of the courts were incontestable.

Sentences were sometimes translated into German but written out in Cyrillic, making them impossible for the accused to read. Prisoners were sometimes forced, after severe beatings and other kinds of torture, to sign documents they couldn't understand. For example, Wolfgang Lehmann, aged fifteen, unknowingly signed a document stating that he had blown up two trucks. Some of those arrested really had been Nazis, although not necessarily important Nazis. Little attempt was made to separate real criminals from small-time bureaucrats or opportunists. In addition to the Nazis, the arrests soon swept up thousands of people too young to have been Nazis, usually under the charge of belonging to the Werewolf.[15]

Using the authority in the Allied Control Council decrees #24 and #38, the Soviet authorities, including the NKVD/MVD, NKGB (People's Commissariat of State Security), MGB (Ministry of State Security), and SVAG (Soviet Military Administration in Germany), arrested most any German, even those who were not in the immediate arrest categories. Even standard Soviet minimal legal protection of the accused was ignored and the practices of the Soviet Security services in the USSR were employed in the Soviet Zone of Occupation in Germany.[16]

At the beginning, trials were directed against war criminals, but by the end of 1946, 17,175 members of the SS and other Nazi security formations had been convicted by the SMTs.[17] However, starting in 1946, most trials were for crimes against the "new democratic order," members of democratic parties, youth in opposition, social democrats, and even opponents from within the SED. The usual verdict was 25 years in prison. Under SVAG order #160, crimes against the economy carried a verdict of up to 15 years or even the death sentence. Thus, even poor economic performance could be labeled sabotage with the consequent penalties.[18]

There were a few public trials by the Soviet Military Tribunals, such as those of 245 members of the 9th Berlin-Spandau Police Battalion or 14 guards and members of the Sachsenhausen camp administration in October/November 1947. There were also trials held in Moscow in a special court of the NKVD/MVD. Those Germans so charged were inevitably deported to the USSR.[19] These distant tribunals held in Moscow usually consisted of three MVD officials, the number of officials being set according to the importance of the antecedents of the accused. Judgment was based solely on the examination of the files. The basic reason for such trials in Moscow was that details of the arrest and conditions of the accused were strictly secret (e.g., whether the accused previously had connections with the Soviet security services or special knowledge of the internal workings of the security services). Most of the sentences were ten years in the Gulag in the Soviet Union. These distant trials were eliminated after Stalin's death in 1953.[20]

Prisoners sentenced to 25 years were sent to prisons in Strelitz and Torgau, as well as to special camps, Bautzen and Sachsenhausen. Beginning in1948, all Germans sentenced to 15 years prison went to Sachsenhausen, and those with more than 15 years were sent to the Bautzen penitentiary. Soviets reported that by September 1948, the Soviet Military Tribunals (SMT) had sentenced 13,873 prisoners to East German special camps. According to German sources, from 20,000 to 25,000 Germans from the Soviet Zone of Occupation were also sent to GULAG camps in the Soviet Union, Siberia, and Central Asia. These individuals were mostly those sentenced to 25 years in prison for espionage. Some did not return until the middle 1950s.[21] According to the West Berlin opposition group, KgU *Kampfgruppe gegen Unmenschlichkeit* (Combat Unit against Inhumanity, see chapter 6) , the SMTs convicted, between 1945 and 1955, 30,000 Germans in the SBZ/GDR. Other Germans cite this figure at between 40,000 and 50,000, while Russian sources in 1996 recorded the total arrested and convicted Germans at 40,000.[22] Those convicted by the SMTs were not freed until the beginning of 1950 when 5,400 were released, 190 were deported to the USSR, and 10,000 were handed over to the East German prison system.[23]

All those condemned to death by the Soviet Military Tribunals had to have their conviction reviewed by the legal department of the Soviet Army of Occupation in Germany. Appeal to the Supreme Court of the USSR also existed.[24] These convicts were deported to the Soviet Union and shot in the NKVD prison, at Butyrka in Moscow. Their ashes were interned in the Moscow cemetery, at Donskoje, in anonymous graves.[25] Between 1945 and 1955, the Soviet Military Tribunals condemned 3,000 Germans to death.[26]

Figure 2. A German Translation of an SMT Sentencing Document Copy.

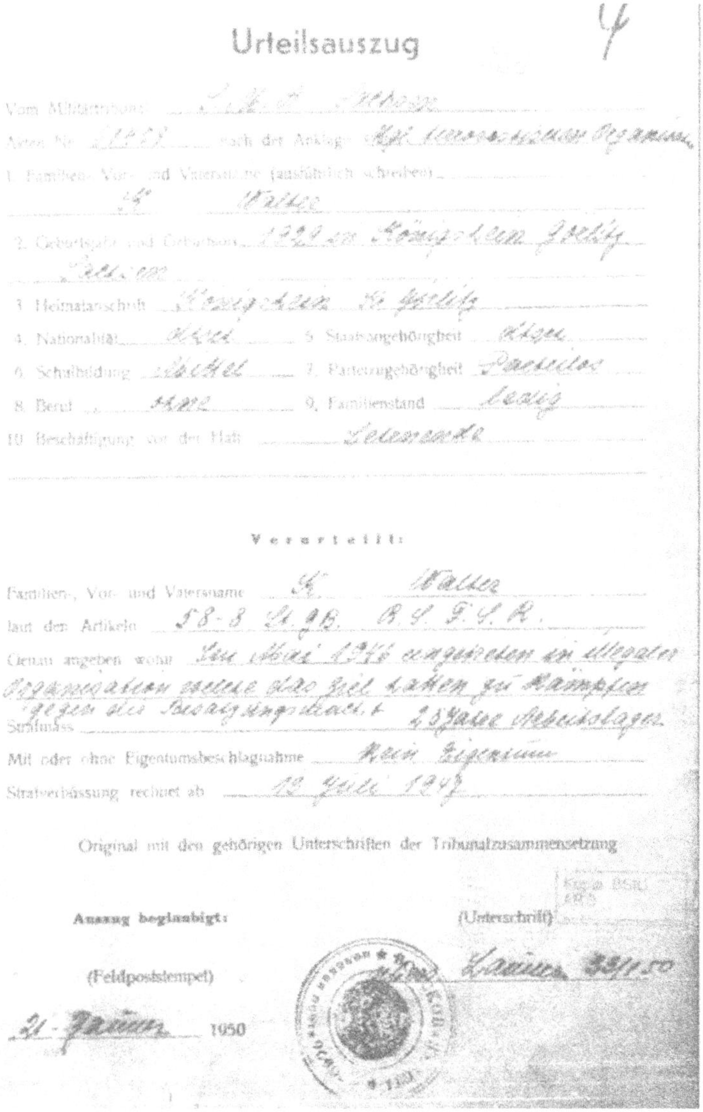

Urteilsauszug

Vom Militärtribunal

Akten Nr. nach der Anklage

1. Familien-, Vor- und Vatersname (ausführlich schreiben) K. Walter

2. Geburtsjahr und Geburtsort

3. Heimatanschrift

4. Nationalität 5. Staatsangehörigkeit

6. Schulbildung 7. Parteizugehörigkeit

8. Beruf 9. Familienstand

10. Beschäftigung vor der Haft

Verurteilt:

Familien-, Vor- und Vatersname K. Walter

laut den Artikeln 58-8 St.GB. R.S.F.S.R.

Genau angeben wofür Im Mai 1946 eingetreten in illegaler Organisation welche das Ziel hatten zu kämpfen gegen die Besatzungsmacht

Strafmass 25 Jahre Arbeitslager

Mit oder ohne Eigentumsbeschlagnahme Kein Eigentum

Strafverbüssung rechnet ab Juli 1947

Original mit den gehörigen Unterschriften der Tribunalzusammensetzung

Auszug beglaubigt: (Unterschrift)

(Feldpoststempel)

21. Januar 1950

Figure 2. shows a German translation of an SMT Sentencing Document Copy, in the name of Walter K., issued by the Soviet Military Tribunal of Sachsen,(Province Saxony); convicted on July 13, 1947 to 25 years imprisonment for belonging to an illegal organization whose aim was to fight the Soviet occupation of Germany. He was convicted under Article 58 of the RSFSR Penal Code on Crimes against the State, on February 25, 1927.[27]

Figure 3. A German Translation of a Rehabilitation Certificate.

ÜBERSETZUNG
(Vordruck u. Inhalt)

(Wappen)
Generalstaatsanwaltschaft
der Russischen Föderation
HAUPT-
MILITÄRSTAATSANWALTSCHAFT

MITTEILUNG
über eine Rehabilitierung

10.November 1997
Nr. 5 uk - 29428-51

103160 Moskau, K - 160

Der(die)Bürger(in TÖPFER, Fritz Karl-Julius

Jahr und Geburtsort geboren 1899 in der Stadt Jauer, Schlesien

Bürger(in) welchen Staates Deutschland

Nationalität Deutscher Wohnort bis zur Verhaftung

im Dorf Naundorf, Land Sachsen

Arbeitsplatz und Amt/Art der Beschäftigung/ bis zur Festnahme

landwirtschaftlicher Pächter

Festnahmedatum: 23.Mai 1951

Wann und durch welche Organe verurteilt/verfolgt/
am 26.November 1951 durch das Militärtribunal des Truppenteiles 48240

Tatbezeichnung und Strafmaß/grundsätzlich und ergänzend

Art. 58-6, Teil 1, zum höchsten Strafmaß der Erschießung

Datum der Freilassung Das Urteil ist am 22.02.1952 vollstreckt worden

Auf der Grundlage des Art.3 des Gesetzes der Russischen Föderation "Über die Rehabilitierung der Opfer politischer Verfolgungen" vom 18.Oktober 1991 ist der (die) Bürger(in)
TÖPFER, Fritz Karl-Julius rehabilitiert.

Militärstaatsanwalt
der Abteilung Rehabilitierung
der Hauptmilitärstaatsanwaltschaft

gez.: L.P.KOPALIN

F.d.R.d.Übersetzung
53177 Bonn, den 10.01.1999

(Heini Fritsche)

Figure 3. shows a German translation of a Rehabilitation Certificate issued by the state prosecutor's office of the Russian Federation on November 10, 1997, stating that Fritz Karl – Julius Töpfer was condemned to death by the Soviet Military Tribunal of Army section #48240, on November 21, 1951. He was executed on February 2, 1952. On the basis of Article 3, of the laws of the Russian Federation for the Rehabilitation of the Victims of State Persecution of October 18, 1991, he was rehabilitated.[28]

The overwhelming majority of prisoners, however, were arrested without charges or court verdict. Many had no idea why they were arrested. These were known as administrative arrests and deportations, an NKVD procedure by which individuals or groups were arrested without any legal process whatsoever. The individual was arbitrarily seized and sent to the Gulag or prison. The prisoner had absolutely no legal recourse. This procedure was used extensively against the Kulaks, at the time of farm collectivization in the early 1930s, during the Stalin purges of the late 1930s, and especially during the war, when many ethnic groups such as German Russians or people from the Caucasus were deported to the GULAG.[29] Almost 90% of all arrests by the Soviets in Germany were administrative, and detainees were sent to the special camps without trial.[30]

According to the Soviet legal system, belonging to a certain adversarial social class made one automatically a class enemy and liable to be charged and condemned. This criterion had a double function: first, to eliminate any opponent of the Soviets and secondly, to provide scapegoats for failures of the Soviet system.[31] The basis of Soviet legality was that Soviet power never arrested the innocent. Thus, to be arrested meant that one was automatically guilty, that is, that the arrested already had a presumption of guilt. Proof of innocence, therefore, had little influence in Soviet legal procedure, and the role of the defense was, thus, irrelevant.[32]

CREATION OF THE CAMP SYSTEM—THE FIRST CAMPS

The first camps and prisoner settlements were established on the Island of Rügen in the Baltic Sea. (See Map #6.) Not only the Junkers (large, traditional land owners) from the Prussian estates but all German larger landholders were held there as a result of the land reform law instituted by SVAG on September 2, 1945. All farms over 100 hectares were confiscated without compensation. Not only were the owners' farms taken from them but all their other property was as well. Similar to the anti-*Kulak* purges of Stalinist Russia in the early 1930s, the NKVD sent landholders from all the Eastern German states to camps and settlements on the Island of Rügen, where they lived in terrible conditions without proper shelter or food, leading to high death rates.

These large landholders were mostly from the states of Mecklenburg and Pomerania, where most German large estates were located. They were taken by train to Stralsund and from there were forced to trek to the Island of Rügen, where they were then distributed to the various towns on the island. Forbidden to leave, they had to report regularly to the Soviet military commander. Nevertheless, many escaped to the West and an unknown number died. Wilhelm Pieck, Communist Party Leader and later President of the German Democratic Republic, said on announcing the collectivization of farms in September 1945, *"All these individuals responsible for the war and war criminals, now have to be made forever harmless. One has to take away from them the basis of their power, their landholding, and their wealth."* [33]

(Refer to http://www.thegulagineastgermany.comforMap #6, The island of Rügen in the Baltic Sea. Source: Polish History, Heraldry and Genealogy)

The Building of The Special Camps

More infamous than the camps on Rügen island, were the many *Spezlager* created by the NKVD in the Soviet Zone of Occupation. Some of these, such as Sachsenhausen and Buchenwald, had been simply carried over from the Nazi era. As the Russian general Dratvin explained to some British visitors, *"The [Nazi] camps have been liquidated, but the buildings are being used for housing fascist criminals who have committed crimes against our country."* The traditional Nazi camps were joined by new sites like Hohenschönhausen in Berlin, which was also in a Soviet residential enclave. It was here that Otto Grotewohl (SPD head in the Soviet Zone and later SED leader and Prime Minister of the German Democratic Republic) lived, surrounded by Russians and barbed wire. Then there were Jamlitz in Brandenburg; Frankfurt-an-der-Oder and Ketschendorf,

Neubrandenburg in the province of Brandenburg; Mühlberg on the Oder river, in Sachsen; Bautzen, a former Gestapo penitentiary, in Sachsen; and the old POW camp at Torgau which had been turned into a political prison. Hardened cases, senior Nazi leaders, and later those Germans sentenced for espionage, were normally transferred to the Soviet Union (see map #1 of the locations of the camps).

The former concentration camp Sachsenhausen, near Oranienburg, north of Berlin was placed in operation on August 16, 1945, as Special Camp No. 7. The first two thousand inmates were drawn from the concentration camps Weesow, in Brandenburg and Hohenschönhausen in the eastern part of Berlin. The average number of prisoners at Sachsenhausen ranged from eleven to seventeen thousand.[34]

In the summer of 1937, the SS had established the Concentration Camp Buchenwald near the city of Weimar in Thüringen. This camp consisted of 15 two-story stone barracks and 32 single-story wooden barracks. In August 1945, the NKVD took over Buchenwald and turned it into NKVD/MVD Special Camp No. 2. This camp, whose population averaged 10,000 to 12,000 prisoners, drew its new arrivals from Thuringian prisons or from other camps. In Buchenwald, the majority of the prisoners were interned, that is, sent there without a court judgment, whereas in the Sachsenhausen camp, at the end of its existence, most prisoners there had been sentenced by the Soviet military courts.[35]

In January 1949, a group of journalists from the United States wanted to visit *Buchenwald* in order to record the Nazi atrocities committed in the camp. The Soviet forbade them to visit the concentration camp, explaining that it was now the site of an important military facility where Soviet troops were stationed.[36]

Jamlitz, which the Nazis, at one time, used to house imprisoned Jews, was located in the province of Brandenburg, near Frankfurt-an-der-Oder. In September 1945, the NKVD established a prison camp there as a transit camp for prisoners from the towns of Guben and Cottbus and then as a transit camp for those being moved from Frankfurt-an-der-

Oder, Posen (Poznan, Poland) and Ketchendorf to other destinations. The camp averaged 6,000 prisoners.[37]

From May 1945 to February 1950, cell blocks of the prison buildings in Bautzen in Sachsen, as well as the barracks along the inner courts, served as Soviet concentration camp facilities. The prison got its name, "Yellow Misery," from the yellowish whitewash on its walls. On the average, Bautzen housed 7,000 internees and convicts, sentenced by Soviet military tribunals. Approximately 28,000 people passed through the camp. They were transferred to Bautzen from other prisons and camps and then integrated into transports leaving Bautzen again. The Bautzen Committee for the Investigation of Stalinist Crimes reported that some 9,000 to 16,000 people starved to death or died of tuberculosis in Bautzen between 1945 and 1950. Many were also said to have been executed. The dead were dumped into shallow graves originating from former anti-aircraft ditches both inside and outside the camp, as well as on a nearby mountain north of the site.[38]

On arrival of the prisoners in the Mühlberg Special Camp #1, the prisoners were greeted with the slogan, "ORDER, DISCIPLINE, CLEAN-LINESS." This was similar to the slogans greeting prisoners in the Nazi concentration camps, These orders were the following:

-Any contact with the world outside the camps is prohibited.

-Ownership of pencils, paper, knives, scissors, sharp instruments, writing material, and money is prohibited.

-Talking with women prisoners is prohibited.

-Soviet officers and soldiers must be greeted militarily.[39]

Figure 4. Special Camps and Years of Operations.

Name of Special Camp	Number	Period of Operation
Mühlberg by Riesa	No. 1	September 1945 until November 1948
Buchenwald by Weimar	No. 2	August 1945 to February 1950
Hohenschönhausen in Berlin	No.3	May 1945 to October 1946
Bautzen	No.4 (from 1948, No. 3)	June 1945 to January 1950
Ketschendorf by Fürstenwalde	No. 5	May 1945 Until February 1947
Jamlitz by Lieberose	No. 6	September 1945 to April 1947
Sachsenhausen (Oranienburg)	No. 7 (from 1948, No. 1)	August 1945 to March 1950
Torgau	No. 8	From September 1945 in Fort Zinna, then from March 1946 in Seydlitz-Kaserne, liquidated in January 1947
Fünfeichen bei Neubrandenburg	No. 9	April 1945 to October 1948
Torgau	No. 10	May 1946 to October 1948 (except in Fort Zinna)

Figure 4. is a list of the special camps and their years of operation.[40]

In all the years of existence of the special camps, the NKVD/MVD maintained strict control of prisoners and guards through a system of special Operational Groups.[41] The leaders of the NKVD/MVD Operational Groups in the special camps were generally captains, occasionally majors. They received their instructions from the NKVD heads in Berlin, under the command of General Serov. These instructions emphasized the creation of a wide network of informers among the prisoners and, above all, for the complete isolation of the prisoners. NKVD headquarters insisted on periodic reports from the Operational Groups on the security situation, the prisoners' mood within the camps, the examination of individuals subject to further punishment, the discovery of escape plans, and the quality and behavior of the prison guards.[42]

On June 25, 1946, the NKVD/MVD issued the following instructions to the Operational Groups in the camps, entitled, Temporary Instructions to the Operational Groups on the Activities of Agents in the MVD Special Camps on German Territory:

> *The principal work objectives of the Operational Groups regarding agent activities among the prisoners in the special camps of the MVD are these:*

(a) To secure and isolate the prisoners completely from the outside world; to prevent escape and any disturbance of the camp order.

(b) To secure active Nazis among the prisoners, agents of the military intelligence, Nazi security organizations, and any individual who was eligible for trial before military courts.

(c) To discover and prevent prisoner attempts to organize enemy activities in the camps.

Beginning in 1947, with the increase in Cold War tensions, the discovery of enemy agent activities received a greater emphasis. Also, with the decrease in food rations in 1946/1947, prevention of prisoner escape attempts received more priority from the Operational Groups. For example, from Buchenwald camp, five prisoners succeeded in escaping on December 12, 1946, but this was an exceptional case.[43]

Every camp Operational Group had the responsibility to recruit and organize informers in their respective camps. Former agents of the German military intelligence and former members of the German security services were considered especially apt for this service. Soviet records reveal that by October 31, 1946, there were 890 informers in the special camps. Nevertheless, there were constant complaints about the quality of the information gathered. The NKVD recommended an increase in agent compensation by offering more tobacco and food to improve the quality of the information. Headquarters also found the reports often overly optimistic in regard to the prisoners' feelings about the USSR. Obviously, reports of prisoners' very positive opinions and interest in the Soviet Union were, of course, completely untrue, and were merely attempts to win approval from the Berlin NKVD.[44]

Other reports to the NKVD/MVD in Berlin were realistic and honest, like this example:

The prisoners who are held in the barracks of the 2nd zone, complain about the policies of the Soviet occupation troops in Germany. About the

Berlin question, they say that everything is the fault of the Russians and that everything that the Russians write in the press is a lie, such as shown by the results of the elections of December 12, 1948. That the population of Berlin does not want to know anything about the Russians.(Editor's note: this referred to the October 1946 elections; in this election 85% of the population in Berlin voted against the SED). Grotewohl (PrimeMinister of the German Democratic Republic) and Pieck (President of the Germans Democratic Republic) are Russian agents. If there is a war (against the Soviet Union) all the prisoners would wish to fight against the Russians.

Or this from a sentenced prisoner of the second court who stated the following:

I know the Russians very well and I know that they only want to completely annihilate us. Whoever falls into the hand of the GPU,(predecessor of the NKVD) he is, so to say, really lost. We should not hope for an amnesty. In Russia there are also people who are against Bolshevism, but the GPU is so terrifying that no one will ever dare to revolt against them. I only wish that as soon as possible war begins between America and Russia; then I would be free and communism would come to an end.

Prisoners expressing such ideas had them inserted in their personal documents as enemies of the State, were transferred to other barracks, received additional punishment or even executed. All information from the informants was gathered twice a month, either through the NKVD or SVAG, and sent to Moscow.[45]

It should be noted that prisoners quickly learned to identify informers. If someone returned from a visit to the *Kommandantur* with extra rations, it was immediately evident that he had denounced someone to the Russians. Most everyone was frightened by a call to the *Kommandantur*, but if someone went calmly, it was clear that he was called to make a report. Such persons were avoided at all costs by the other prisoners.[46]

By the winter and spring of 1945/1946, all NKVD special camps and prisons were over-filled with inmates. Order #00461, which authorized the arrest and incarceration of a variety of Nazi offenders and others opposed to the Soviet occupation, made these crowded conditions even worse. Prisons were so full in the provinces of Thüringen and Sachsen-Anhalt, for example, that the Soviet security services there could not fulfill their orders.[47]

ARREST, INTERROGATION, AND DEPORTATION

The interrogation of prisoners took place in all major cities and towns, in all provinces of the SBZ. In the early occupation of East Germany, the NKVD/MVD in all the larger communities confiscated large houses whose cellars could be converted into prison cells. They preferred isolated houses with high fences around them; the NKVD/MVD also took over some prisons for use as interrogation centers.[48]

The NKVD initially controlled interrogations, but after the ministerial change in May 1946, they were placed under the control of the MGB, the Ministry of State Security. The Soviet security services installed torture chambers in their Berlin Hohenschönhausen central command, but mental and physical torture was common in all interrogation centers. Physical force was used to extract confessions and guilt was assumed of all those arrested; any evidence to the contrary was not admitted. Interrogations were usually at night; both physical and psychological torture was used and all prisoners quickly understood that they were in the complete power of their captors as to whether they lived or died. The denunciation by fellow prisoners was common. Sleep and food deprivation, simulated firing squads, and the threat of arresting family members were all common torture methods. In the case of prisoners arrested in groups, one member was always played off against the other. These interrogations could go on for a year or sometimes longer. Under these circumstances, most prisoners were prepared to confess whatever was demanded of them in order to stop their torments. The final interrogation protocol had to be signed by the prisoner, and it was always in Russian, which none of them could read. Translators were usually present at the interrogations. None of the accused ever received a charge sheet or conviction from the NKVD.[49]

To be arrested and charged required only a minimum amount of suspicion. Many were arrested as a result of denunciations by others, sometimes made in order to save themselves and sometimes in order to receive benefits from the Soviet occupation authorities. The disappearance of family members, friends, and colleagues without a trace created a great climate of fear and uncertainty about the Soviet secret police, which was of assistance in imposing their police state on East Germany.[50]

After interrogation in the NKVD cellars, the prisoners were then sent to a special camp: One prisoner stated; *"For us, Buchenwald (special camp) was as a salvation. Some, who had only been two or three days in an NKVD prison could not understand this feeling. He could not understand it at all, the relief we now felt (in Buchenwald). Oh well!"*[51]

Another report tells us that after a short period under interrogation, prisoners were taken by truck to the special camps. There, they met prisoners who had never been interrogated. One witness from the town of Neu Brandenburg, reports:

At this time, in the summer of 1945, groups of arrested persons, both former soldiers and civilians, were taken by the Mecklenburg Road to the camp at Fünfeichen. These groups were each formed by 50 to 150 individuals. When these marching columns were reduced by individuals fleeing or collapsing from exhaustion, then passers-by were taken and pressed by force into the columns so that the complete number were delivered to the special camp.[52]

EXECUTION OF PRISONERS

In most interrogation prisons, there were special cells for those to be executed; they were mostly cellar cells without daylight, dirty, damp, and full of vermin. Normally, there was no possibility to wash. The execution candidate sometimes had to wait months until the fulfillment of the verdict. The candidate for execution was typically undernourished and unkempt, dressed in rags. Food and waste were handed in and out through a small hole in the door; there was no contact with the outside world. The prisoner was taken out of the cell at night, not knowing whether he would be executed or receive a reprieve in the form of a prison sentence (usually ten years). If he was to be executed, he would be told to leave his clothing in the cell. If he could take it with him, that meant a reprieve. The execution candidate had to undress and could only take a blanket in which his body would then be wrapped for burial. In some cases, the executions took place in cellars of empty houses; one example was House #4, in the Bautzen camp.[53]

NKVD INTERROGATION CELLARS

Personal Narrative of Willi T. born May 28, 1914

Attempting to drive home with my mother and mother in law, I was accosted by a person in Russian uniform who told me that I was under arrest and must go with him to be interrogated. My initial reaction was to resist, but desisted immediately as I saw that I was surrounded by a number of people. I went to the Kommandantur. After awhile, a Russian Major came in, whom I later found out was the commander of the MVD unit in the town of Mahlow. He ordered me to get into an automobile. Without my being able to say goodbye to my family, I was driven to the Birkenstrasse headquarters of the MVD. I was relieved of my personal possessions and was sent by a Russian civilian into a prison, located in a small house with only a cellar and a first floor. I first was imprisoned in a small, barred room, on the ground floor, but later confined to a prison cell in the cellar. In this small room, the electric light was on day and night. There was graffiti on the walls, made by former prisoners, saying to only tell the truth and to trust in God.

After a few hours, I was taken to the first interrogation. At first, I was only asked why I did not immediately follow orders, without complaint of the person who arrested me. Then my personal history was written down.

I had to counter sign each page, which was written in ink and in Russian. An interpreter translated what I had signed. It was difficult, however, for me to follow the interpreter, especially as the interrogation lasted for hours. My answers were basically treated as lies, and with threats that I would be sent to Siberia, and would never see my wife and children again. The interrogators wanted me to tell all and confess. When they realized that this had no effect on me, I was hit on the head, they twisted my head and kicked me in the stomach so that I fell off the chair...A captain who came often into the interrogation room kicked me in the shins with his boots so that I was soon practically completely crippled. They were furious, but I could not understand their words of anger.

They wanted to have me confirm that I said in a meeting in Jütchendorf on August 1,1946, that the CDU (Christian Democratic Party) was the only party that would ensure that the millions of refugees from the East would receive their homes again; that I also stated that the SED (Socialist Unity Party) is a reactionary party. Also, why was I employed by a company active in the British sector? It was not an insurance company, but one active in the black market and a spy agency. What did the English officers want in our company and how often did they visit my manager?... I should tell all and then I could go home again, already tomorrow. Every one of my answers was characterized as a lie. They said, "We know all about you; we have our informants. We don't need your witnesses! We will not shoot you or hang you, but you will die of hunger. We have confiscated all your possessions, your house, horse, and goats and everything else.. We will also arrest your family. They will also go to Siberia."

I was continuously asked why I engaged in propaganda against the SED. My reply was that I did nothing against the SED but only tried to defend myself against their constant attacks. Their reply was blows to my face, kicks on my shins and in the stomach. Also, my explanation that as a member of a democratic party, the duty of a party leader was to participate in meetings and to dispute the ideas of other parties was met with a cynical laugh and brutal mistreatment. Why did I, on May 1, 1929 as a leader of the former Stahlhelm (a reactionary German veterans organization), march to the houses of socialist comrades and sing slanderous songs such as "Thälmann (head of the German communist party) to the gallows" and "Rosa Luxemburg swims in the Canal" (a founder of the German communist party who was assassinated and her body found in a canal)?.My reply was that on May 1, 1929 I was not yet 15 years old and was not a member of Stahlhelm or any sort of leader in my community. My replies were answered with the most horrible mistreatment. One also did not believe me that at this time I did not live in Thyrow-Trebbin (Brandenburg), but with my parents in Berlin-Charlottenburg.

For nine days these questions were directed at me for hours on end, day and night. But as I always stubbornly stuck to the truth, they tried with increasingly unpleasant methods to force me to confess. I was hit on the ears with the sharp edge of a ruler; one threw heavy objects at me, and kicked me on the shins with iron edged, pointed boots.

On the night of March 30/31, 1947, I was transported with another prisoner to Bernau. There we were jailed in a cellar cell. On the second day, precisely at 9:00 PM,I was taken out for interrogation. This interrogation again lasted several hours. The same questions were again put to me.... The interrogating officer drew on a piece of paper a coffin and said that I would be buried in Siberia and no one would know what happened to me. This interrogation suddenly ended at 0:30 AM with his comment that if at the next interrogation I did not confess I would greatly regret it. He did not think that I would survive this encounter.

After several days, I was suddenly taken out of the cell and on the way to the interrogation room kicked and beaten without interruption. . . .During the interrogation, the officer brought out from an adjoining room a cudgel and beat me 17 times so that my entire body became bloody and totally black and blue.

On April 23, 1947 a charge sheet was read to me, that I had to sign. When I refused, the officer told me that evidently I could only be managed with a cudgel and that I would be going to another interrogation again. I then signed the charge sheet in order to be finally left in peace.[54]

Every prisoner who passed through the NKVD/MVD cellars spoke of mistreatment. In the opinion of the prisoners, one should sign the protocol of the interrogations as soon as possible in order to bring the tortures to an end as soon as possible. Most prisoners collapsed quickly under the physical and psychological tortures. After the prisoners had signed the protocol under coercion, which was always in Russian and without a German translation, the prisoners had no idea what they had signed; the head of the MVD unit then decided whether the prisoners would go before a Military Tribunal for trial or be detained administratively and sent to a special camp.[55]

(Refer to http://www.thegulagineastgermany.com for Illustration #10. A Soviet prison train. In such cattle cars, the prisoners were taken to the *Spezlager* or to the Gulag camps in the Soviet Union. Source: Finn, Gerhard, Die Politischen Häftlinge der Sowjetzone, 1945-1959)

NOTES

1. Giles Macdonogh, *After the Reich: The Brutal History of the Allied Occupation,(New York,2007)*, 214–215.
2. Mironenko, Niethammer, and von Plato, eds., *Sowjetische Speziallager in Deutschland 1945 bis 1950 Band I*, 32.
3. Helmut Barwald, *Terror als System*, in Scholz, Günther, Ed.,*Verfolgt-Verhaftet-Verurteilt; Demokraten im Widerstand gegen die rote Diktatur-Fakten und Beispiele,*(Berlin,Germany, 1990,), 19.
4. Ibid.
5. Jan Von Flocken, and Michael Klonovsky, *Stalin's Lager in Deutschland 1945–1950,* (Berlin, Germany, 1994), 22–23.
6. Frederick Taylor, *Exorcising Hitler; The Occupation and Denazification of Germany,* (New York, 2011), 240.
7. Mironenko, Niethammer, and von Plato, eds., *Sowjetische Speziallager in Deutschland 1945 bis 1950 Band I*, 29.
8. Ibid.
9. Ibid., 30.
10. Norman M. Naimark, *The Russians in Germany, A History of the Soviet Zone of Occupation, 1945–1949,* (Cambridge, Massachusetts, 1995), 360–361.
11. Jan Lipinsky, "Mobilität zwischen den Lagern," in *Sowjetische Speziallager in Deutschland 1945 bis 1950 Band I,* eds. Sergej Mironenko, Lutz Niethammer, and Alexander von Plato (Berlin: Akademie Verlag, 1998), 226–227.
12. Nikita Petrov, "Die Apparate des NKVD/MVD und der MGB in Deutschland (1945-1953), Eine Historische Skizze," in *Sowjetische Speziallager in Deutschland 1945 bis 1950 Band I,* eds. Sergej Mironenko, Lutz Niethammer, and Alexander von Plato (Berlin: Akademie Verlag, 1998), 147.
13. Mironenko, Niethammer, and von Plato, eds., *Sowjetische Speziallager in Deutschland 1945 bis 1950 Band I*, 29.
14. Peter Erler, "Zur Tätigkeit der Sowjetischen Militärtribunale (SMT) in der SBZ/DDR," in *Sowjetische Speziallager in Deutschland 1945 bis 1950 Band I,* eds. Sergej Mironenko, Lutz Niethammer, and Alexander von Plato (Berlin: Akademie Verlag, 1998), 179.
15. Lutz Niethammer, "Alierte Internierungslager in Deutschland nach 1945, Ein Vergleich und Offene Fragen in *Sowjetische Speziallager in Deutsch-*

land 1945 bis 1950 Band I, eds. Sergej Mironenko, Lutz Niethammer, and Alexander von Plato (Berlin: Akademie Verlag, 1998), 102–104.

16. Erler, "Zur Tätigkeit der Sowjetischen Militärtribunale (SMT) in der SBZ/ DDR," in *Sowjetische Speziallager in Deutschland 1945 bis 1950 Band I*, eds. Sergej Mironenko, Lutz Niethammer, and Alexander von Plato (Berlin: Akademie Verlag, 1998), 175.

17. Ibid., 176.

18. Ibid., 33–34.

19. Peter Erler, "Zur Tätigkeit der Sowjetischen Militärtribunale (SMT) in der SBZ/DDR," in *Sowjetische Speziallager in Deutschland 1945 bis 1950 Band I*, eds. Sergej Mironenko, Lutz Niethammer, and Alexander von Plato (Berlin: Akademie Verlag, 1998), 180.

20. Gerhard Finn, *Die Politischen Häftlinge der Sovjetzone* (Pfaffenhofen, Germany, 1960), 29.

21. Erler, "Zur Tätigkeit der Sowjetischen Militärtribunale (SMT) in der SBZ/ DDR," in *Sowjetische Speziallager in Deutschland 1945 bis 1950 Band I*, eds. Sergej Mironenko, Lutz Niethammer, and Alexander von Plato (Berlin: Akademie Verlag, 1998).

22. Ibid., 173.

23. Bettina Greiner, *Verdrângter Terror* (Hamburg, Germany, 2010), 15.

24. Ibid., 183.

25. Ronny Kabus, *In der Gewalt Stalins und der SED,*(Norderstedt, Germany, 2011), 208.

26. Ibid., 72.

27. Ibid., 183.

28. Ibid., 215.

29. Anne Applebaum, *Gulag, A History* (New York, 2003), 422–423.

30. Ronny Kabus, *In der Gewalt Stalins und der SED*, 30.

31. Von Flocken and Klonovsky, *Stalin's Lager in Deutschland 1945–1950*, 29.

32. Ibid., 31.

33. Greiner, *Verdrângter Terror*, 113.

34. Adrian Preissinger, *Death Camps of the Soviets, 1945–1950*, (Ocean City, Maryland, 1994), 46.

35. Mironenko, Niethammer, and von Plato, eds., *Sowjetische Speziallager in Deutschland 1945 bis 1950 Band I*, 14.

36. Preissinger, *Death Camps of the Soviets, 1945–1950*, 138.

37. Ibid., 51.

38. Ibid., 140–141.

39. Achim Kilian, *Einzuweisen zur volligen Isolierung, NKWD Speziallager Muhlberg, Elbe,* (Leipzig, Germany, 1992), 82.
40. Mironenko, Niethammer, and von Plato, eds., *Sowjetische Speziallager in Deutschland 1945 bis 1950 Band I,* 32.
41. Ibid., 34.
42. Ibid., 64.
43. Ibid., 65.
44. Ibid., 66.
45. Ibid., 66–67.
46. Ibid., 68.
47. Naimark, *The Russians in Germany, A History of the Soviet Zone of Occupation, 1945–1949,* 386.
48. Finn, *Die Politischen Häftlinge der Sovjetzone,* 15.
49. Erler, "Zur Tätigkeit der Sowjetischen Militärtribunale (SMT) in der SBZ/DDR," in *Sowjetische Speziallager in Deutschland 1945 bis 1950 Band I,* eds. Sergej Mironenko, Lutz Niethammer, and Alexander von Plato (Berlin: Akademie Verlag, 1998), 178–179.
50. Jan Von Flocken and Michael Klonovsky, *Stalin's Lager in Deutschland 1945–1950,* 26.
51. Mironenko, Niethammer, and von Plato, eds., *Sowjetische Speziallager in Deutschland 1945 bis 1950 Band I,* 63.
52. Jan Von Flocken and Michael Klonovsky, *Stalin's Lager in Deutschland 1945–1950,* 28.
53. Uwe Greve,*Lager des Grauens: Sowjetische KZs in der DDR nach 1945* (Kiel, Germany, 1990), 124–125.
54. Finn, *Die Politischen Häftlinge der Sovjetzone,* 23–25.
55. Ibid., 20, 22.

CHAPTER 6

THE PRISONERS:
WHO WERE THEY?

Communists are only red-painted Nazis.

The above was a remark from Kurt Schumacher, first head of the Social Democratic Party (SPD) in the Federal Republic after the war, a member of the Bundestag, and leader of the opposition. Before 1933, he was a strong critic, in the Reichstag, of Hitler and of the Nazi Party for which Hitler sent him to concentration camps, including Dachau, for ten years. After the war, he became a leading opponent of the East German communist party and of the German Democratic Republic.

(Refer to http://www.thegulagineastgermany.com for Illustration #11; Kurt Schumacher, Head of the Social Democratic Partyof Germany. Source: Wikimedia Commons)

CATEGORIES OF PRISONERS

Immediately after the war, the Soviets interned nominal SS and Nazi party members, i.e. Nazis with little importance, such as judges, teachers, and many young people accused of Werewolf activities. Major Nazi war criminals were sent to the Soviet Union. Shortly thereafter, however, the only Nazis arrested and interned in the special camps were minor Nazis, such as block or cell leaders. Even these arrests ceased by the beginning of 1946.[1]

After the initial arrests of Nazis, the Soviets then concentrated on punishing those accused of political crimes, especially terrorist acts against Soviet authorities. As mentioned, young people were especially singled out as members of the Werewolf; also targeted were individuals who had contacts with the political opposition in the West, such as the Eastern bureaus of the SPD, CDU, LDPD, and in West Berlin with the KgU (see below), and RIAS (the West Berlin-based radio station directed at communist East Germany). All were considered "spies and agents" and subject to arrest and incarceration. Reading forbidden newspapers, magazines, and leaflets from the West led to internment, as did accusations of Trotskyism and Titoism.. Starting 1947, members of the Liberal Democrats (LDPD), Christian Democrats (CDU), Social Democrats (SPD), and student opposition groups were also arrested. They were joined by unreliable members of the official party SED, the FDJ (communist youth group), former members of the KPD (Communist Party of Germany), or left splinter groups of the communist and socialist parties, and other anti-fascists; even former prisoners of the Nazi concentration camps were included.[2]

When the Soviets first marched into Germany in April and May of 1945, aside from the arrests of Nazi Party members, they were most greatly concerned with the radical left. These communists strove toward an immediate "peoples' revolution" and a German Soviet state, as opposed to the so-called Soviet style "party of the new type," Walter Ulbricht's fusion of socialists and communists into the SED. The KPD leadership, Ulbricht in particular, and NKVD agents cooperated in making these sectarian groups harmless. At the time, they became the NKVD Operational Groups' most serious targets and the greatest threat to Soviet authority. They consumed much of the energies of the Operational Groups. The KPD finally brought them under political control and made it clear to them that it was ideologically incorrect to work for a Soviet Germany, as this played into the hands of the reactionaries. Many hard line, disgruntled communists left politics altogether; a number fled to the West; and some were arrested and sent to the camps for their opposition. However, by far the greatest number of them submitted to the Moscow line. While the Soviets continued to complain of sectarian elements in the SED, they realized that the SPD, the social democrats, presented a far more serious challenge to the military government and to the German communists.[3]

Also of special concern to the Soviet authorities were the many young people whom they thought had all been brainwashed in the Hitler Youth and BDM (*Bund Deutscher Mädchen*), and were, thus, prime raw material for recruitment into the Werewolf (see chapter 1) and for anti-Soviet activities in general. Their main crimes seem to have been painting anti-Soviet graffiti on walls and circulating flyers attacking the Soviet occupying authorities. In general, however, these activities were not common. There were rare cases of youth gangs attacking Soviet soldiers, incidents of sabotage, and bombs exploding in factories or SED party houses. In 1948, police reported 51 explosions in factories and 500 cases of other kinds of sabotage, such as unexplained fires and equipment damage. However, there were never fully documented cases of serious acts of sabotage, either by the Werewolf or other counter-revolutionary groups in the period of 1947 through 1949.[4] Nevertheless, many youths were arrested by the NKVD/MVD and sent to the special camps as suspected members of the Werewolf.[5]

Between 1948 and 1951, some 300 East German high school and university students were arrested and sentenced to hard labor in the Soviet Union, many for pranks committed against the East German regime. A group of young boys in Jena received ten years each for throwing stink bombs at school officials during a formal celebration of President Wilhelm Pieck's birthday. By 1950, East German camps and jails held 800 boys and girls under the age of 17. Some were even being held for having made faces during a lecture about Stalin, or for having scribbled an "F" for *Freiheit* (freedom) on city walls at night.[6]

The fact that many young people simply disappeared into the Soviet security apparatus, with no charges ever brought, greatly upset not only the general populace, but also some in the SED leadership. In December 1947, Wilhelm Pieck, later President of the GDR, protested, without success, to the Central Committee of the Communist Party, the arrest and disappearance of many innocent young people based on unfounded Werewolf charges, requesting that an orderly procedure be introduced to judge them correctly.[7]

Also, in early December 1947, the Evangelical (Lutheran) Bishops of East and West Germany sent a letter to the four Allied Military Governors claiming that 2,000 young people had been arrested and imprisoned in East Germany during one year. This number included 157 under the age of 15 and another 500 from 16 to 18. The letter noted that many of the young people were sent to the old Nazi concentration camps of Sachsenhausen, Buchenwald, and Bautzen.[8]

When the Soviets legalized both the KPD and the SPD in June 1945, they harbored visions of the Communists outpolling the social democrats in future elections and, as a result, dominating the antifascist democratic bloc of parties. The Operational Groups were used to intimidate the SPD in the hope that the party would accept its Soviet-designed role as junior partner to the Communists. In August 1945, Otto Grotewohl, then leader of the SPD in the East, noted that any time the SPD protested problems with the occupation authorities, they did so "under threat of not coming home from these discussions."[9]

The strongest terror measures in the SBZ were used by the Soviets and their German Communist allies against the Social Democrats, their members, officers, and even fighters against the Hitler regime who had just been released from the concentration camps in May 1945. Many were sent to the special camps in the same year; some even to the same former

Nazi camps. The Soviets considered them the most uncompromising opponents to the Soviet attempt to communize East Germany and to make it into a satellite of Moscow. The Soviets and the East German Communists especially resented the influence of SPD members on the East German labor unions.[10]

This persecution of the socialist party reached a high point in April 1946, during preparations to join the two parties, SPD and KPD into one party, called the SED. Members and officers of the SPD largely opposed this merger, as it would mean the disappearance of social democracy in East Germany. Many who opposed it were then arrested and sent to the camps. Even some of the delegates to the joint party congress, which was to approve the new party, were arrested on their way to the congress, if they were considered opponents.

Yet in 1948, after the SED was established, the socialists continued to be a main target of repression. The motto was *"Be alert for the agents of Schumacher."* Thousands of SPD members were arrested and incarcerated in the special camps. Socialists became the main object of Soviet and SED defamation and persecution. The social democrats nonetheless remained the main clandestine opposition to the Soviet/SED Communist government in East Germany.

Not surprisingly, Erich Mielke (head of the secret police in East Germany) looked to K-5 (see chapter 4) as an incipient East German office of state security. Its job, he stated, was *"to defend democratic institutions, their further development, and the economic rebuilding of the SBZ from (Störversuche.)" destabilization attempts. Enemies had made their way into the political parties and mass organizations."* Mielke continued, *"Schumacher agents"* were everywhere, trying to undermine the democratic rebuilding. The task of K-5 was to uncover their plans and disrupt their activities.[11]

According to the *Ostbüro* (Eastern Office) of the SPD, founded by Kurt Schumacher in May 1946, for the purpose of collecting political information on the Soviet occupation zone as well as maintaining contact with social democrats in East Germany, it reported that from December 1945 to April 1946, before the fusion of the two parties, at least 20,000 Socialists in East Germany were thrown out of their homes, dismissed from their jobs, arrested, and incarcerated for shorter or longer periods; and some were even executed. Of those arrested after the formation of the SED, at least 5,000 SPD members were sentenced by the SMTs as "Schumacher Agents," most for 25 years; 400 died in the camps and 1,000 died after their release as a result of their incarceration.[12] Most SPD members and supporters of the *Ostbüro* were interned in the *Bautzen* penitentiary in Sachsen and in the Brandenburg camps, passing through the *Roter Ochse* (Red Ox) interrogation center in Halle (Province Sachsen-Anhalt).[13]

In order to counteract internal opposition from former SPD members, the SED in 1948 established the *PPA-Pesonalpolitische Abteilung*, "personnel political department," to verify the personal political position at all levels of government officials in East Germany. They divided former SPD members into these three categories: 1. Fellow travelers; 2. Doubtful members (in 1949, thousands of former SPD members were expelled from the SED; they lost their jobs and then most fled to the West); 3. Opponents (these were then reported to the Soviet security services and arrested).[14] In 1950/1951 this number increased to 150,000 SED party members purged; they were mainly former socialists, but some were former KPD members as well.[15] Most of the 5,000 SPD members convicted by the SMTs were freed in 1956, as a result of Chancellor Adenauer's state visit to Moscow in September 1955, when, in return for establishing diplomatic relations with the USSR, the Soviets promised to release all German war prisoners and interned German civilians.[16]

The number of NKVD/MVD arrests became so great that SED leaders began to fear a loss of legitimacy for their party. In March/April 1948, both SED heads Pieck and Grotewohl complained to Soviet leaders in Moscow and Berlin that Western propaganda was successfully undermining the confidence of the East German populace in the Soviet Union and the SED by these acts of violence and disappearances.[17]

PERSONAL NARRATIVE

Fritz Schenk was a young Social Democrat who fled in September 1957 to West Germany. He relates the following in his book, *Im Vorzimmer der Diktatur, 1962,"* (In the Anti-chamber of the Dictatorship, 1962):

"I personally experienced a terrible circus. My friend Hermann Polenz was arrested at night. The Russians went through his home thoroughly, through all drawers and closets. They also arrested and took with them our county commissioner, evidently for interrogation. When Polenz' wife went to the local Soviet Army headquarters (Kommandantur), the next day, they expressed ignorance of his arrest. The local head of the party (SPD), did everything possible to have him freed or at least to find out what happened. The Soviets also did not give any information to the local party head. After further arrests of SPD members became known, there was a party meeting with resolutions demanding the freeing of all party members as well as to present an official, party protest to the Soviets. The Russians replied with much misleading information. For example, they documented with letters attempting to prove that Hermann Polenz moved to the West with his girlfriend. In other cases, they constructed incriminating evidence that he was arrested by German authorities (Volkspolize-Peoples' Police) because of alleged acts of corruption, bribery and fraud. Because these accusations were false, the local Volkspolizei involved in his arrest had a conflict of conscience even though the majority of the VPs were members of the SED. Under pressure from their fellow officers, they finally admitted that the Russians, under threats of retaliation, ordered them to confirm this false misinformation.

By and by, the details of the fate of those arrested became known. The majority were in interrogation cellars of the main Red Army regional headquarters of Halle, Leipzig, Dresden Magdeburg, Görlitz, Bautzen and other cities. Many were deported to the Soviet Union and charged with alleged espionage against the Red Army resulting in long prison sentences. Only many years later were the prisoners allowed to write and receive mail. Hermann Polenz was a prisoner from 1947 to 1954 in the special camp Bautzen. After his release he fled to the Federal Republic.[18]

(Refer to http://www.thegulagineastgermany.com for Illustration #12: Prisoner being led away by a Soviet guard, Sachsenhausen Camp. Source: Sachsenhausen bei Berlin, Speziallager #7, Günter Agde.)

Members of the CDU (Christian Democratic Party) also were frequently subject to arrest. After the forced elimination of Jakob Kaiser as head of the CDU in East Germany in December 1947, by the Soviets, there was a mass arrest the next year of CDU officials at the provincial, county, and city levels, as well as of local party leaders. Arrests were also extended to LDPD (Liberal Democratic Party) leaders. Ulbricht said both bourgeois parties were a hiding place for reactionaries, and *"that there was no peaceful union for them with socialism."* For example, on June 24, 1948, the SMTs began a criminal process against 25 active CDU members. All were convicted of espionage, anti-Soviet propaganda, and illegal group formation; they were each sentenced to 25 years imprisonment.[19] In university student elections of 1948/1949, in all six universities in the SBZ, the CDU and the LDP, parties won 50-70% of the vote. Consequently, the Soviet security apparatus undertook a purge of these organizations, with 400 to 500 leaders arrested, tried by the SMTs, jailed, and some even executed. After these police actions, both parties were banned in the universities.[20]

Soviet security organization also attacked leaders of Christian Socialist trade unions, arresting and imprisoning them.[21] In 1950, when the SED decided to make the CDU into a "front" party, an instrument of the SED, and a member of the "block of democratic parties" supporting the GDR, many remaining independent CDU members were arrested and thousands of members left the party. Some leaders were able to escape to the West. [22] Many arrests of CDU leaders were based on denunciations by informers working for the Soviet Security Services.[23] In August 1952, 70 members of the Thüringen CDU, reacting to this wave of harassment and arrests, sought refuge with the CDU *Ostbüro* in West Berlin.[24] (Contact with the *Ostbüros* of any of the democratic parties was grounds for arrest in the GDR.) [25]

Those German POWs were also arrested by the NKVD Operations Groups; they had been processed in Western POW camps and allowed to return home in the SBZ. According to British intelligence sources, some groups of returning POWs had their documents confiscated at the border and were sent to Erfurt for five weeks of quarantine and political re-education. The majority were then interned in the Sachsenhausen special camp, with the healthy ones sent to the Soviet Union for forced labor. On arriving in East Germany, returning POWs were sometimes not even allowed to go home but sent directly to the Soviet Union as slave laborers.[26]

RESISTANCE IN THE SOVIET ZONE OF OCCUPATION

Chief among the opposition groups that gathered and distributed information on conditions and abuses in the special camps were the *Ostbüro* of the CDU, the *Ostbüro* of the SPD, *Kampfgruppe gegen Unmenschlichkeit* (KgU) (Combat Unit against Inhumanity), and *Waldheim-Kameradschaftskreis* or the group *Opfer des Stalinismus* (Victims of Stalinism).[27]

Both the FDP (German Liberal Democratic Party), whose affiliated party in the East was the LDPD, as well as the DGB, (*Deutschergewerkschaftsbund*) Confederation of German Trade Unions, had *Ostbüros*. Their function was the same as those of the SPD, that was to aid political refugees coming from the East, sending anti-communist material to the SBZ, gathering information on conditions there for their headquarters in West Germany, and vetting refugees from the East to ensure that they were not spies for the Soviets. The DGB and the FDP worked closely with the *Ostbüros* of the SPD and CDU. However, neither had the organizational capacity and support in the SBZ/GDR as did the two other organizations.

KAMPFGRUPPE GEGEN UNMENSCHLICHKEIT (KgU) (COMBAT UNIT AGAINST INHUMANITY)

Rainer Hildebrandt founded the KgU in West Berlin in 1948 as a militant opposition organization against the Sovietization of East Germany with unconfirmed reports of some CIA financing. It served as an information service about the SBZ (Soviet Zone of Occupation) and, as such, was in the front line of the Cold War.[28] Hildebrandt and his partner Ernst Tillich were active anti-Nazis, both of whom had been imprisoned by the Nazi regime. Hildebrandt had connections to the July 20th assassination attempt on Hitler. Tillich, a well known Lutheran clergyman, was active in the "confessing church," the anti-Nazi Lutheran church which had split from the official German Lutheran, church which had not opposed the regime. The KgU motto was, "*Silence is suicide; inaction is murder.*"[29]

One of their major initiatives was to break the Soviet information blackout on the special camps by reporting on them, including names of prisoners and locations where they were being held, names of informers in the camps, and names and locations of those who denounced the prisoners. When the Soviets made a partial release of special camp prisoners in 1948, Hildebrandt considered himself and his organization vindicated, because they had exposed the existence and injustice in these camps.[30]

Their search service, the purpose of which was to find the location of those arrested and deported, was of particular irritation to the Soviets. They were among the first to find out about the high death rates in the camps. Their many sources of information included released prisoners, who could be interviewed at that time in West Berlin; this occurred before the construction of the "wall" in 1961.[31]

Advising the relatives of those arrested of the fate of their family members was not the only task of the KgU. Their reports were also designed to destabilize the political system of the SBZ and later the GDR. They published the names and death notices of the prisoners in the West Berlin press and were assisted in this work by the RIAS (Radio in the American Sector), a radio station established and run by the US Military Administration in their sector of Berlin. In 1953, the KgU, in collaboration with the organizations of Free Jurists and Victims of the Nazi Regime, published a brochure for the East Germans on what to do in case of arrest by the NKVD.[32]

Between 1949 and 1954, more than 250,000 East Germans traveled to Berlin to visit the KgU offices to find out about their family members in the camps or to report new arrests and give information on informers. All this information was then published. Although it was still possible for East Germans to visit West Berlin, such visits to the KgU were very dangerous and could lead to arrests by the NKVD.[33] The KgU generally did not ask their informers the reasons for their arrests. Evidently, the organization did not want to become involved in the politics of the denazification programs.[34]

In the early 1950s, the KgU did become involved in sabotage activities in the German Democratic Republic, such as bombing railway lines or railway bridges. In terms of damaging the GDR economy, these actions had a very limited effect. The major impact, however, was the significant increase of the fear of the Soviets and GDR of an organized upheaval against the regime.[35]

In 1959, the KgU principals, having experienced serious strategic differences, disbanded in March of that year, at the request of the Berlin Senate (legislature) and of the German Federal Government.

THE *OSTBÜRO* OF THE SOCIAL DEMOCRATIC PARTY (SPD)

The *Ostbüro* of the SPD originated in April 1946, after the forced merger of the SPD and KPD into the SED, which took place against the will of the majority of the SPD members in the SBZ. After the merger, the SPD was virtually banned in the Soviet Zone. In the West, the leader of the SPD, Kurt Schumacher, disapproved of and rejected the merger. The SPD then decided to oppose the East German Communist system, just as they had the Nazi regime. This was to be led by the *Ostbüro* and headquartered in Hannover, with its principal office in West Berlin.

Schumacher conceived the *Ostbüro* as a resistance group in the SBZ, led by the Western SPD, so that once the Soviets were gone, the SPD would be a fully functioning political party there. Its first duty was to help fleeing SPD members from the East. At the beginning, the *Ostbüro* also sent couriers to the Eastern Zone to establish contact with SPD members there and to give them current information from the West, as well as to check on refugee members from the East to ensure that they were not Soviet agents. These confidential agents in the East were to maintain the opposition to the communist regime and act as a reserve for the recreation of the party, once the Communist system was gone.

Their first efforts included publication of lists of SPD members who were arrested by the Soviet security services. The first such list appeared on October 30, 1947.[36] When an SPD member was released from prison or a camp, the other SPD members gave him lists of SPD prisoners, the reasons for their arrest, and addresses of family members. These were sent to the *Ostbüro* in Berlin for their further transmittal, along with requests for food and clothing packages to family members of those arrested. Some of these were then forwarded to the prisoners themselves by family members, which was permitted until 1955. Thereafter, only gifts of money were allowed.[37]

The *Ostbüro* also reported on SBZ/GDR conditions. The SPD couriers were frequently shadowed and when they met their SPD contact, the whole group was arrested. In 1948–1949, as a result of lack of care in their work, as well as denunciations, there was a mass arrest of SPD members in the SBZ. Over 1,000 key SPD members were deported to the camps or else to the Soviet Union. It was evident that the *Ostbüro* was ill prepared for illegal work.

A major disaster occurred on February 8, 1949, when an *Ostbüro* officer, Heinz Kühne, was kidnapped, taken to East Berlin, interrogated, and tortured there. He divulged many names and contacts of the SPD, which led to another wave of arrests. They were known as "Agents of the *Ostbüro*" or "Schumacher Agents."

Thereafter, the *Ostbüro's* work became more professional, emphasizing security consciousness; it functioned as a center of democratic opposition, working against the Communist system. The courier program was revamped, involving increased caution. As a result, only 10- 15 couriers were arrested yearly. Their work of the *Ostbüro* now concentrated on sending flyers and brochures to the East by balloons. For example, in 1950, 670,000 flyers and brochures were sent to the SBZ.[38] In addition, the *Ostbüro* had four radio programs monthly on RIAS (The Radio In the American Sector, a US government station). The GDR Ministry of State Security stated, "*the publications of the SPD-Ostbüro are especially dangerous because they were written in the language of the workers, and, in specific instances, foretold future developments in the GDR.*"[39]

These were the principal duties of the *Ostbüro* (SPD), after the forced merger in 1946 of the SPD with the KPD into the SED:

-To maintain contact with former SPD members.
-To send information from the SPD in West Germany to the SBZ.
-To prevent the infiltration of Communist agents into the SPD leadership apparatus.
-To inform the West about conditions in the SBZ/GDR.

Only after several years did they commence direct action to undermine the East German Government. For example, the *Ostbüro* forged shipping papers of the East German Railway in the fall of 1950, so that refrigerated cars full of butter, a rarity in the SBZ, were on a siding in Rostock; thus, the butter would not be delivered to Leipzig, as intended, which caused great unrest in that city. A similar incident occurred in the winter of that year, when potatoes were not delivered to consumers, but froze in railway sidings in East Germany.[40]

During this time, the leadership of the *Ostbüro* was frequently criticized as being amateur, due to their lack of professionalism in their underground work in the Eastern Zone and the GDR, leading to the arrest of many couriers and members of the opposition. The security and information services of the German Federal Republic considered the *Ostbüro a* "kindergarten of laymen," due to their lack of skills for such operations. After the construction of the Berlin Wall in August 1961, information from East Germany practically dried up, obviating the need for this group.

Not until Chancellor Willi Brandt introduced his eastern policy's opening to the Eastern Bloc in 1967 was the operation closed. It became a study/research institute for Pan-German issues, *Referart für gesamt-deutsche Fragen*, a project of the *Bundeszentrale für Politische Bildung an der Robert-Havemann-Gesellschaft e.v.* Berlin.[41]

Personal Narratives of Several SPD Members Undertaking Anti-Communist Resistance Work in the Soviet Zone of Occupation (SBZ)

Some SPD members were engaged in underground, anti-Communist resistance actions immediately following the fusion of the two parties, KPD and SPD, into the SED in April 1946. In this case, one SPD dissident group in Halle (Sachsen-Anhalt) was composed of six anti-merger SPD members. Prior to the fusion of the SPD with the SED, they met to plan an anti-Communist strategy in case the merger of the two parties succeeded. Once the SED had been created, one of the members of the group made a long trip to the *Ostbüro*'s SPD information center in West Berlin, to obtain brochures and newspapers for illegal distribution in the eastern zone. Only at the end of 1946 did a courier from the *Ostbüro's* head office in Hannover contact him directly. Soviet security forces, however, brought the activities of this group to an end, by arresting a member of this group at his apartment early on the morning of April 9, 1947, and delivering him to the underground interrogation cellars in a prison in Halle, nicknamed the Red Ox by the inmates. Red Army officers beat him almost daily for over five months in an attempt to obtain the names of others in the group. After his sentencing to ten years in a special camp, he was deported to Sachsenhausen, the former Nazi concentration camp just north of Berlin, converted into a "*Spezlager*" by the NKVD following the war. The prisoner complained about the lack of food and the harshness of conditions in the barracks that the Nazis had built for opponents of the Third Reich.

In a more violent case in Rostock, (East Germany) in May 1946, the NKVD arrested five former secretaries of the SPD in the province of Mecklenburg-Vorpommern. One was immediately shot, while the others were each sentenced to 25 years in a special camp. One escaped to the West.

This episode shows that the *Ostbüro* was no match for the seasoned veterans in the Soviet NKVD. Indeed, it appears that the NKVD penetrated the *Ostbüro* in Hannover at an early stage. The various SPD dissidents and resisters were mostly all caught and sentenced to the usual 25 year prison term under Article 58 (RSFSR Penal Code).[42]

THE *OSTBÜRO* OF THE CHRISTIAN DEMOCRATIC PARTY (CDU)

Similar to the SPD *Ostbüro,* the CDU office in West Berlin organized illegal opposition work in the SBZ, such as putting up wall posters; they also distributed leaflets and Western newspaper articles, as well as other information. Additionally, CDU leaders and members in the

SBZ held public meetings criticizing the Soviet occupation and SED, but these were mostly broken-up by the East German police and NKVD with the leaders arrested.[43] These arrests increased after the founding of the GDR in October 1949.

Another objective in opening the *Ostbüro* in West Berlin was to support the exiled CDU leaders from East Germany, expelled by the Soviet Military Administration (SVAG). These individuals were strongly influenced by the illegal work in the SBZ of the SPD *Ostbüro*. Initially directed by Jakob Kaiser, head of the CDU in East Germany until he was deposed by the Soviets in December 1947 and then exiled,[44] the *Ostbüro* was designed to be a liaison office between the exiled CDU heads and those members remaining in the SBZ. This included observing the further development of the CDU in East Germany, but its main responsibility was the vetting of refugee CDU members from the East to ensure they were not Soviet spies or infiltrators.[45]

Until the summer of 1948, contacts between the *Ostbüro* and representatives of the CDU were strong.[46] The *Ostbüro* attempted to convince the active members still in the SBZ to stay, in anticipation of the day the party would be free to take an active part in the politics of the country. The SVAG/GDR however, criminalized any contact between the local party and the *Ostbüro,* as well as the CDU in the Federal Republic. The *Ostbüro* only occasionally sent couriers to the East. Normally, CDU visitors from the East would pick up material at the *Ostbüro*'s West Berlin office. For example, in February 1950, 12,000 editions of the CDU newspaper was distributed in East German railway stations—1,120 by mail and 6,000 by couriers to the East. Sometimes they were even able to put up CDU posters on walls in Eastern cities.[47]

In 1950, the GDR Ministry of State Security, MfS, began to take draconian measures against CDU propaganda activities. Thousands of CDU members were abruptly dismissed from their work and forced to flee to the West; many others were arrested. Ten of the 14 heads of the CDU in the GDR fled to the West. All CDU directors of the provincial councils were removed, arrested, and incarcerated or executed by the summer of 1950. In the years 1948–1950, 597 CDU members in the East were arrested and jailed.[48] Their places were taken by those CDU members cooperating with the East German Government.[49]

The CDU in the SBZ was originally formed in June 1946 and entered the Soviet-sponsored Block of Anti-fascist Democratic Parties, together with the SPD, and LDPD (Liberal Party). In the local elections of September 1946, the CDU, in opposition to the SED, won an important victory. On December 19, 1947, the Soviet military commander, Marshal Sokolovskii, dismissed the leadership of the party because he felt that they were becoming too popular.[50]

There were two phases of the CDU in East Germany. 1. From1945 to 1949, it exerted some independence of action, with many of its own leaders, and basically exhibited a strong, nuanced anti-Communist position. For example, they opposed the agrarian reform's expropriation of those farms of more than 100 hectares, because the owners, even if they were not Nazis, were not compensated. Also, many farms were confiscated, that were less than 100 hectares. 2. From 1950 to 1989, it was just a Communist front party with some leading members in the GDR government, but with no independence of action.[51]

When the CDU could no longer function as an independent political party in 1950, an opposition CDU was formed in West Berlin, called Exil CDU. It was a fully functioning and accredited element of the CDU in West Germany. It was treated by the CDU in the Federal Republic as a representative of the CDU in East Germany. It was made up of leaders of the party in the East, who had escaped from the SBZ/GDR.

The CDU *Ostbüro* functioned as a general secretariat for the Exil-CDU. All members of the CDU in the East who had contact with the *Ostbüro* were persecuted and arrested, even the Foreign Minister of the GDR, Georg Dertinger, who was a leading member of the CDU in East Germany. He was arrested in January 1953 as a spy and traitor and sentenced to 15 years in prison. The arrested were all tried by the SMTs.

The CDU *Ostbüro* was dissolved in February 1959, as it was considered pointless to maintain it in the light of the persecution of its members by the Soviets and GDR security services.[52]

THE *OSTBÜRO* OF THE FDP (LDPD) IN THE SOVIET ZONE

Due to the limited membership and activities of the LDPD in the Soviet Zone of Occupation, compared to the two major democratic parties, their opposition to the Soviets was also more circumscribed. Just like the SPD and CDU, the LDPD was legalized by the Soviet authorities in June 1945, and it entered the block of the Soviet sponsored, Anti-fascist Democratic Parties. In April 1948, LDPD went into opposition against the SED and threatened to leave the Anti-fascist Block. The Soviets then threatened to close the party, and their security agents began a wave of arrests of party members, particularly in the provinces of Brandenburg and Mecklenburg-Vorpommern.[53]

Between 70 to 100 members of the LDPD were arrested at this time, fewer than their counterparts in the SPD. This was due to the fact that the LDPD concentrated chiefly on opposition to the collectivization of agriculture and to the nationalization of industries in East Germany, rather than in political work among the working class, like the SPD. After these arrests, the LDPD practically disappeared the Soviet zone.[54]

As a reaction to Soviet repression of its membership, the *Ostbüro* of the FDP was formed in 1948 in West Berlin more to assist its members in the SBZ than to conduct anti-Soviet activities. It operated under the name of *Hilfsdienst Ost* (Help Service East) to help and support members still in the Soviet zone, as well as to receive reports from them of developments in the East.[55]

In addition, it was expected to execute these responsibilities:

-Provide opinions on refugees from the Soviet zone, especially higher officials.

-Observe and report on Communist infiltrators to the West.

-Continually monitor Communist front organizations.

-Identify individuals involved in anti-Western activities.[56]

As is shown, activities of the FDP *Ostbüro* emphasized informa-
tion-gathering on Soviet/GDR intelligence penetration of West Germany
rather than on anti-Soviet activities in their zone. This reflected the
growing fear in West Germany of Communist infiltration of the West
German government and political parties. By the mid 1950s, it became
increasingly difficult to receive information from the GDR, which made
the existence of this information service superfluous.

NOTES

1. Jürgen Danyel, "Zwischen Repression und Toleranz: Die Politik der SED zur politischen Integration der ehemaligen NSDAP-Mitglieder in der SBZ/DDR," in *Speziallager in der SBZ* Ritscher, eds. Peter Reif-Spirek and Bodo Ritscher (Berlin, Germany, 1999), 222.
2. Peter Erler, "Zur Tätigkeit der Sowjetischen Militärtribunale (SMT) in der SBZ/DDR," in *Sowjetische Speziallager in Deutschland 1945 bis 1950 Band I*, eds. Sergej Mironenko, Lutz Niethammer, and Alexander von Plato (Berlin: Akademie Verlag, 1998), 176–177.
3. Norman M. Naimark, *The Russians in Germany, A History of the Soviet Zone of Occupation, 1945–1949*, (Cambridge, Massachusetts, 1995), 386.
4. Ibid., 382–383.
5. Frederick Taylor, *Exorcising Hitler, The Occupation and Denazification of Germany*, (New York, 2011), 324–325.
6. Anne Applebaum, *Iron Curtain, 1944–1956*,(New York, 2012), 414–415.
7. Naimark, *The Russians in Germany, A History of the Soviet Zone of Occupation, 1945–1949*, 384.
8. Richard Prittie, *Germany Divided: The Legacy of the Nazi Era*,(Boston, Massachusets, 1960), 115.
9. Naimark, *The Russians in Germany, A History of the Soviet Zone of Occupation, 1945–1949*, 386.
10. Ibid., 389.
11. Uwe Greve, *Lager des Grauens: Sowjetische KZs in der DDR nach 1945*, (Kiel, Germany, 1990), 115–116.
12. Ibid., 21.
13. Uwe Greve, *Lager des Grauens: Sowjetische KZs in der DDR nach 1945*, 115–116.
14. Ibid., 22.
15. Greiner, Bettina, *Verdrângter Terror* (Hamburg, Germany, 2010), 125.
16. Ibid., 25.
17. Naimark, *The Russians in Germany, A History of the Soviet Zone of Occupation, 1945–1949*, 391.
18. Greve, *Lager des Grauens: Sowjetische KZs in der DDR nach 1945*, 75–77.
19. Richter, Michael, "Vom Widerstand der christlichen Demokraten in der DDR," in *Verfolgt-Verhaftet-Verurteilt; Demokraten im Widerstand gegen die rote Diktatur-Fakten und Beispiele*, ed., Günther Scholz, *Verfolgt-Ver-*

haftet-Verurteilt; *Demokraten im Widerstand gegen die rote Diktatur-Fakten und Beispiele* (Berlin,Germany, 1990), 35–36.
20. Ibid., 36–37.
21. Ibid.
22. Ibid., 40.
23. Ibid., 47.
24. Ibid., 49.
25. Ibid.
26. Naimark, *The Russians in Germany, A History of the Soviet Zone of Occupation, 1945–1949*, 384–385.
27. Mironenko, Niethammer, and von Plato, eds., *Sowjetische Speziallager in Deutschland 1945 bis 1950 Band I*, 48.
28. Greiner, *Verdrângter Terror*, 343.
29. Ibid., 345.
30. Ibid., 344.
31. Ibid., 345.
32. Ibid., 347.
33. Ibid., 348.
34. Ibid., 372.
35. Ibid., 345.
36. Mironenko, Niethammer, and von Plato, eds., *Sowjetische Speziallager in Deutschland 1945 bis 1950 Band I*, 32.
37. Buschfort, *Das Ostbüro der Parteien in den 50er Jahren*, (Berlin, Germany), 65–66.
38. Ibid., 43
39. Bluschfort, *Das Ostbüro der SPD*, (Bavaria, Germany.,2008), 2–3.
40. SPD-Ostbüro Kartoffeln erfroren, Der Spiegel, July 11, 1996. Retrieved from: http://www. spiegel.de/Spiegel/print.html
41. Ibid.
42. Gary Bruce, *Resistance with the People, Repression and Resistance in Eastern Germany, 1945–1955*, (Lanham, Maryland, 2003), 40–41.
43. Richter, *Vom Widerstand der christlichen Demokraten in der DDR*, in *Verfolgt-Verhaftet-Verurteilt; Demokraten im Widerstand gegen die rote Diktatur-Fakten und Beispiele*, ed. Scholz, Günther (Berlin, Westkreuz Verlag), 38–39.
44. Buschfort, *Das Ostbüro der Parteien in den 50er Jahren*, 34.
45. Ibid., 35.
46. Ibid., 47.
47. Ibid., 48.

48. Ralf G.Jahn,. *Christlich-Demokratische Union Deutschlands, (CDU) (Ost),* retrieved from:http://www.adel-genealogie.de/CDU-Ost.html, 5–6.
49. Ibid., 49–50.
50. Ibid., 33.
51. Jahn, *Christlich-Demokratische Union Deutschlands, (CDU) (Ost),*1,4.
52. Ibid., 19.
53. Buschfort, *Das Ostbüro der Parteien in den 50er Jahren,* 36.
54. Wolfgang Buschfort, "Die Ära Adenauer," in *Sowjetischen Speziallager in der gesellschaftlichen Wahrnehmung, 1945 bis heute,* eds. Petra Haustein, Annette Kaminsky, Volkhard Knigge, and Bodo Ritscher (Göttingen, Germany, 2006), 38–39.
55. Ibid., 37.
56. Ibid., 53.

CHAPTER 7

LIFE AND DEATH
IN THE SPEZLAGER

"Katyn is not only located in Russia" is a saying in Germany, on discovering mass graves near the former Soviet special camps in East Germany.

SURVIVAL IN THE SPECIAL CAMPS

The explicit goal of the Soviet special camps in eastern Germany was not labor or murder but isolation: The special camps were meant to cut off any opponents of the Soviets from the rest of the population. In this sense, they were preventive and not punitive but NKVD arrest charges were always based, usually falsely, on anti-Soviet acts. During the first three years of their existence, special camp prisoners could not send or receive letters, and they had no news from the outside world whatsoever. In many cases, their families did not know what had happened to them or where they were. They had simply disappeared.[1] The Cheka, the first Soviet security service (see chapter 4), called this system of isolation and preventive incarceration, "social prophylaxis."[2]

One could, however, also call the *Spezlager* death camps to the extent that, like the camps of the Gulag in the Soviet Union, little effort was made to ensure the physical well-being of the internees. In Sachsenhausen, for example, daily rations were normally one and three-fourths liters of the thinnest soup and 450 grams of bread, just enough, remembered one survivor, to keep internees alive but truly hungry. They had to sleep on wooden bedsteads without blankets and, at first, without straw mattresses, live under leaking roofs, wash in ice-cold water even in the dead of winter, half starved and with no change of clothes. They were kept on parade for five hours at a stretch, and were kicked and bullied for the least offenses such as, for example, possessing pencil and paper.[3]

As a result of the hunger and cold, thousands of prisoners suffered from tuberculosis. In Sachsenhausen, 10 to 20 internees died every day from the disease, forcing the camp to build special barracks to hold the overflow of tuberculosis patients. Internees also suffered from a wide array of other diseases, the most common being dysentery and malnutrition. In Bautzen, during the very cold winter of 1946-47, 50 to 60 internees died every day. Tuberculosis again took a terrible toll. In one Bautzen compound, more than 400 prisoners lay sick with the disease; on one day it was reported that 14 young prisoners died in the barracks.[4]

Next to hunger, sickness, and cold, the complete isolation of the prisoners had a very negative impact on their moods. As said, prisoners were prohibited from writing to their families or friends and were not allowed to receive mail. The families did not know where they were and the NKVD did not give out this information to them. No news escaped from the camps and until the first releases in 1948, the prisoners were hermetically sealed off from the outside world.[5]

Completely opposite to the purpose of the GULAG camps in the Soviet Union, prisoners were not allowed to work, except for tasks maintaining the camp. (Occasionally prisoners were taken out of the camps to work for the Soviet Security services or the Soviet Military Government as translators, scientists, or even nuclear specialists. In the latter two cases, they were usually sent to the Soviet Union.)[6] They were not allowed to listen to the radio and until the fall of 1947 or to read newspapers. Nor were they allowed to sing, write, paint, read books, attend lectures or poetry recitals or play cards. Although chess was permitted, watches, mirrors, pictures and writing materials were forbidden. Prisoners were likewise forbidden to lie on the cots during the day, leave the barracks without permission, or discuss political events or Soviet policies. There was no denazification education or effort to win prisoners over to communism.[7] Any violation of these regulations resulted in punishment by isolation in the "bunker" (see below), where only one-half of food rations were given and one had to sleep on the concrete floor. This meant the end for many prisoners. Regulations were only eased somewhat in 1948. Overall, a climate of lethargy and hopelessness prevailed among the prisoners.[8]

Despite the prohibition of any entertainment, very exceptionally, some prisoners were still able to hold lectures or stage plays or even have secret political discussions. In later years, after 1948, the NKVD camp commanders permitted plays. For example, the well-known actor Heinrich George, who died in the Sachsenhausen camp, staged Goethe's Urfaust in the Hohenschönhausen camp as well as Pushkin's The Postmaster in the Sachsenhausen camp.[9]

The reason the local Soviet administration did not improve the conditions of the special camps in the first few years is that they were run by the NKVD and directly under the GULAG administration, beginning August 1948, which considered the rights of prisoners as a bourgeois institution. The elimination of state enemies was their revolutionary obligation: better to eliminate too many rather than too few. The life of an individual was worth little in Stalin's time. Further justification in Soviet thinking, derived from the opinion that the Nazi German security services were much more violent, is, however, a moot point. Revenge was also a factor and it accounted, in part, for the violent arrests and interrogations by the Soviet Secret Police. Some German writers have speculated that revenge was not necessarily a reason for Soviet behavior, but rather bureaucratic indifference, although this is a disputed position. The fact is that a large majority of internees in the Western internment camps had been released by 1946; the conclusion of their denazification program had absolutely no effect on the Soviet security services managing the camps.[10]

Ironically, for many prisoners, their arrival at the camps was a relief. Having lived for weeks alone in interrogation cells, without daylight, coming to the camps where there were other people and movement in fresh air was an improvement. Above all, the torment, interrogations, and torture ceased. However, during the period of their incarceration, on average between three to five years, prisoners had to continuously deal with hunger, sickness, and death. They also had to cope with their total isolation from the outside world and an uncertain future. They suffered from depression and hopelessness, as well as a constant fear of deportation to the Soviet Union as slave labor.

One prisoner reported the following:

> *The first winter of 1945/1946 was the worst. We slept on boards, Bunks were only built later. I ran around with my short pants until November. Then we took the clothing from the dead for our personal use. The dead were then buried in packing paper. In that winter, which was very cold, there was hardly any heat in the barracks. On some days, even the meals were cold due to lack of coal. I was very undernourished and had a strong condition of water in the legs. We suffered greatly from lice, resulting in ulcers. My rear end was full of puss with ulcers and ulcers on the lower thighs. I wanted to give up soon.*[11]

Conditions were not necessarily the same in all the camps. In many, prisoners lived in crowded, humid, and poorly heated rooms, and slept on bunks with straw which was rapidly overrun with vermin, often without blankets and no change of clothes. Sicknesses such as skin irritation, dystrophy (a sign of poor nourishment), dysentery, typhus, and tuberculosis were common and often of epidemic proportions. Frequently there were no medicines to fight these diseases and no doctors or else only poorly educated ones.

For example, in the Buchenwald camp, which was among the best equipped, there were latrines outside the barracks, but in some others there were only barrels in the barracks which were emptied from time to time. There was no toilet paper in any of the camps.

Bathing arrangements were scarce in most camps. There were no showers or bathtubs in any of them. Every few weeks, the prisoners were allowed to wash themselves in wash basins with no water pressure and always harassed by the guards to hurry.

The prisoners had to double or triple up on bunks, so that during the night, if someone had to turn over, all had to do so on command. The feeling of constriction was increased in some camps, such as Buchenwald, where each barrack was surrounded by a barbed wire fence, limiting prisoners' ability to circulate outside.

But the most dramatic suffering was caused by the lack of food. The older prisoners always talked about food, trading recipes for example. In the first months the camps were established, food was adequate, but in November of 1946, there was a drastic reduction in rations. A gradual increase began only in the fall of 1947. Prisoners spoke of meeting old acquaintances in the camps whom they could no longer recognize because they had lost so much weight.

One prisoner wrote of their anxiety concerning lack of rations:

> Once when we were working on the camp grounds, the food for the pigs arrived. The Russians kept their pigs there, which they then slaughtered on site. All the kitchen garbage was used to feed the pigs. There were noodles and barley mixed in with the waste from the kitchen. We then ate it, even though it was becoming sour. But we survived after eating this waste.

Distribution of food among the prisoners was a most important occasion and became a ritual of closely watched sharing. Anyone attempting to take more than his share was punished by the other prisoners. Sometimes the German internal barracks administrators—all prisoners—would take advantage of their position by receiving more food or other privileges, but often they would also confront the Soviet guards to defend the prisoners. There was very little direct contact with the Soviets because of the self-administration in the camps. The guards came into the barracks only when there was a search, when Soviet doctors came to determine who was able to go to work in the Soviet Union, or when labor was needed to work outside the camp.[12]

From time to time there was a general roll-call of the entire camp:

> *The general roll-call was especially feared. Immediately we had to drop whatever we were doing and the barracks had to march as one unit to the roll-call square. Here one had to wait a long time until the entire camp arrived. Finally, there was movement in the masses of people waiting there, and under strict security came at last "our women," fellow prisoners. These women shone with such a strong will that they gave many men the support they needed to survive. Once the women joined the group, then the march began and the camp gate opened and we had to march through the gate in groups of five with arms locked. There, six Russians stood to count us. For each group they made a mark. Hours passed until all were counted, and then we had to return to the barracks. During this time, the entire camp was empty except for the infirmary, boiler room, and kitchen, where prisoners worked. The Russians also went there to count them. We were always pleased to return to the barracks after marching and standing, often for five hours. The longest general roll-call we experienced was eight hours and forty minutes. During that time the old and weak often collapsed, which did not bother the Russians in the least. They were only Germans.[13]*

The indifference of the Russians was clearly seen by all, in making the prisoners stand for roll call for hours, without caring about the fact that many could no longer do this without collapsing, due to their state of malnutrition. When it rained, the prisoners suffered especially, always causing a number of deaths due to inadequate clothing and malnutrition.

Many thought the Soviets did this on purpose to reduce their numbers. For them, the roll-calls demonstrated the arbitrariness and terror of the NKVD camp administrators. The prisoners felt completely helpless against their harassment and the suspected murderous intent of the Soviets; they felt they were being treated like animals. The inmates were, therefore, especially incensed by a Christmas visit in 1949 to Sachsenhausen camp by a bishop of the Lutheran Church, who stated publicly that the prisoners were well treated, and certainly better than the Nazis treated theirs.[14] (See endnote below for the controversial 1949 Christmas visit of Lutheran Bishop Otto Dibelius to the Sachsenhausen special camp.)

Below is a personal narrative from Erwin Krombolz. Erwin Krombolz was born in Vienna, Austria and a member of the Luftwaffe since 1936. Shot down over the Soviet Union while on a reconnaissance mission, he was badly wounded. He returned to Germany where he was hospitalized and released after two years with a crippled left hand. Arrested by the NKVD as a result of a neighbor's denunciation in May 1945, he was sent to the Weesow special camp (Brandenburg province) via the collection camp at Biesdorf near Berlin. The Weesow camp was established northeast of Berlin by the NKVD as a provisional camp composed of farm buildings. The civilian prisoners had to build the watch towers and barbed wire fences. From the temporary camp, the prisoners were then sent on to camps at Landsberg, Frankfurt/Oder, Sachsenhausen, and Fünfeichen. Of the 10,000 prisoners who passed through Weesow, some 1,000 died and were buried in a nearby forest.

Weesow was a village in a very rural region. Our exhausted group tramped, with difficulty, to Weesow. Fear of physical collapse pushed us on. Uncertainty as to our fate was felt especially by the older men who considered their situation tragic.

The camp, consisting of many barns and other farm buildings, was encircled by barbed wire. Our guards were Poles in civilian dress. Our stay became a torment as a result of beatings, harassment, and plundering.

However, as a foreigner who was an Austrian, I was not beaten. But the Germans suffered greatly.

Our reception was terrible. As soon as we stepped into the first farm, we were disinfected and our clothing boiled in many large vats, placed in the middle of the farm. We had to squat naked on the ground until the disinfection was finished. Our clothing was returned, destroyed, ruined, shrunken and mostly unusable. During this waiting period, our guards went among us, searching for valuables, but after being previously searched by the NKVD, we no longer had anything of value. However, the next group of prisoners who came from the immediate area, still had some valuables such as a watch, of which they were relieved.

After the disinfection, we were hurried to our quarters, by blows as well as by a fear of further violence. I found myself in a group of former Vlasov soldiers (Russian volunteers for the Wehrmacht, considered traitors by the Soviets), with whom I established friendly relations. One came to my defense when a Polish guard attempted to take my hiking shoes. He was driven away by blows from my Russian friend.

Our quarters were unbearable. We slept on straw sacks, in over-crowded conditions. The sanitary installations became continuously worse. The uncertainty of our fate was a horrible weight on us. Cries and screams during the night made clear to us the system we were in.

On the subject of deaths in the Weesow camp, I was also aware that well-nourished peasant prisoners became victims of these new conditions. Diarrhea set in rapidly and under these circumstances, death soon came.

Every day was a day of misery, beginning with sun-up and ending with sun-down. Then one was happy that a day of torment was behind. The problem of justice in life concerned us greatly, unaware of any guilt and just waiting and vegetating.

Our stay in the Weesow camp suddenly and unexpectedly ended when we were driven in a column to be transported by rail to Bernau. Soviet soldiers surrounded us, while marching together, tired, dusty, and in rags, *dragging along a country road. However, we were happy to be rid of the Polish guards, but concerned what future awaited us. During this march, an unforeseen event occurred. A former German soldier in a tattered uniform was watching us from the roadside. His misfortune was that he had a bag of bread and a canteen. One of the Soviet guards demanded that he hand over the canteen. He refused saying he was a released war prisoner on the way home and had a valid release certificate. The guard kicked him in the rear and took his canteen. He was then forced to join the marching column of prisoners. He protested but the guard pointed his machine pistol at him, and that was that.*

Although we were not allowed to talk, I was able to slip a short written note, explaining my situation to my family to a passer- by. Fortunately, they received it. My further stay then was in the NKVD special camp, Buchenwald.

Erwin Krombolz remained in Buchenwald until January 1950. There-after, together with many others, he was sent to Waldheim, Saxony, for trial. In the Waldheim "war crimes" trials, he was sentenced to fifteen years in prison. As a result of an amnesty, commemorating the three year existence of the German Democratic Republic, he was released on October 5, 1952.[15]

INTERNAL GERMAN CAMP ADMINISTRATION

For internal security purposes, the Soviet assigned prisoners to internal camp leadership and police posts. In turn, every barracks had its German "elder," an inmate responsible to the internal camp administration to keep order.[16] It turned out that in many cases the Nazi prisoners were able to form cliques that monopolized these positions which were desirable because they came with extra rations and benefits. In the Mühlberg camp, these positions were even held by officers of the Waffen SS (this was prior to their deportation to the USSR in 1946). In order to maintain these positions and privileges, each camp leader had to make three denunciations monthly of fellow prisoners to the NKVD camp administration. The Soviets successfully played the Germans off against each other.[17]

One prisoner relates the following:

> We all were unanimous in our opinion that the Russians deliberately chose such superiors (Waffen SS) for us of whom they knew that they would do their jobs well and with German thoroughness. That is why, in our daily contact with them, we suffered more from those who often were still decked out in their old uniforms than from the Russian guards. . . . NKVD psychology was based on the realization that "the German is the German's own worst enemy, so let them stew in their own juice!"[18]

Another example was, in the camp at Ketschendorf, a number of opportunistic prisoners who switched sides and joined the Soviets, when the camp received its own German internal camp administration in early November 1945. It consisted mostly of former police officers and all ex-members of the NSDAP. This German administrative staff enjoyed important privileges, one of which was extra rations at a time when the food situation for the rest of the inmates was catastrophic.

For example, the internal camp commandant in the Ketschendorf camp, was Kasimir, also an inmate. An ethnic German from the Baltic, he was a very serious appearing man, of average build and middle-aged. He wore a standard dress hat of the day, a neat, clean suit, and an overcoat with a fur collar. This was how other inmates saw him every day in the course of countless trips through the camp. The Soviet Camp Commandant who was his superior, a gigantic and obese army major actually respected him because Kasimir spoke Russian.

Starting with the wave of arrests that began in July of 1945 and lasted until February of 1946, conditions in the Ketchendorf camp worsened markedly. Rations became even smaller and now consisted of seven ounces of bread and a cup of the thinnest possible gruel. A temporary improvement in provisions and hygiene is credited to the actions of a young Russian female doctor who was sent from Karlshorst, the Soviet occupation headquarters.

Again and again, former inmates reported acts of harassment by the German camp internal leaders who were always answerable to the Soviet camp commander. Some mornings, the German administration heads conducted a roll- call. Every evening the Soviets did theirs, in which the inmates had to stand in groups of five, arms linked together. The utterly enfeebled prisoners were forced to stand at attention in the courtyard for up to five hours, even in the bitterest winter months. Inmates who had been arrested in the summer months were still only wearing their light clothes when the snow came.[19]

PUNISHMENT IN THE CAMPS

A typical punishment for the infringement of regulations was an isolation cell or "bunker," (see map of Ketchendorf Camp # 5) where one remained on half rations for days or weeks, according to the seriousness of the violation. In winter, the unheated cells often became death chambers. Prisoners usually received no physical punishment, except for arbitrary acts by guards. The Isolator was a special barracks to isolate prisoners suspected of planning to escape, or for former German internal camp leaders in whom the Soviets had lost confidence or who had committed a transgression. Conditions in these barracks were poorer than in the regular barracks.[20]

(Refer to http://www.thegulagineastgermany.com for Illustration #13 - Interior of the Women's Gulag Barracks. Source: Wikimedia Commons.)

(Refer to http://www.thegulagineastgermany.com for Map #7- Ketschendorf Camp #5, Province (Land) Brandenburg with Index. Source: *Die Strasse die in den Tod Führte, Renate und Jan Lipinsky, Initiativgruppe Internierungslager Ketschendorf e.V, Skpeziallager Nr. 5.*)

DEPORTATION OF GERMAN PRISONERS TO THE SOVIET UNION FOR FORCED LABOR

From time to time, Soviet doctors came to the camps to determine who was healthy enough to be sent to the Soviet Union for hard labor.

A prisoner who witnessed this procedure reports the following:

> The entire camp was divided into four groups; numbers three and four contained those who could no longer work, entirely beyond hope. Numbers one and two included those capable of working. I was always classified as number two, even though I was only skin and bones. When the Soviet doctors' delegation arrived, the procedure was as follows: The doctors all sat behind a table in a large room, in uniforms covered by white smocks. We had to undress and approach them, stand still and be examined as though in a cattle auction. I was pushed aside very rapidly. Whoever appeared somewhat healthy went to one side, the sickly ones to the other. The first group was then loaded onto a freight train for transport to south Siberia.[21]

According to MVD Order #001196, of December 26, 1946, all special camps had to furnish 27,500 Germans who were capable of working for deportation to the Soviet Union. They were to be sent to the enterprises of the USSR Ministry for Coal Industries to work in the coal mines of the eastern regions of the country. (15,500 went to the Kuzbass, Karaganda, and Kizel in the Urals; the rest were sent to factories in Central Asia.) They were to replace German POWs who were no longer capable of work and had to be returned to Germany. According to Soviet records, at that time there were 74,256 prisoners in the special camps, of whom 25,189 were judged capable of work, including 4,442 sentenced by SMTs. But by January 19, 1947, Soviet doctors could only find 2,030 able-bodied Germans to send to the Soviet Union, the result of poor sanitary conditions in the camp and the hunger winter of 1946/1947.[22]

During 1947, the MVD also required all camps to provide technical specialists for deportation to the Soviet Union; specifically these were electricians, automobile mechanics, locksmiths, radio repair, etc., who were then transported to the Soviet Union at the end of that year. However, the head of the GULAG in Moscow, at the beginning of July 1949, rejected all prisoners who were sentenced to over 15 years by the SMTs, probably for security reasons. Deportations of German prisoners continued, although in smaller numbers, until the liquidation of the camps in 1950.[23]

In the winter of 1946/1947, in the Mühlberg special camp there was a call for workers for the Soviet Union. A general physical examination of all prisoners determined who were capable of hard labor. From a total of 10,000 Mühlberg prisoners, 900 were selected. They were then quarantined and received winter clothing, which were second hand *Wehrmacht* uniforms. In mid-winter, February 8,1947, the transport left for West Siberia, a trip of five weeks, in a cattle car. They were sent to the GULAG camp at Anshero-Sushensk to work in the Kuzbass coal mines where in the first year, 20% of the prisoners died. Thereafter, the death rate decreased. The last prisoners were released in 1955, as a result of Chancellor Adenauer's visit to the Soviet Union.

One of the prisoners reported the following about this trip:

> *Our car was provisionally outfitted with two tier wooden bunks, a small oven in the middle and a wooden urinal. Heating material was wood and some coal. In the town of Brest (Belarus) the train halted, by coincidence, next to a freight train full of coal. The guards told us to take coal and after working for one hour, we were entirely covered with coal dust. Later we realized that we took too little coal, because on arriving shortly after in Moscow, we had used up all our coal and wood including our bunks. Our meals were dried bread and fish as well as five liters of water per day. We suffered greatly from thirst. Several of us died of colds, pneumonia, and diarrhea. There were no doctors or nurses and the bodies were thrown out of the train on its daily stop. Their burial garment was the snow.*
>
> *The trip was unending and lasted until the middle of March. After arriving, we had to tramp a kilometer in the snow to GULAG camp #7503/11. Many did not make it, as they could no longer walk. The*

camp itself was buried in four to six meters high snow drifts. The
primitively outfitted infirmary was soon overflowing.[24]

HUNGER, SICKNESS, AND DEATH

In 1945, on the opening of the special camps, rations in the camps should
have followed the "norms" for prisoners of war, according to regulation
#64 of Soviet State Security. However, these were reduced according
to Soviet documents because the Soviet army of occupation received
responsibility for providing food for the camps, which was not prepared
for this task, with funds coming from the NKVD budget.[25] In addition,
corruption in the Soviet camp administration and guards was rampant
(with food sold on the open market); there was also a great deal of stealing
food destined for the prisoners.[26]

Aside from insufficient food, a lack of clothing for the prisoners also
led to increased mortality in the winter of 1945/46. Many people were
arrested on the street and went to prison with the clothes they had on,
which were insufficient for winter. They had no change of clothing.
General Serov, concerned about the high death rate, in August 1945,
ordered that all arrested individuals sent to the interrogation cells have
proper clothing and shoes, ie: a winter coat, two changes of underwear,
two pairs of socks and two handkerchiefs as well as a blanket and
pillow. Most were arrested without even a minimum of this clothing,
but families at this time were allowed to provide the missing items. This
rarely happened, however, as relatives usually had no idea where the
prisoners were held. As it turned out, the Special Camp Administration
in January 1946 ruled that General Serov's order could not be carried out,
as prisoners were no longer allowed to receive packages with food or
clothing or family visits. Prisoners' clothing was also frequently stolen
by Soviet prison personnel.[27] Eventually there was an improvement in
clothing provided to the camps when the prisoners began to receive cast-
off clothing from German and Russian soldiers.[28]

Due to lack of rations, many prisoners, in the winter of 1945/1946, developed illnesses, the most serious being typhus and diphtheria.[29] Also prevalent were skin infections and stomach sicknesses followed by pneumonia, epidemics of dysentery, and especially tuberculosis. There were no real infirmaries in the camps, only stations for the very sick.[30] The Soviet doctors in the camps, the majority of whom were military doctors, tried to alleviate this situation but were unable to do so as they had neither medicines nor medical instruments. Hunger also effected the prisoners mentally; with many suffering from loss of memory or vision.[31] A Soviet camp physician once explained it to a German doctor in this way, "In our camps, everyone dies twice! First mentally, and then physically."[32]

In the Jamlitz camp, for example, hungry prisoners ate the bark from trees in the camp, dying from horrible stomach cramps. One prisoner was quoted as saying, "The mass deaths in the NKVD camps were based on a sinister program of promoting prisoner suicide." The dead were taken by the burial commands as far away as possible from the camps for internment in mass graves. This was done generally late at night or in the early morning hours so that those living near the camps did not know what was happening. The graves were then often planted with trees.[33]

An October 30, 1946 order, signed by General Serov and a member of the SVAG, strongly reduced food rations beginning November 1946. Results were not long in coming; The death rate reached its highest point in February 1947, when 4,156 prisoners died in the special camps, a 10% increase. (Soviet death statistics were normally understated.) In January 1947, of the 2,030 prisoners slated to be shipped to the Soviet Union, only 318 were found capable of working. In another camp, 2,200 were selected for deportation to the Soviet Union in December 1946, and even received better rations, but by the end of January, only 833 were capable of work.[34]

The reduction in rations was due to the October 1946 transfer of the responsibility for feeding the camps to the SVAG from the Soviet army of occupation. Security services in the SBZ were also transferred about this time from the MVD (Ministry of Internal Affairs) to the MGB

(Ministry of State Security). However, the NKVD/MVD continued to administer the special camps. Apparently surprised by the order, the SVAG was unprepared for its new duties. Prisoners reportedly came to the conclusion that the reduction of food rations was an attempt by the Soviets to kill them all.[35]

The Soviets justified their reduction of rations to the camps as due to administrative problems as stated previously, because they were increasing rations to the East German populace. In July 1946, as a result of pressure from the nascent SED, prior to local and provincial elections in 1946, rations were temporarily increased by the SVAG. The Soviets said this was the positive results of the land reform in East Germany.[36]

By the end of December 1946, the administration of the special camps was forced to consider increasing rations not only because of the increasing death rate, but also because of possible flight attempts. They believed that massive flight attempts were being discussed in a number of camps, and, in fact, five prisoners did escape from Buchenwald. There was no more flight of prisoners, but security was nevertheless increased in all camps.[37] On January 1, 1947, a small increase in rations for the camps was ordered. On December 5, 1946, Colonel General Serov and the Military Governor of the Soviet Zone of Occupation, Marshal Sokolovskii, wrote to Stalin and Beria recommending that 35,000 of the 80,000 prisoners in the special camps be released in order to deal with the food problem. These were considered only nominal Nazis. They stated in this letter that "We assume that it is not necessary to continue to incarcerate this category of prisoners (nominal Nazis) and to continue to feed them unnecessarily as their freedom does not represent any danger for us." In any event, the freed prisoners would have to report monthly to the local Military Command. This letter never received a reply.[38]

Not only was there a serious problem of lack of rations in the camps in the winter of 1946/1947, but of medicines, soap, and fuel as well. Nothing was done, however, by the Soviet camp administration to reduce the death rate.[39] For example, no efforts were made until the middle of 1947 to fight the tuberculosis epidemic. The only step taken was to isolate the sick.[40] In the summer of 1947 rations increased and the impression among the prisoners was that corruption among Soviet personnel decreased a little. The prisoners also noted that the Soviet doctors were more interested in helping the sick and in advising headquarters of the actual disastrous health conditions in the camps. This occurred despite the fact that deaths from the tuberculosis epidemic had increased. There was even talk of a special camp for tuberculosis patients, but no strong measures were ever taken to fight the disease.[41]

Consequently, the most difficult years for the prisoners, especially the elderly, were from December 1946 to July 1947. Death began with those over 60, who died from dysentery. When they had gone, it was the turn of the 50 year-olds. In the winter of 1946 to 1947 even the 40 year olds died in large numbers.[42] An additional reason for the food shortages was that new prisoners were constantly being sent to the camps without a corresponding increase in the overall food rations.[43] As a result of malnutrition, many prisoners succumbed to illnesses complicated by the lack of resistance to the cold, depression, and vermin. Starting in early 1947, as noted above, there was a slight improvement in food rations as well as in medical support, which, however, did not help the weakened prisoners very much.[44]

At the request of General Serov, and in anticipation of the takeover of the special camps by the GULAG administration, a GULAG inspection team came in February 1948, and inspected most of the camps. One of their conclusions was that the camp administration did not recognize the seriousness of the tuberculosis and dystrophic epidemics and did not take the correct measures to contain them. As a result of these visits, in March 1948, food rations for sick prisoners were increased with the justification that prisoners could not be released in their present condition, as it would reflect negatively on the Soviet Union. Medicinal supplies were also increased for camp infirmaries.[45]

In the fall of 1948, the GULAG administration formally took over the special camp administration and attempted to introduce forced labor, as in the Soviet Union, but had little success due to the poor health of the prisoners. Soviet camp leaders in Germany also objected to forced labor because of the lack of tools, machines, and translators plus the fact that aside from poor health, the prisoners lacked experience for the work required. They insisted that the GULAG administration in Moscow did not know of these problems and Moscow's idea that prisoners working would bring in funds to increase food rations was not realistic.[46] Despite some positive changes, severely inadequate food rations for the majority of prisoners essentially remained the same. Even those sick with tuberculosis had to appear for roll call twice daily; and the stoves in the barracks of the sick were only heated during the day.[47]

In the spring of 1949 the death rate from tuberculosis increased, so that 98% of all deaths in the camps resulted from tuberculosis. In 1948, 15% of all prisoners died, but in the first five months of 1949, this was reduced to 9.6%; (these are all Soviet statistics and often contradictory). In the summer of 1949, the Soviets introduced some "liberalizing" ordinances. For example, in the Sachsenhausen and Bautzen camps, prisoners sentenced by the military courts could receive packages and money transfers, just as in the GULAG camps in the Soviet Union. Stores were also introduced where the prisoners could buy toiletries and clothing. On the other hand, those prisoners not sentenced by military court, but arrested administratively, still more than one-half of all prisoners, did not receive these privileges. In February 1950, the camps were dissolved. The sick were either released or turned over to the *Volkspolizeil* (Peoples' Police).[48]

According to some sources, the high death rate in the special camps was due not so much to a calculated, cold-blooded intention of eliminating the prisoners but rather as the result of bureaucratic mismanagement and indifference as to their fate. The high rate of deaths was not welcomed by the Soviets but they did nothing about it. On the other hand, they did not want the many deaths known outside of the camps, particularly in the West. Only under pressure from political forces in East and West Germany did the Soviets liberalize camp conditions and release many, but certainly not all prisoners in 1948.[49]

A report from the Ketschendorf Camp relates the following:

> In the Ketschendorf Camp a great many German prisoners died. When our comrades went to the camp infirmary and when they said good bye to us, we already knew that they would never return. In the camp, there was even the rumor that in the Russian infirmary one could be cured with the help of injections, i.e. poison.. That we survived the Ketschendorf Camp allows us to spread to the Free World this excellent anti-Soviet propaganda. We were fed for many months with only groats. Everyone's legs became sickly swollen. We called the groats the white death.[50]

Russian statistics indicated that about 122,000 to 123,000 German prisoners passed through the camps in the period of 1945-1950, with a mortality number of about 43,000 or about a 30% death rate. German figures, mostly calculated after the collapse of the GDR, including the uncovering of many mass graves at the special camp sites, showed a much higher incarceration number of 240,000 with 95,643 deaths, or about a 40% rate. (See chapter 1 for further details including a list of the number of prisoners and deaths per camp.)[51]

In order to maintain the secrecy of the high death rate, burials were mostly carried out at night, with internment far from the camps, whenever possible. For example, more than 20,000 prisoners died in the Sachsenhausen camp. They were buried in three areas: in a grove along the road leading to the town of Schmachtenhausen, under the former Commandant's courtyard, or outside of the north corner of the camp.[52] More than 5,000 inmates were said to have perished in the Jamlitz camp. Their bodies were buried on the far side of the railway track in the woods along the road to the town of Guben.[53]

All camps had their corpse details, so-called B-Kommandos. These work groups had to load all the dead onto carts at night and bury them in limed pits. Usually it was 600 bodies per pit. In Sachsenhausen, during the worst of the winter of 1946–47, there were as many as 120 corpses every day.[54]

One prisoner who witnessed these corpse details recalls the following:

> The sight of these carts of dead bodies made me shudder in horror, and I had seen plenty as a soldier. But that was war and this was the 'peace from the East. The stretchers consisted of two wooden poles nailed together with boards and carried by two men. The lifeless bodies were covered with blankets. Sometimes, arms and legs dangled over the sides. A frightful consignment!

> As I found out later from a corpse bearer, the dead ended up in mass graves near the rifle range. They were just dumped like garbage into these graves and covered over with dirt. But the covering over part was difficult at this time of year because of the frozen ground, so the pits stayed open until the last frost was past. None of the relatives ever received word of the death of their loved ones.[55]

Although execution of prisoners was not usual in the special camps, members of the burial squads were often executed on the spot in order to maintain the secrecy of the high death rate. For the same reason, many others were deported to the Soviet Union. Although members of the burial commands received extra rations, death or deportation awaited them at the end. For example, the entire burial command of the Buchenwald special camp was deported to the Soviet Union in early 1950, before the closing of that camp. There is no evidence that they survived.[56]

(Refer to http://www. thegulagineastgermany.com. for Illustration #14: The Cemetery at Fünfeichen Special Camp #9, Containing Mass Graves of Prisoners. *Source: Speziallager in der SBZ, Bodo Ritscher, Editor, Gedenkstätte Buchenwald und der Landszentrale für politische Bildung, Thüringen.*)

Note: Christmas service, December 1949 at the Sachsenhausen Special Camp by the Lutheran Bishop of Berlin, Dr. Otto Dibelius

On December 25, 1949, the Superintendent of the Lutheran Church in Berlin – Brandenburg, Dr. Heinrich Grüber, together with the Lutheran bishop of Berlin, Dr. Dibelius, held a Christmas service in the Sachsenhausen special camp. This was with the permission of the Soviet camp authorities. On arriving in the camp, they were accosted by many inmates who requested them to contact their relatives who had not heard from them in four years.

Two services were held, one before 1,000 men and the other before 350 women. Heinrich Grüber was previously a prisoner in the Nazi Sachsenhausen concentration camp. He stated publicly that contrary to the Nazi camps, the prisoners were not in prison uniform but in their own clothing, well groomed, and well nourished. Women even used cosmetics. There were no signs of concern in the prisoners and relations with the guards were normal and without expressions of fear. He stated that it was not correct to compare these camps to those of Hitler.[57] He said, *"It is an unforgivable injustice to equate these camps with Hitler's concentration camps, or to say, 'it's just as it was under the Nazis, or even worse' ... Here we are dealing with incarcerated people, but there, under Hitler, with constantly abused and tortured people. Here, people are being kept from outside life, but their lives aren't being made any more difficult than they have to be."*

He continued saying that granted that the prisoners were isolated, but they were not living in terror and constant harassment as were those in the Nazi camps. The Soviets did not systematically liquidate or torture the prisoners. Grüber did state that the Lutheran church requested the Soviet authorities to release young people, since prison was particularly hard on their well-being. Aside from that, however, he did not want to criticize the Soviets as we (the Germans) all felt collectively guilty for the atrocities committed against Russians, Poles, and Jews. When asked what could be improved in the camps, he mentioned the need for fair court trials, freedom to correspond with their families, and the release of young people. He also stated that food rations were better here than in many refugee camps in the West. Superintendent Grüber also said that *"Life in the Soviet camps is much better and more pleasant, more humane than life in the so-called refugee camps in West Germany. I was able to verify this personally."*[58]

Grüber published these comments in the official communist press of the GDR, *Neues Deutschland,* which, of course, gave them maximum publicity. But all these views and comments were heavily criticized by the Western press and radio, especially in West Berlin which stated, among other points, that these positive comments about camp conditions by the two religious authorities were a condition by the Soviets for their permission to hold Christmas services in the Sachsenhausen camp. Other commentators alleged that the two clerics saw only one small part of the camp, and with just a limited number of prisoners allowed to participate in the Christmas service; (and these were members of the German internal camp administration, their followers, and friends). The majority, however, were in the main part of the camp and not permitted to leave their barracks during their visit.[59]

In response to the statements of the two religious authorities about the Soviet camps, the anti-Communist and human rights group *Kampfgruppe gegen Unmenschlichkeit (KgU)* located in West Berlin reported in the West Berlin newspaper *Tagesspiegel* on January 6, 1950, that the two clerics should look at the list of all those who had perished from hunger and disease in the Soviet special camps. It added that Grüber should interview former special camp inmates to hear the truth about life in the camps and that his views were either lies or he saw a "Potemkin village," that is, that the entire scene was staged for his benefit by the Soviet authorities. It also stated that Grüber should answer the questions why youths of 15 and 16 were still being imprisoned in the concentration camps after four or five years; and why, after all these years of imprisonment, the inmates still could not correspond with their families.[60]

As a result of this controversy, the Lutheran church in East Germany declared its official position as having always opposed all concentration camps, whether Nazi or Soviet, particularly as most inmates in the special camps never had a court trial and could not correspond with their families. It also noted that the Lutheran church was instrumental in the large 1948 prisoner release by the Soviet Military Administration. It confirmed that the opinions of the two clerics were their own and did not represent the official position of the German Lutheran Church in East Germany.[61] Furthermore, it was stated that both Christian churches, Catholic and Protestant, made their membership aware of the abuses in the special camps and criticized them publicly in their bulletins, sermons, and other communiqués.

NOTES

1. Anne Applebaum, *Iron Curtain, 1944–1956*, (New York, 2012), 168.
2. Adrian Preissinger, *Death Camps of the Soviets, 1945–1950*, (Ocean City, Maryland, 1994), 147.
3. Richard Prittie, *Germany Divided: The Legacy of the Nazi Era,*(Boston, Massachusets, 1960), 175.
4. Norman M. Naimark, *The Russians in Germany, A History of the Soviet Zone of Occupation, 1945–1949* (Cambridge, Massachusetts, 1995), 377–378.
5. Jan Von Flocken and Michael Klonovsky, *Stalin's Lager in Deutschland 1945–1950*, (Berlin, Germany, 1994), 41.
6. Jan Lipinsky, *Mobilität zwischen den Lagern*, in *Sowjetische Speziallager in Deutschland 1945 bis 1950 Band I*, eds. Sergej Mironenko, Lutz Niethammer, and Alexander von Plato (Berlin: Akademie Verlag, 1998), 230.
7. Mironenko, Niethammer, and von Plato, eds., *Sowjetische Speziallager in Deutschland 1945 bis 1950 Band I*, 36.
8. Von Flocken, and Klonovsky, *Stalin's Lager in Deutschland 1945–1950*, 41–42.
9. Ibid., 43.
10. Lutz Niethammer, "Alleierte Internierungslager in Deutschland nach 1945, Ein Vergleich und Offene Fragen," in *Sowjetische Speziallager in Deutschland 1945 bis 1950 Band I*, eds. Sergej Mironenko, Lutz Niethammer, and Alexander von Plato (Berlin: Akademie Verlag, 1998), 109–110.
11. Eva Ochs, "Erfahrungsgeschichtliche Aspekte des Lagerlebens," in *Sowjetische Speziallager in Deutschland 1945 bis 1950 Band I*, eds. Sergej Mironenko, Lutz Niethammer, and Alexander von Plato (Berlin: Akademie Verlag, 1998), 266.
12. Ibid., 267–268, 271.
13. Ibid., 271.
14. Ibid., 272–273, 276.
15. Von Flocken, and Klonovsky, *Stalin's Lager in Deutschland 1945–1950*, 168–171.
16. Mironenko, Niethammer, and von Plato, eds., *Sowjetische Speziallager in Deutschland 1945 bis 1950 Band I*, 36.
17. Von Flocken, and Klonovsky, *Stalin's Lager in Deutschland 1945–1950*, 44.
18. Preissinger, *Death Camps of the Soviets, 1945–1950*, 159.

19. Ibid., 123–125.
20. Gerhard Finn, *Die Politischen Häftlinge der Sovjetzone*, (Pfaffenhofen, Germany, 1960), 36.
21. Eva Ochs, "Erfahrungsgeschichtliche Aspekte des Lagerlebens," in *Sowjetische Speziallager in Deutschland 1945 bis 1950 Band I*, eds. Sergej Mironenko, Lutz Niethammer, and Alexander von Plato (Berlin: Akademie Verlag, 1998), 274.
22. Lipinsky, "Mobilität zwischen den Lagern," in *Sowjetische Speziallager in Deutschland 1945 bis 1950 Band I*, eds. Sergej Mironenko, Lutz Niethammer, and Alexander von Plato (Berlin: Akademie Verlag, 1998), 228.
23. Ibid., 228, 229.
24. Achim Kilian, *Einzuweisen zur völligen Isolierung, NKWD Speziallager Muhlberg, Elbe* (Leipzig, Germany, 1992), 125–127.
25. Natalja Jeske, "Speziallagerstatistik," in *Sowjetische Speziallager in Deutschland 1945 bis 1950 Band I*, eds. Sergej Mironenko, Lutz Niethammer, and Alexander von Plato (Berlin: Akademie Verlag, 1998), 196–197.
26. Ibid., 201.
27. Ibid., 202–203.
28. Von Flocken, and Klonovsky, *Stalin's Lager in Deutschland 1945–1950*, 37–38.
29. Jeske, "Speziallagerstatistik," in *Sowjetische Speziallager in Deutschland 1945 bis 1950 Band I*, eds. Sergej Mironenko, Lutz Niethammer, and Alexander von Plato (Berlin: Akademie Verlag, 1998), 204.
30. Von Flocken, and Klonovsky, *Stalin's Lager in Deutschland 1945–1950*, 37.
31. Ibid., 40.
32. Preissinger, *Death Camps of the Soviets, 1945–1950*,145.
33. Von Flocken, and Klonovsky, *Stalin's Lager in Deutschland 1945–1950*, 39.
34. Jeske, "Speziallagerstatistik," in *Sowjetische Speziallager in Deutschland 1945 bis 1950 Band I*, eds. Sergej Mironenko, Lutz Niethammer, and Alexander von Plato (Berlin: Akademie Verlag, 1998), 206–207.
35. Ibid., 208–209.
36. Ibid., 210.
37. Ibid., 212.
38. Mironenko, Niethammer, and von Plato, eds., *Sowjetische Speziallager in Deutschland 1945 bis 1950 Band I*, 39.
39. Jeske, "Speziallagerstatistik,"in *Sowjetische Speziallager in Deutschland 1945 bis 1950 Band I*, eds. Sergej Mironenko, Lutz Niethammer, and Alexander von Plato (Berlin: Akademie Verlag, 1998), 212.
40. Ibid., 215.

41. Ibid., 216–217.
42. Giles Macdonogh, *After the Reich: The Brutal History of the Allied Occupation,(New York,2007)*, 213, 215.
43. Mironenko, Niethammer, and von Plato, eds., *Sowjetische Speziallager in Deutschland 1945 bis 1950 Band I*, 38.
44. Niethammer, *Alleierte Internierungslager in Deutschland nach 1945, Ein Vergleich und Offene Fragen*, in Von Plato, Sergej Mironenko Eds. *Sowjetische Speziallager in Deutschland 1945 bis 1950*, 108.
45. Ibid., 219.
46. Ibid., 221.
47. Ibid., 220.
48. Ibid., 222–223.
49. Jeske, "Speziallagerstatistik," in *Sowjetische Speziallager in Deutschland 1945 bis 1950 Band I*, eds. Sergej Mironenko, Lutz Niethammer, and Alexander von Plato (Berlin: Akademie Verlag, 1998), 223.
50. Mironenko, Niethammer, and von Plato, eds., *Sowjetische Speziallager in Deutschland 1945 bis 1950 Band I*, 66.
51. Macdonogh, *After the Reich: The Brutal History of the Allied Occupation*, 214–215.
52. Preissinger, *Death Camps of the Soviets, 1945–1950*, 46.
53. Ibid., 51.
54. Mironenko, Niethammer, and von Plato, eds., *Sowjetische Speziallager in Deutschland 1945 bis 1950 Band I*, 19–20.
55. Preissinger, *Death Camps of the Soviets, 1945–1950*, 110–111.
56. Von Flocken, and Klonovsky, *Stalin's Lager in Deutschland 1945–1950*, 40.
57. Agde, Gunter, *Sachsenhausen bei Berlin,Speziallager Nr. 7,1945–1950*, (Berlin,Germany, 1994), 161.
58. Ibid.
59. Ibid., 168.
60. Ibid., 162.
61. Ibid., 171, 175.

CHAPTER 8

PRISONER RELEASE AND THE CLOSING OF THE CAMPS

The presence and protection of the Soviet Army contributed decisively to the success of revolutionary renewal on largely peaceful paths, which does not mean that, due to the machinations of Reactionaries, the class struggle did not sometimes take on very harsh forms, even of a military nature.

This statement reflects the official position of the government of the German Democratic Republic on the *Spezlager*. Source: Stefan Doernberg- a writer, secondary school teacher, and researcher of contemporary history, as well as the final Director of the International Relations Institute for the Academy of the State and Jurisprudence for the German Democratic Republic. He served as East German Ambassador to Finland from 1981 to 1987.[1]

THE FIRST RELEASE OF PRISONERS

The increasing complaints from the East German populace, regarding the disappearance of individuals, particularly children, began to concern

Soviet occupation authorities as well as the SED, and was a leading motivation for the release of prisoners in 1948. The whereabouts of their missing children caused the SED to petition SVAG, which resulted in the release of 500 detained youths. Popular hostility to the NKVD was very clear to the Soviet authorities in Germany. In November 1947, General Major I.S. Kolesnichenko, head of SVAG in the province of Thüringen, stated in a letter to General-Lieutenant Makarov that the activities of the NKVD were a main reason behind the hostile attitude toward the Soviet occupiers. The SED also could sense the impact of Soviet conduct on their political standing with the people of East Germany. In April 1948, SED leader Grotewohl brought up the problem of the special camps by blaming the West: "*Western propaganda about the supposed wave of arrests and lack of freedom seriously undermines the SED's authority in the zone and in Germany as a whole.*" The disregard for basic rights which characterized the Soviet occupation clearly undermined the legitimacy of the SED.[2]

The complaints from soviet officers about the arrest and disappearance of Germans had no immediate effect on the Operational Groups of the NKVD/MVD. Nevertheless, the Soviet authorities understood that the continuing arrests and incarcerations were damaging their legitimacy and that of their SED allies. The military government, therefore, undertook a number of measures in 1948 and early 1949, to improve the situation and reorient their denazification program toward rehabilitation of Nazis. The SED also acknowledged that "*we must try to win over former nominal members of the Nazi Party and educate them for active cooperation in democratic construction.*"[3]

Incarceration policies did change somewhat in 1948 and early 1949, when the military government decided there was little to be gained from the continued arrests and jailing of former Nazis. On March 8, 1948, the Council of Ministers of the USSR determined that the cases of all prisoners who had not been sentenced by the Military Courts, should be reviewed, and the minor and harmless Nazis released. The head of the GULAG administration in Moscow, Georgy P. Dobrynin, on

March 30, 1948, recommended to Colonel General Ivan Serov that the Mühlberg and Buchenwald special camps be closed. A special commission in Moscow proposed releasing 27,749 unimportant and nominal Nazis, members of the various security services, *Volksturm,* and other Nazi party organizations. The Politburo decided on June 30, 1948, to release those prisoners and close all camps except Bautzen, Buchenwald, and Sachsenhausen.[4]

There was opposition to the release of prisoners, especially of the young men who had been arrested for supposed Werewolf activities. The head of the MGB (Ministry of State Security) in Germany, Colonel Gerneral N.K.Kovalcuk, advised MGB Moscow of the many young Germans not yet sentenced who were still imprisoned.

Regarding the groups of young people up to the age of 20: these include active members of the now liquidated, illegal opposition and terror organization, Werewolf, and other illegal fascist groups which were created by the Germans even before their capitulation. In view of their proven enemy actions, this is not the moment to release them from arrest [5]

The denazification commissions were, nonetheless, formally disbanded in Februaryof 1948. The military government in the Soviet Zone declared an amnesty on March 18, 1948, on the centennial of the 1848 German Revolution, for Nazi prisoners who were serving less than one year, as well as those accused of minor crimes but who had not yet been indicted. For the most part, the prisoners affected were precisely the "nominal party members," whom the Soviets were trying to integrate into their political and economic structure of the zone.[6]

In mid-April, Marshall Sokolovskii, head of the Soviet Military Government at the time, also agreed to expand the amnesty to include a large number of youths who had been arrested for minor crimes and to provide Germans who had been arrested for more serious crimes with the opportunity to appeal their cases to SVAG judicial boards. At the April 14 and 15 plenums of the SED, Party Executive Grotewohl took credit for the release of "political prisoners and youth." The Soviet occupation zone newspaper, *Tägliche Rundschau,* also gave credit for the releases to the "repeated requests" of SED leaders Pieck and Grotewohl to Sokolovskii.

In preparation for the release of large numbers of prisoners, conditions in the internment camps improved dramatically. There was finally an increase in the prisoners' starvation-level rations; the tuberculosis barracks were cleaned up; medicines were made available; and the death rates substantially declined. Before their actual release, inmates were moved into quarantined barracks and provided with new clothes and a higher level of rations. On May 13, the Soviets announced a prisoner release. This only involved those arrested administratively and not those sentenced by the SMTs, i.e. practically all minor Nazis or members of Nazi affiliated organizations. Those released were all considered by the Soviets to be harmless to the Soviet zone of occupation.[7] The Soviets later announced that approximately 28,000 prisoners had been released in the summer of 1948; however, the total number for the spring and summer may have been as high as 46,000. Some prisoners were released right away, while some, for unknown reasons, were detained and quarantined for a longer period of time. To avoid releasing particular categories of political opponents, the military authorities deported thousands of prisoners to the Soviet Union, but the exact number of those is unknown. By the fall of 1948, enough prisoners had been either released or deported to the USSR that the Soviets could close down eight of the special camps; only Buchenwald, Bautzen, and Sachsenhausen remained open, holding, respectively (on May 5, 1949), 6,481, 10,110, and 11,901 prisoners each.[8]

As a result of recommendations from Serov and Sokolovskii, it was decided in Moscow that burial commandos were not to be released.[9] After the closing of the camps, most of them were sent to the Soviet Union and executed; some were executed on the spot. After this release, about 50% of the remaining prisoners were those sentenced by the SMTs. This included many younger prisoners who were convicted for belonging to the Werewolf as well as those engaging in anti-Soviet activities. With the increase in Cold War tensions, the Military tribunals increasingly convicted individuals for such anti-Soviet activities.[10] At this time, total prisoners remaining in the three camps was 28,983.[11] After the closing of most camps, those prisoners who were interned without trial were sent to Buchenwald; to Bautzen were sent those convicted by the Military Courts with long penalties of over 15 years. Those who were convicted with shorter penalties were sent to Sachsenhausen. In August 1948, after the first release, the camps came under the direct control of the GULAG –the Main Camp Administration, which was also a part of the MVD/NKVD. Previously they had been directly under MVD/NKVD control.[12]

(Refer to http://www.thegulagineastgermany.com for Illustration #15, an illegally taken photograph of the Special Camp #1, Sachsenhausen in 1949. Source: Brandenburg Memorial Foundation.)

THE CLOSING OF THE CAMPS

In the summer of 1949 the question of the special camps and their prisoners became acute for the Soviet Union and the East German government because of the establishment of the GDR in October 1949. What to do with the 13,539 prisoners who were never convicted and the 16,093 who were convicted by the military tribunals. The German communists wanted to close the camps because they considered that they negatively affected their image. The camps were no longer necessary because the security apparatus of the GDR could now exercise internal control.[13]

In September 1949, SED leaders Ulbricht, Pieck, and Grotewohl traveled to Moscow to discuss with the Soviet communist party leadership the formation of the GDR. Present were Malenkov, Beria, Bulganin, Molotov, Mikoyan, and Kaganovich. In a September 19th letter to Stalin, East German leaders requested, among others things, the following:

1. *The Return of all German prisoners of war: Inasmuch as the German Provisional Government has to take a position on the issue of the return of the prisoners of war, we request that by the end of 1949, all war prisoners in the Soviet Union be released.*

2. *The closing of all punishment camps: We think it is useful that the existing special camps in the Soviet zone of occupation be liquidated, and those prisoners sentenced by Soviet courts be sent to the Soviet Union. The rest should be turned over to the German authorities.*[14]

On October 19, 1949 two MGB ministers of the state security drafted this resolution regarding those prisoners in the special camps who had not been sentenced by the SMTs:

1. *Persons will be released who were arrested for minor crimes and who are no longer a danger to the democratic order in Germany.*

2. *Persons will be released to the German Democratic Republic whose criminal activities can be investigated by German state security.*

3. *Especially dangerous criminals, former leading and operational members of the German secret services, spies, dissidents, and terrorists, as well as agents of the American, English, and French secret services, who were involved in undermining work against the USSR, will be turned over to the MGB authorities in Germany for interrogation and then turned over to the courts.*

4. *The underlying arrest documents of especially dangerous criminals, whose activities are not sufficiently documented, will be turned over to the MGB for further investigation.*

Those convicted by the SMT, depending on the degree of their danger to the state, will be turned over to the prisons of the GDR (Ministry of the Interior) or the MGB.[15]

The resolution was adopted by the Central Committee of the CPUSSR on October 31, 1949.[16]

On December 30, 1949, the Politburo of the USSR Communist Central Committee decided on the complete liquidation of the special camps of the NKVD/MVD; this measure would apply to 29,632 prisoners; 15,038 prisoners with a minimum sentence would be released; and 10,513 prisoners sentenced by the SMTs would be transferred to the GDR for further incarceration; 649 of the most serious criminals were to be transferred to the MGB for further legal proceedings. The 10,513 prisoners transferred to the GDR would be handed over to the GDR's Peoples' Police Force and sent to prisons in the GDR, except for those who represented a particularly serious danger, and those would be transferred to the USSR.[17]

On the orders of General V.I. Chuikov, Sokolovskii's successor as military governor in the SBZ, (after the creation of the GDR he became Soviet High Commissioner), the Soviets closed down the special camps of Bautzen, Sachsenhausen, and Buchenwald in January and February of 1950. On January 17, 1950, *Neues Deutschland*, the newspaper of the central committee of the SED, published an exchange of letters between Walter Ulbricht, General Secretary of the Central Committee of the SED, and the Soviet General Chuikov, with the headline, "*The Closing of the Internment Camps.*" In this letter, Chuikov advises Ulbricht that, "*according to a decision of the government of the USSR, all internment camps under the control of the Soviet authorities in Germany, Buchenwald, Sachsenhausen, and Bautzen, will be liquidated.*"[18] In his reply, Ulbricht thanked the Soviet General for this information, stating that this measure had the full concurrence of the Government of the GDR. *Neues Deutschland* called this decision an " *act of magnanimity which showed trust and confidence (in the GDR government) on the part of the Soviet government.*"[19]

After the January 6, 1950, Order #0022, by the Minister of Internal Affairs, Colonel General Kruglov, liquidating the special camps, it was followed on January 13, 1950, and on February 4, 1950, by directives of the Berlin NKVD/MVD giving instructions on the closing of the camps and on the delivery of the prisoners, both those with court judgments and those without, to the Ministry of the Interior of the GDR.[20] The approximately 10,500 special camp prisoners, who were turned over to the GDR *Volkspolizei* and who were previously sentenced by Soviet Military Tribunals, were sent to prisons in Torgau, Hoheneck, and Bautzen.[21]

In the case of the Bautzen camp prisoners, 5,400 were turned over to the German police, 700 were sent to Waldheim to face trial by the German court authorities, and an unknown number were deported to the Soviet Union; among them were members of the burial battalion, who otherwise might have exposed the existence and even location of the mass graves. Buchenwald and Sachsenhausen camps were turned over to Soviet military authorities for their own use. The Bautzen prison, which was given to the German authorities had the worst reputation for brutality at that time. They treated the inmates, many of whom were angry and frustrated at not being included in the amnesties, no better than their NKVD/MVD warders had. In early March 1950, the prisoners staged a series of protests against conditions in Bautzen and subsequently negotiated with both the Soviet and the German authorities about improving them. On March 31, 1950, the prisoners attempted one more protest, but this time the People's Police reacted violently and hundreds of prisoners were badly beaten, ending all Bautzen demonstrations.[22]

One prisoner, on being transferred from the Sachsenhausen camp to a GDR prison, remembers this account of his experience: *Our hopes and expectations of finding human rights and justice were destroyed when we marched through the gates of the Soviet concentration camp at Buchenwald and were received by German communist police. They were accompanied by bloodhounds and armed with machine pistols. We were treated as hardened criminals, even though none of us had ever committed a crime, nor were we ever accused of one. Another "via crucis" began which our fellow Germans imposed on us. This new reality hit everyone very hard. We felt robbed of any understanding of the injustice that was done to us. Many of our comrades felt a spiritual and bodily death blow at having fallen into the jaws of the communists.* [23]

PRISONER RELEASE

On their release, prisoners received new clothing which had been made in the camp workshops. Prior to their release, food rations were also increased. These inmates generally did not speak about their incarceration, as they were too afraid of being arrested again. They only received a release certificate, but indicating nothing more, omitting information like the dates of the period of their imprisonment or reasons for arrest. No information as to the names of the dead prisoners was ever released by the Soviets/GDR, nor were death certificates issued to the families. The most families ever received from the authorities for missing family members, who disappeared in the special camp system, was a statement of "missing and presumed dead," similar to messages that German families received during the war from the *Wehrmacht*. Occasionally, families found out about the fate of their members from fellow prisoners who were released. Only after the collapse of the GDR were German State authorities able to construct detailed death lists from Russian and GDR archives and from the mass graves found near the camps.[24]

Figure 5. A Discharge Certification.

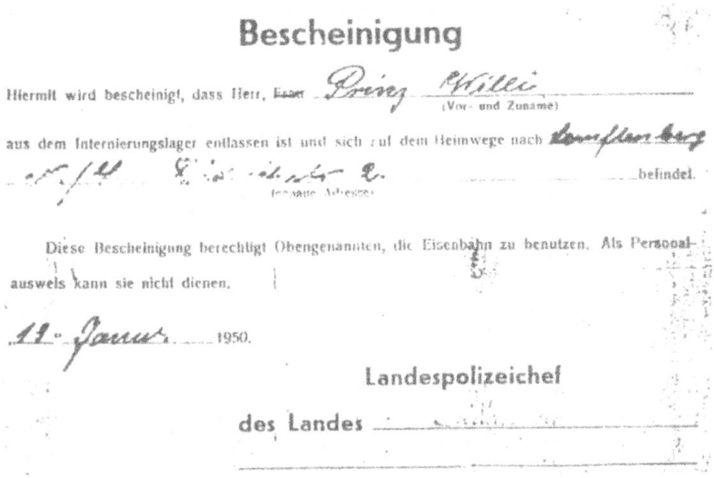

A Discharge Certificate example from a special camp; the first line states, "This will certify that Mr._____." The second line states "has been released from the internment camp and is on the way home [to] _____." [full address is given]." The third and fourth lines state, "This certificate gives the above named individual the right to use the railway. This certificate cannot be used as a personal identity document." After the date, it is signed by the head of the provincial police of the province of _____. This is the only document that a prisoner ever received upon being released.[25]

The majority of the prisoners had a very difficult time adjusting to society after their release and overcoming the trauma of their imprisonment. Not only were they physically weakened, but they also had large gaps in their civilian careers, having lost years of schooling or years in their stated profession. In the GDR, the subject of the special camps was forbidden territory. One could not write about them or even speak about them, without incurring punishment by the authorities. The Stasi (GDR Ministry of State Security) enforced this silence. However, if anyone did publicly speak of these things, revealing that from 1945 to 1950, the same sort of concentration camps existed as had been common under the Nazis, then the person was charged with 'inciting a boycott' and was sentenced to several years in prison.[26] For this reason, people did not disclose their incarceration in the camps until the collapse of the GDR. Even those former prisoners who escaped to the West did not talk about it, in order not to endanger families still living in the East.[27]

Former prisoners who continued to live in the GDR were constantly viewed as being guilty of illegal activities; people on the outside thought they had been in re-education camps. The majority of the people in the East never imagined or believed that special camps existed in the Soviet Zone of Occupation, especially in former Nazi prison camps, such as Buchenwald or Sachsenhausen.[28] After their release, many prisoners felt a certain pride that they survived and that they did not surrender. One former prisoner said, "*After my release I had the feeling that nothing could bother me in the future, after having survived all that. I will be able to overcome anything that I will encounter in the future.*" However, many also felt guilty that they lived when so many died. Others believed that they had done penance for the evils of the Nazi regime and felt absolved by the years of imprisonment.[29]

Finally, as to those few prisoners in the special camps who were also prisoners of the Nazis in their concentration camps, their general opinion was that, not withstanding the horrors of the special camps, the Nazi–SS camps were worse. In the special camps, the guards generally did not harass the prisoners, nor were they beaten or shot at. To survive in the special camps, however, was just as uncertain as it was in the Nazi camps.[30]

PERSONAL NARRATIVE – HELMUT KIND

Helmut Kind was born in 1922 and had to go to war when he was 17 years old. He was lucky and survived the difficult years until 1945. Originally apolitical, he belonged to the founders of the Liberal Democratic Party (LDPD) in Halle, (Province Sachsen-Anhalt) in July 1945. (This was a sister party of the FDP in West Germany, and officially sanctioned by the Soviet occupation authorities.) This fact took him to several special camps, including the Hohenschönhausen camp near Berlin. This camp was established by the NKVD in May 1945 on the property of a former community kitchen in Berlin-Hohenschönhausen, as Special Camp #3. It was established to be a collection station for all German civilians arrested in the Berlin area. The prisoners were either held in the cellar rooms of a dairy, in part of the kitchens, or in newly built barracks. In August 1945, the camp had to be expanded to include the buildings of a neighboring machine factory. On September 13th, 1945, a transport of 1,500 men and 200 women were assembled there to march on foot to the Sachsenhausen concentration camp. The participants in this column called it "The March of Horrors, Without any Humanity." The maximum number of individuals housed at any one time in Hohenschönhausen was 2,000. A total of 10,000 prisoners passed through Hohenschönhausen, who were then sent on to other special camps. This camp was dissolved in October 1946. Incarceration in Hohenschönhausen cost more than

3,000 prisoners their lives during the period when it operated. After closing in 1946, the Soviet security organizations continued to use the camp as an interrogation prison until March 1951. It was then turned over to the GDR, Ministry of State Security – Stasi.[31] The other camp where Helmut Kind was imprisoned was Sachsenhausen. It was an important Nazi concentration camp rebuilt by the NKVD in August of 1945 as Special Camp #7. The first prisoner transport of 2,000 men came from the Hohenschönhausen and Weesow camps. Initially it was for leaders of the SA, SS, and Hitler Youth, but later more and more political prisoners were interned there. In 1946, the camp was divided between Zone 1, for interned prisoners, that is, people arrested administratively, without a warrant, and Zone 2, for prisoners tried by Soviet military courts. Two important release actions came in July/August 1948 and in January 1950 when 3,800 and then 5,000 prisoners, respectively, were released. In January 1950, 1,200 female prisoners were sent to the jail in Hoheneck and 4,000 male prisoners were sent to the Torgau prison The last prisoners left the Sachsenhausen concentration camp on March 10, 1950. The largest number of deaths in any special camp occurred in the Sachsenhausen camp. One estimate is that in four and one-half years over 25,000 prisoners died. The bodies were buried in a forest on the road to Schmachtenhausen.[32]

Helmut Kind writes his recollection of this period:

After a short period as a prisoner of war, I became a gate keeper in a chemical factory in Halle. During the war, I was an officer in the armored corps. I was shortly released from this job with the explanation that, as a former officer, I could not control any members of the working class. In July 1945, I was among the first members of the LDPD in Sachsen-Anhalt and worked, since that September as a provincial leader of the party. In this work, I traveled extensively in towns and villages in order to promote the LDPD. I had to receive prior approval from the Soviet occupation authorities for all my speeches.

In the fall of 1945 I was arrested four times by the Soviet secret police. During interrogation, always held in NKVD prisons in Halle or Merseburg, I always had to hear their accusations for founding a new middle class political party. This surprised me very much because Soviet occupation authorities permitted the LDPD as a democratic party. I was always correctly treated, but also was subjected to penetrating questions about the character of my party. Somehow, they always saw in me a former Wehrmacht officer or perhaps even a member of the Werewolf. But I was never a member of the Nazi party.

These interrogations never disturbed me very much as one was always released after a short while. My view about my legal situation was that as I was not guilty of anything, I had nothing to fear.

When I was arrested again in November 1945, and delivered to the police prison in Halle, I had no idea that I was to be imprisoned for four years. I had to spend six months in the police prison where indescribable conditions existed. In a two man cell there were twelve people. We practically had to lie one above the other. There was only one slice of bread daily and a little soup. Many were so weak that they could not even sit up. There was even a murderer in our cell. Today it is difficult for me to understand how a normal person could get used to living in such conditions, even though he had no choice.

After it was decided that I was a political prisoner, I had to move into a one man cell. At the end of April 1946, we were sent to the prison in Halle, known as the Red Ochs. That was a collection station for the various Soviet concentration camps. The transport through Halle was very demeaning. We had to march through the city, in rags, unshaven and manacled. From the Red Ochs, I was transported twice by cattle car to the special camp in Torgau. But as it was always completely full, we had to return each time to Halle where the authorities harassed us with police dogs on the railway platform.

One day the Russian commander of the prison in Halle called me in and said that as I was "panzer" officer," that is, I was a specialist. "In the

Hohenschönhausen camp we need people who can drive and repair cars."
Thus started my life in the Hohenschönhausen camp.

There, behind walls and barbed wire was a special work shop of the Red
Army. Stolen cars from the West were repaired there and given new motor
numbers and so on. I had to work in this shop with 50 other 'specialists,'
repairing and fixing stolen cars. I had a number of opportunities to flee
from the camp but did not as I did not want the Soviets to seek retribution
from my family. Also, as I thought I was innocent, I [assumed that I] would
be released as soon as I could prove my case.

In the summer of 1946 more prisoners came to Hohenschönhausen, so I
had to help in converting a large church into prison cells. There were, for
example, cells so small that a prisoner could only stand in them. The work
bosses were German criminal prisoners who behaved disgustingly.

Death was ever present in Hohenschönhausen. It existed in the burial
squads that had to take away bodies several times weekly. We lived in
unheated factory rooms; hygienic conditions were deplorable, and food
rations poor. Most prisoners looked like skeletons. There were no medicines
or medical help. No clothing was given to the prisoners so that in the winter
of 1946/1947 many prisoners died of cold. I was among the lucky ones as
I was able to get hold of a Russian military coat. In the entire camp there
was only one place to wash and the prisoners looked accordingly. There
was hunger dystrophy. Men lost their sanity due to lack of food. Many
fantasized and imagined the most elaborate meals. I saw how some people
really became crazy and not only the young but many of the very educated.

At the beginning of 1947, my time in Hohenschönhausen was over. During
this period, I was never interrogated or accused of any crime by the Soviets.
More dead than alive, many hundreds of prisoners were forced into cattle
cars and transported to the Sachsenhausen Concentration Camp.

I had to stay in the Sachsenhausen Camp for the next three years No
matter how bad conditions were there, compared to Hohenshönhausen, there
were improvements. For example, we received new prison clothing. Hygienic

conditions were also better. I worked in the bath and the disinfection stations. Every day I had to chop wood for two hours in order to heat the disinfection ovens. In this camp, everyone did their utmost in order to remain alive. Whoever was able to work found this a great blessing. To survive was a question of luck, as hunger increased steadily. I remember especially the continuously re-cooked sauerkraut. If one became sick to one's stomach, one either died or recovered. That I survived these tortures can only be ascribed to lucky coincidences.

If one was to be released, one was sent to a special barracks. There new clothing was given and the prisoners received increased rations, so that they would be released in a better condition. This day came for me on January 17, 1950, after four years and two months of imprisonment. I was given 20 marks and a release certificate. Why I spent so much time behind bars and barbed wire no one has ever told me. On my return, I was immediately rehired by my political party, the LDPD in Sachsen-Anhalt. In 1987, when I attempted to receive my pension, the communist authorities wanted to convince me that I did commit a political crime, but fortunately they were set straight, in time.[33]

NOTES

1. Adrian Preissinger, *Death Camps of the Soviets, 1945–1950*, (Ocean City, Maryland, 1994), 96.
2. Ibid., 49.
3. Norman M. Naimark, *The Russians in Germany, A History of the Soviet Zone of Occupation, 1945–1949*, (Cambridge, Massachusetts, 1995), 394–395.
4. Mironenko, Niethammer, and von Plato, eds., *Sowjetische Speziallager in Deutschland 1945 bis 1950 Band I*, 40–41.
5. Nikita Petrov, "Die Apparate des NKVD/MVD und der MGB in Deutschland (1945–1953), Eine Historische Skizze," in *Sowjetische Speziallager in Deutschland 1945 bis 1950 Band I*, eds. Sergej Mironenko, Lutz Niethammer, and Alexander von Plato (Berlin: Akademie Verlag, 1998), 151–152.
6. Gary Bruce, *Resistance with the People, Repression and Resistance in Eastern Germany, 1945–1955*, (Lanham, Maryland, 2003), 95.
7. Ralf Possekel, ed., "Sowjetische Dokumente zur Lagerpolitik," in *Sowjetische Speziallager in Deutschland 1945 bis 1950 Band I*, eds. Sergej Mironenko, Lutz Niethammer, and Alexander von Plato (Berlin: Akademie Verlag, 1998), 84.
8. Ibid.
9. Ibid., 87.
10. Mironenko, Niethammer, and von Plato, eds., *Sowjetische Speziallager in Deutschland 1945 bis 1950 Band I*, 42.
11. Ibid., 43.
12. Ibid., 89.
13. Jan Von Flocken, and Michael Klonovsky, *Stalin's Lager in Deutschland 1945–1950*, (Berlin, Germany, 1994), 49.
14. Possekel, ed., "Sowjetische Dokumente zur Lagerpolitik," in *Sowjetische Speziallager in Deutschland 1945 bis 1950 Band I*, eds. Sergej Mironenko, Lutz Niethammer, and Alexander von Plato (Berlin: Akademie Verlag, 1998), 93.
15. Ibid., 94.
16. Ibid., 95.
17. Peter Erler, "Zur Tätigkeit der Sowjetischen Militärtribunale (SMT) in der SBZ/DDR," in *Sowjetische Speziallager in Deutschland 1945 bis 1950*

Band I, eds. Sergej Mironenko, Lutz Niethammer, and Alexander von Plato (Berlin: Akademie Verlag, 1998), 184–185.

18. Mironenko, Niethammer, and von Plato, eds., *Sowjetische Speziallager in Deutschland 1945 bis 1950 Band I*, 19.

19. Ibid., 20.

20. Ibid., 44.

21. Von Flocken, and Klonovsky, *Stalin's Lager in Deutschland 1945–1950*, 196.

22. Ibid., 197.

23. Ibid., 194–195.

24. Ibid., 49.

25. Hanno Muller, ed., *Recht oder Rache? Buchenwald 1945–1950*, (Frankfurt/Main, Germany, 1991), 57.

26. Preissinger, *Death Camps of the Soviets, 1945–1950*, 110–111.

27. Mironenko, Niethammer, and von Plato, eds., *Sowjetische Speziallager in Deutschland 1945 bis 1950 Band I*, 69, 70.

28. Ibid., 71.

29. Ev Ochs, "Erfahrungsgeschichtliche Aspekete des Lagerlebens," in *Sowjetische Speziallager in Deutschland 1945 bis 1950 Band I*, eds. Sergej Mironenko, Lutz Niethammer, and Alexander von Plato (Berlin: Akademie Verlag, 1998), 278.

30. Muller, ed., *Recht oder Rache? Buchenwald 1945–1950*, 252.

31. Von Flocken, and Klonovsky, *Stalin's Lager in Deutschland 1945–1950*, 163.

32. Ibid., 91.

33. Ibid., 164–167.

CHAPTER 9

THE WALDHEIM TRIALS
AND LAST THOUGHTS

Does it make any sense to have all these pitiful prisoners subjected—in the wildest style of Nazism and its people's courts, in the exact style of Roland Freisler, (president of the Nazi People's Courts) who assuredly went to hell—to precisely the same prison and death sentences those courts imposed? Thus, providing the non-Communist world with a bloody spectacle that is an incentive for hatred?

The above is an excerpt from a letter, dated July 1950 from Thomas Mann to SED Chief Walter Ulbricht, asking for clemency for those special camp prisoners sentenced at the GDR Waldheim trials. This letter was never answered.

THE WALDHEIM TRIALS

When in January/February 1950, the Soviets closed the last three special camps, not all prisoners were released. About 10,500 prisoners were turned over to the GDR Interior Ministry for further interrogation and trials or to fulfill their sentences.[1] Of these, the GDR Ministry of the

Interior received 3,432 former special camp prisoners for additional trials for criminal acts that were considered the most serious. In cattle cars, enclosed by barbed wire, guarded by *Volkspolizei*, with guard dogs, rifles, machine pistols, and illuminated by searchlights, the prisoners arrived at the Waldheim, Sachsen prison on February 15,1950.[2]

One prisoner relates this experience:

> *The majority of us were convinced that we would experience real justice in order to be set free. At that time none of us knew about the September 19, 1949 letter of Pieck, the president of the so called GDR, to Stalin with the request to liquidate the punishment camps in the Soviet zone of occupation for practical reasons. Also, not known to us was the letter from General Chuikov, commander of the Soviet army in East Germany, to Walter Ulbricht, Deputy Prime Minister of the so called GDR and General Secretary of the East German SED, regarding the closing of the camps. Somewhere the train halted, and the door of the cattle car was opened. Uniformed guards brusquely ordered us to leave the cattle cars. We climbed down without help and found ourselves in the furthest part of a train station. We are in Waldheim, Saxony. Our truck took us to the gate of a building. When it halted we climbed down and marched with our baggage through a neighboring small gate. The first thing I saw was a large, old linden tree. Behind the tree, almost in a wall, was a chapel, more akin to a small church. We thought, at that time, of the many men and women, who had already been four years in the Soviet special camps and at the beginning February 1950, that is, after the founding of the GDR, were then sent to the prison in Waldheim, Saxony.[3]*

Even before the trials, one of the chief prosecutors said that these prisoners had to be isolated from society in the interest of building a democratic state in the GDR. The regional court in Chemnitz established 12 sub-courts for these trials. All trials were closed to the public, including the press. GDR propaganda broadcasts said that these were the Nürenberg trials of the GDR, when, in reality, very few former Nazis were tried and those that did belong to the party were only nominal or followers. The legal basis of the charges was SVAG Order # 201 of August 16,1947, which was based on CC Directive #38, calling for the arrest and trial of major Nazi offenders.[4]

Everyone saw these procedures as sham trials. Witnesses for the accused were not permitted. Although the accused could speak in their own defense, it had to be short. Then the judges would meet and "decide" on the previously agreed-upon guilty verdict. This normally did not take more than half an hour. Previous years of incarceration in a Soviet special camp were not taken into consideration in sentencing. Most guilt was not established for individual illegal acts, but rather for collective guilt for having belonged to a political party or organization. No specific charges were made by the courts and no proof was submitted of any charges. Indicted prisoners included former *Wehrmacht* officers, jurists, police, public servants, journalists, and teachers. Many of the convicted had already spent over four years interned in the special camps, and more than half were emaciated and sick.[5]

Members of the *Volkspolizei*, judges, and prosecutors were under the impression at the beginning of the trials that they were to try Nazi war criminals. Many of the judges and prosecutors had even been in Nazi concentration camps themselves. At the beginning of the trials, there was an atmosphere of unease among some of the judges and prosecutors, who were educated in traditional German law, in light of the fact that defendants could not bring witnesses.[6]

A clearer picture of the legal procedure followed in the Waldheim trials is given by the following public statement from the head of the prosecutor's office of the East German Justice Ministry on April 19, 1950:

> *The coming work cannot in any way be viewed from a formal, legalistic position, but only from a political one. The court sentences cannot be less than those of our "friends" (Soviets) based on the same evidence. It is necessary for the accused....to remain under arrest as they are committed enemies of our construction. Therefore, no consideration should be given to any material evidence (in favor of the accused) in our possession. Sentences under ten years should*

be avoided, and today it is not important to give consideration to time already served.[7]

The original Soviet arrest protocols were used in the trials and the condition of their validity shortly became evident. East German archives stated that the following:

When these prisoners, at their interrogation, came into contact for the first time with German officials, either the Volkspolizei or the state prosecutors, many made it clear that they had signed the Soviet protocols only under pressure of beatings and other tortures.[8]

Four of the trials resulted in verdicts, in June 1950, of not guilty; 43 died during the trials; 33 received death sentences, and 145 got life imprisonment; the rest received between 4 and 25 years of prison time. A total of 3,324 prisoners were tried.[9] Beginning on June 20, the SED attempted to demonstrate to the East German public that all previous sentences were justified by staging show trials of handpicked war criminals from the remaining prisoners. The SED daily bussed in a carefully selected public audience to the Waldheim City Hall, where the trial was being staged. In the period from June 20–29, only 10 of the 20 show trials in the Waldheim Courthouse resulted in a sentence for a major crime.[10]

THE PERSONAL EXPERIENCE OF KURT KRAKOW:

Kurt Krakow was born in 1914. As a youth he joined the Boy Scouts and later became a sales man of technical goods. After his military service from 1936 to 1938, he returned to his profession in Berlin and never belonged to any political party. In 1939/1940 he was drafted for the campaign against France, but then was released and forced to join the *Wehrmacht* Reserves. He worked again in his previous position and demonstrated anti-fascist opinions, scattering homemade anti-Hitler flyers in his company. On the basis of a denunciation, he was arrested on October 15, 1942, by the Gestapo and condemned on August 27, 1943, by a Berlin court, to two and a half years in prison for high treason for distributing anti-Nazi propaganda. Imprisoned in Magedeburg, (Province Brandenburg), he was freed in 1945, and worked in the municipal administration of a Berlin suburb where he participated in the "Save the Children" humanitarian organization. At the end of 1945, he also began to work with youth groups, organizing "home evenings," where he taught the history of the rise of youth movements. Denounced again, on May 20, 1946, he was arrested by the Soviets with no specific charge, and interned in the Soviet special camp, Hohenschönhausen #3, near Berlin. Despite documents indicating his incarceration for his anti-Nazi activities and his official designation as a "Victim of Fascism" number 471, he remained in prison. Later, he was transferred to the Sachsenhausen camp #7, where he stayed until June 1949. Although suffering from tuberculosis, he was nonetheless transferred to Waldheim (Sachsen) in February 1950. His Soviet arrest protocol of January 18, 1950, charged him with resistance to the Soviet occupation, making anti-Soviet propaganda among youths, and attempting to organize an underground Boy Scout movement.

Although his court interrogation, according to him, was legally correct, he was sentenced on June 19, 1950, in accordance with CC Directive #38 to eight years prison stating "propaganda for militarism which threatened the peace of the German people."

He declared himself "not guilty" on the basis of his illness. On July 6, 1950, he went into the prison hospital at the Bautzen prison (Sachsen) where he remained until his pardon on October 6, 1952. He spent very difficult years there due to his illness and was several times on the verge of dying. Despite his efforts during the period of the GDR government, including support from his friends who wrote a statement for his trial relating his anti-Nazi activities, the "Victim of Fascism" designation was only returned to him in September 1992.[11]

According to most people in the West, the Waldheim trials had nothing to do with a judicial process in a legal state. Although the GDR press only covered the public trials, many individuals and even some organizations in the GDR attempted to help the condemned. Family members, some lawyers, church ministers and priests, and the leader of the Jewish community in East Germany, and Probst (Dean) Heinrich Grüber of the St. Mary's Lutheran church in Berlin offered free legal service to the convicted. (See chapter 7 for comments on Probst Grüber .) Thomas Mann wrote a letter in July 1950 to Walter Ulbricht asking for clemency for the sentenced individuals, while, at the same time, condemning the totalitarian state. He requested an act of mercy, generosity, hope, *détente,* and reconciliation to free the condemned. The letter remained unanswered. (See introduction for an excerpt of this letter.) Even the GDR State Secretary of Justice Hermann Brandt criticized the trials and requested a revision of the sentences. In return, he was arrested in September 1950 and sentenced to 14 years prison.[12]

On June 10,1952, the Politburo of the SED ordered a review of all files of convicted persons due to the increasing criticism of the process, principally from the West. As a result, in October 1952, 996 were pardoned and 1,024 had their sentences reduced. In 1954, a renewed examination of files resulted in 693 pardons. In 1955 and 1956, additional prisoners were pardoned with the last prisoners being released in the spring of 1964. The death rate in the prisons of the Waldheim condemned was estimated at 600 during this period of incarceration.[13]

Of the 10,500 who remained in prison after the closing of the special camps and had not been sent to the Waldheim trials, the largest number were those convicted by the Soviet Military Tribunals, under Article 58 of the RSFSR Penal Code on Crimes Against the State, of February 25, 1927. Throughout the 1950s, the majority of these were released as a result of amnesties of both the GDR and Soviet governments. After the death of Stalin in 1953, just as in the Soviet Union, many prisoners were released; 6,150 prisoners convicted by the SMTs were released on August 28, 1953, as a result of a decision by the Politburo. However, as of September 1954, 5,628 SMT convicted prisoners still remained in East German prisons. The majority were amnestied in 1956/1957, after a great deal of pressure by GDR president Wilhelm Pieck on the Soviet High Commissioner in the GDR. Pieck was concerned that their continuing imprisonment was one of the main reasons for the opposition to the Communist government. The last remaining SMT convicted prisoners were amnestied by 1964.[14]

The Soviets insisted that the prisoners sent to Waldheim for trials were to be sentenced by the spring of 1950, as soon as possible after the closure of the camps; this was done in order to justify the retention of so many prisoners without any trial or sentence in the camps. In any event, the SED made every effort to fulfill the Soviet order. The Waldheim trials became a symbol of Soviet "law," introduced in East Germany under the pretense of a new "anti-fascist-democratic order," a police state repressing opponents during all the years of the GDR. The Waldheim trials also ushered in the vigorous use of the judicial system as an instrument of political repression.[15] In its years of existence, the GDR never acknowledged the injustices and illegality of the Waldheim trials.[16]

After the release of political prisoners, Erich Mielke, GDR Minister of State Security (Stasi), said, "Our state power and state order is assured that the release of a part of those sentenced ... is no danger [to us]." By the beginning of the 1950s, the GDR's police and Stasi assumed responsibility for political repression in East Germany, though the Soviets, the MVD, and the MGB exercised strong control until the very end of the GDR.[17]

LAST THOUGHTS

On June 17, 1953 the workers in the German Democratic Republic rose up against the Communist regime. The revolt spread immediately to over 400 cities, towns, and villages throughout the GDR, and in all provinces; (they were least effective in Mecklenburg Vorpommern). It had started on the previous day, June 16, when construction workers, who were building a prestigious housing project on the Stalinallee in Berlin, marched down the boulevard calling for a strike, protesting increased work norms of 10% without any increase in pay.[18] The following day, June 17th, between

30,000 to 50,000 workers protested outside of government ministries in the heart of East Berlin, and the strike spread rapidly to other East German industrial cities. The leaders called for a general strike and even though the GDR government cancelled the increased work norms, the strike only increased in scope, becoming a strike against the regime itself and not only against the increased work requirements. The Soviets declared martial law on the 17th, sending an armored division into Berlin, assisted by the *Volkspolizei*. By the 19th the strike was crushed. The cost of the uprising was high with over 500 people killed, of whom 116 were government employees and members of the SED. Of those, 106 were executed under martial law or subsequently condemned to death. More than 1,800 were injured and 5,100 arrested (1,200 were sentenced to an average of five years imprisonment).[19]

Two important aspects of this uprising differentiated it from a normal labor strike. First, not only workers but all German social classes participated, including farmers, , thus making it, in effect, a mass popular uprising against Communism in general and against the SED government specifically.[20] Over 1,000,000 East Germans were reported to have participated in the protests all over the GDR. Second, their demands quickly moved from the economic to the political, basically calling for free elections and the end of the SED government. . Specifically, they demanded reduction of work norms, lowering of consumer prices, removal of farm production quotas, release of political prisoners, institution of free elections, resignation of the SED government, and removal of zonal boundaries.[21] The lessons of this uprising were not lost on the Soviets and their German allies. The government security and repressive apparatus were increased, but the SED government announced measures to improve peoples' living conditions such as more food imports from the Soviet Union, reduction of public transportation prices, and construction of additional housing.[22]

This uprising is notable for the fact that it occurred in this Soviet satellite state, in spite of all the years of repression of the opposition by the Soviet and the GDR state security systems—despite all the abuses of prisoners in the special camps and NKVD interrogation cellars, and generally, the harsh security environment in East Germany. The SPD labor leaders organized the strikes in various factories nationwide, though they appeared spontaneous and unplanned.. This occurred eventhough , the Social Democrats were the special targets of the Soviet repressive system. The June 17, 1953 uprising is, therefore, the underlying narrative of the history of the Soviet special camps.

(Refer to http://www.thegulagineastgermany.com for Illustration #16. Soviet tanks in Berlin, June 17, 1953. Source: Bundesarchiv, B 145, Wikimedia Commons)

It must also be stated that the Soviet special camps violated the Universal Declaration of Human Rights adopted by the United Nations General Assembly on December 10, 1948, but especially the following:

> **Article 3**, which said that everyone has the right to life, liberty, and security of person.

> **Article 5**, which said that no one shall be subjected to torture or to cruel, inhuman, or degrading treatment or punishment.

> **Article 9**, which said that no one shall be subjected to arbitrary arrest, detention, or exile.

When one reads the complete 30 articles of the Universal Declaration, it becomes clear that the Soviets and their German communist allies violated, at one time or another, every one of them during their rule in East Germany.

In 1976, with the adoption of the International Covenant on Civil and Political Rights, a part of the United Nations International Bill of Human Rights, that declaration received legal status and became international law. Although the Soviet Union and its satellite states never signed the declaration, as a member of the United Nations, they were, nevertheless, bound by its terms.

NOTES

1. Jan Von Flocken, and Michael Klonovsky, *Stalin's Lager in Deutschland 1945–1950*, (Berlin,Germany,1994), 49.
2. Ibid., 211.
3. Wilfriede Otto, "Die Waldheimer Prozesse," in *Sowjetische Speziallager in Deutschland 1945 bis 1950 Band I*, eds. Sergej Mironenko, Lutz Niethammer, and Alexander von Plato (Berlin: Akademie Verlag, 1998), 533.
4. Von Flocken, and Klonovsky, *Stalin's Lager in Deutschland 1945–1950*, 213–214.
5. Ibid., 215–216.
6. Otto, "Die Waldheimer Prozesse," in *Sowjetische Speziallager in Deutschland 1945 bis 1950 Band I*, eds. Sergej Mironenko, Lutz Niethammer, and Alexander von Plato (Berlin: Akademie Verlag, 1998), 546.
7. IIbid., 541.
8. Ibid., 541–542.
9. Von Flocken, and Klonovsky, *Stalin's Lager in Deutschland 1945–1950*, 218, 224.
10. Otto, "Die Waldheimer Prozesse," in *Sowjetische Speziallager in Deutschland 1945 bis 1950 Band I*, eds. Sergej Mironenko, Lutz Niethammer, and Alexander von Plato (Berlin: Akademie Verlag, 1998), 548.
11. Ibid., 343–344.
12. Ibid., 551.
13. Ibid., 552.
14. Peter Erler, "Zur Tätigkeit der Sowjetischen Militärtribunale (SMT) in der SBZ/DDR," in *Sowjetische Speziallager in Deutschland 1945 bis 1950 Band I*, eds. Sergej Mironenko, Lutz Niethammer, and Alexander von Plato (Berlin: Akademie Verlag, 1998), 186–187.
15. Mironenko, Niethammer, and von Plato, eds., *Sowjetische Speziallager in Deutschland 1945 bis 1950 Band I*, 72–73.
16. Ralf Possekel, ed., "Band 2: Sowjetische Dokumente zur Lagerpolitik," in *Sowjetische Speziallager in Deutschland 1945 bis 1950 Band I*, eds. Sergej Mironenko, Lutz Niethammer, and Alexander von Plato (Berlin: Akademie Verlag, 1998), 101.
17. Norman M. Naimark, *The Russians in Germany, A History of the Soviet Zone of Occupation, 1945–1949* (Cambridge, Massachusetts, 1995), 397.

18. Gary Bruce, *Resistance with the People, Repression and Resistance in Eastern Germany, 1945–1955,* (Lanham, Maryland, 2003), 170.
19. Report from the 1966 West German Ministry for Inter-German Affairs.
20. Ibid., 197.
21. Ibid., 199.
22. Ibid., 177, 224.

Forced Labor in the Soviet Uranium Mines of Eastern Germany

Forced Labor in the Soviet Uranium Mines of Eastern Germany

Summary

The *Erzgebirge* (ore mountains) have been mined since the 15th century for non-ferrous metals, but by the 20th century they were depleted. The *Erzgebirge* mountains are located in Southeastern Germany in the provinces of Sachsen and Thüringen, on the borders of the Czech Republic. (See Map # 8) The Soviets began mining again in mid-1945 for pitch blend, an oxide of uranium that was necessary to build the Soviet atom bomb, in competition with the United States' nuclear programs. Soviet scientists, geologists, and physicists arrived at that time, followed in early 1946 by conscripted workers. The Soviet labor exchanges drafted young workers, convicts, and even prostitutes and prisoners of war, all transported there under guard. A few were volunteers attracted by the promise of higher wages and more rations. The operation was conducted in great secrecy and its grounds were declared a prohibited zone; nobody could enter or leave without permission. It was under the control of the NKVD/MVD[1] and profound fear prevailed at the core of this uranium mining enterprise. Only flight to the West could spare workers from their fate in the mines.

Wismut AG was the Soviet company that ran the uranium mines. It was under the supervision of Colonel General Serov, head of the NKVD/MVD in the Soviet Zone of Occupation. The uranium shipments to the Soviet Union was a secret operation, and did not count, at that time, as part of East German reparations to the USSR. It was a giant project, employing thousands of workers—a labor intensive project, digging with picks and shovels in primitive working conditions, and with minimal mechanization. The number of uranium miners rose faster than housing could be built for them. In Johanngeorgenstadt, for example, cots were set up in apartment hallways to create sleeping space. In these conditions, laborers' hygiene was non-existent. The miners constantly breathed radioactive dust, with the corresponding high rate of radiation and other sicknesses. Wismut was transformed into a Soviet/ East German joint venture in 1954 with its own police, communications, and transport systems. A huge environmental mess developed, with mountains of waste, lakes of mining slush and residue from the mining operations. Polluted mine shafts, a warren of tunnels and cavities, stretched for many miles under the mountainous landscape, with some as deep as 6,000 feet.[2] With the collapse of the GDR, the German Federal Republic took over the immense task of cleaning up this environmental disaster.

BACKGROUND

In the fall of 1945, about 100 miners began working for the NKVD in several mines. The Soviet mining company began to contract experienced miners in November 1945. On April 4, 1946, the Council of Ministers of the Soviet Union decided to place the uranium mining under the control of the NKVD. Regular mining operation for uranium started in the summer of 1946. Lavrentiy Beria, Soviet Minister of Internal Affairs, chief of the NKVD, who was directly responsible for the Soviet atom bomb project, appointed NKVD Major General Mikhail M. Maltsev, a veteran commander of GULAG labor camps in the USSR and recipient of the highest Soviet decorations, to lead this enterprise. He was under the direct command of Colonel General Ivan Serov, head of the NKVD/MVD in the SBZ and Beria's deputy. The Soviet operating company, Wismut AG, had 26 working mines in East Germany and reached its maximum size in 1949.[3]

On May 26, 1947, the Soviet Zone Military Commander, Marshal Sokolovskii, issued Order #128, transferring six uranium mining operations in the *Erzgebirge* to Soviet control. This was the founding date of Wismut AG. Previously, these properties belonged to the states of Sachsen and Thüringen. The shareholders of Wismut AG were the Main Directorate for Soviet Property Abroad of the Council of Ministers and the state company of the Colored Metal Industry, both located in Moscow.[4]

The Soviet military employees in Wismut, on the other hand, were under the authority of the Ministry of State Security, Minister Viktor Abakumov, who was frequently in conflict with NKVD/MVD chief Serov. Maltsev applied GULAG discipline methods in the early days of the Wismut operation, such as withdrawing food rations from miners who did not fulfill their quotas or the use of military tribunals for those workers accused of alleged sabotage.[5] But unlike the GULAG forced labor camps in Siberia, it was difficult to hide the abuses of labor in the *Erzgebirge*, a fairly densely settled region of East Germany. To maintain secrecy and security, however, in early 1947, the mining districts became closed military zones, banning even the East German government party, SED, from activities there. Wismut, as it was under the political control of the NKVD, dealt with all important issues between the company and its German employees.[6]

Due to shortage of mining supervisors, the Soviets did not hesitate to use former skilled Nazis.

At the beginning, the NKVD opposed the use of former Nazis in the uranium mines; they feared sabotage and espionage by former SS and SA and Gestapo members, but their concern lasted only a few months. As working in the mines was considered punishment for Nazis, the labor exchanges preferred to provide former members of the party. This was also originally opposed by the Soviet mine managers, who criticized the labor exchanges, but the negative attitude diminished with the increasing need for labor in the mines. It also became a way for German workers to avoid the denazification process. It is estimated that about 12% of the miners were former NSDAP members, but this was most likely an inaccurately low number because many hid their past and little effort was made to discover the truth.[7]

For example, at the end of 1948, it was supposed that the majority of the miners at the Annaberg mine were former Nazi party members. Mostly they worked underground and as long as they did their jobs well, no one minded. Nevertheless, the NKVD considered them security risks and kept them under close supervision.[8]

The Soviets originally feared that former Nazis would organize underground operations in the mining district so they organized groups of German informers as a preventive measure. In the first ten months of 1947, for example, the Soviets claimed to have uncovered 2,000 cases of fascist and anti-Soviet groups. Forty seven people were arrested in 1947 for anti-Soviet underground activities, all of whom were interned in the special camps. However, all this organized Nazi activity was finally deemed baseless, and the NKVD then concentrated on maintaining discipline among Wismut employees.[9]

The NKVD maintained a strict security system in the Wismut mines. NKVD/MVD troops guarded not only the mines, but the total Wismut zone of mines as well (see Map #8), having up to 15,000 troops there. These troops were under the command of the NKVD military head of

Wismut. There were additional armed military units stationed in the uranium mining districts. Military and NKVD checkpoints were present at all approaches to this zone. The mines were surrounded by wooden fences and watch towers, and access to them was only through a guarded gate. There were also NKVD posts at district or town levels at the fourteen Wismut mines. A special NKVD group, commanded by a Major Malygin, was very important in its work at all the pits and plants of Wismut. He had the task of investigating all cases of espionage and diversion and reported directly to General Serov.[10]

Maintaining discipline became the major source of Soviet concern, as a large number of the miners wanted to leave as soon as possible. Many of the escaped miners passed on information about the building and production of the uranium project to the West, most frequently to the *Ostbüro* of the SPD in Berlin, and also to the US and British intelligence agencies. To counter the flight problem, the Soviets created a German police called *Bergpolizei* (mountain police), which functioned under the control of the NKVD. They kept a close eye on the miners (particularly the shirkers), dealt with criminal offenses, maintained the peace, and kept order. They submitted lists of miners missing from their jobs to the Soviet authorities and also attempted to catch them. In the early years of the Wismut mines, conditions were relatively chaotic and it was easier to flee, but as the security services in the mines became better organized, the *Bergpolizei* became more effective. Escaped miners were frequently caught and taken to Chemnitz for trial. If the miner was suspected of having visited West Berlin, he was turned over to the East German K5 or the NKVD. Besides guarding the mines, warehouses, and borders of the mining region, the *Bergpolizei* also checked railway stations for wayward miners and those persons wanting to visit the mining region. In September 1949, at the time of the creation of the GDR, this police unit became a part of the East German state police force and eventually part of the *Volkspolizei* in 1957; it reported directly to the GDR Ministry of the Interior. From the mid-1950s, it patrolled the pits and also accompanied uranium transports to the Soviet Union.[11]

Beginning in 1947, a Soviet Military Tribunal SMT was established in Wismut AG. It appeared to have been stricter than those in other parts of the SBZ . In order to discourage flight, it passed about 1,500 sentences on Wismut employees. These trials did not involve Nazi criminals, but rather counter revolutionary crimes, including flight as well as some common criminality. The NKVD executed at least 68 individuals in the Wismut mining complex for espionage, sabotage, or other act of resistance.[12]

The case of Ludwig Hecker, a miner, demonstrates the effort by the secret police and SMT to suppress workers' opposition. Hecker talked about the possibility of a strike with his fellow workers on the night shift. The miners decided to lay down their tools and complain of poor organization and low safety standards at work. They were promised that their complaints would be examined, and the miners made up for the shift they had missed.

That was not the end of the matter. A member of the mines police (*Bergpolizei*) came to wake Hecker up at his house after a night shift and told him "*I have to take you to Bärenstein, into custody ...* " Then the rest followed--solitary confinement and nighttime interrogations. "*'Who asked you to strike?' 'Nobody.'* He said, *'You asshole, Hecker, you asshole! When they had strikes in Germany you were still shitting in your pants. How do you know how to make a strike?' ...* Then he said to me *'I am going on leave. We shall never see each other again. When I return you will not be around here. You are now going to be sentenced.'* I said *'Major, sir, could you please tell me what I shall get? According to German legislation I should not be here at all.'* Then he said to me *'What do you think? You'll be punished.'* So I said *'three months, four months?' 'Oh Hecker'* he replied, *'You are an asshole. We don't reckon in months, we don't reckon in years, we reckon in decades. We decide the fates of men! ....*"

On May 31, 1950, Hecker was sentenced at Kassberg. At the desk in a small room there was an officer who acted as the judge, with an assistant on each side, and an interpreter opposite him. "Behind me by the wall there stood a man with a Kalashnikov. One of the assistants read a book;

the other snoozed. Sentencing was a matter of ten minutes. I had no lawyer. It was clearly and curtly explained to me that I was guilty of an act of sabotage and that I would be sentenced for sabotage according to paragraph so and so, article so and so. It was all rattled off; there was no consultation or anything. The sentence had been agreed upon long before; they brought it with them. And then he said 'Ten years in a labor camp. ' The punishment was thought to have been light, those ten years."[13]

At a meeting on November 26, 1949, between Soviet occupation authorities and heads of the GDR government, Pieck, Ulbricht, and Grotewohl, it was decided to guarantee to the Soviet Union the continued possession of the mines and exclusive access to uranium production. The uranium sent to Russia was not to appear in the GDR export statistics and the GDR agreed on providing Wismut with labor and food on a preferential basis. Deliveries of uranium would be priced in U.S. dollars and charged to the East German reparations account with the Soviet Union.[14]

About 9,500 tons of uranium were delivered to the Soviet Union between 1945 and 1953 for its military and civilian programs, and about $350,000,000 were written off the reparations account with the Soviet Union.[15] In August 1953, the Soviet government announced that reparations payments would be terminated as of January 1, 1954. This was ascribed, in part, to the June 1953 East German uprising. It was later announced that Wismut AG would become a joint stock company in 1954, to be owned equally between the Soviet Union and the East German government. The GDR would participate in management decisions and all costs would be shared jointly.[16]

CONSCRIPTION OF LABOR

In October 1945, the Soviet occupation authorities issued Order #43 to enforce the provision of labor for industrial enterprises. Those unwilling to work were denied ration cards. German labor exchanges in the Soviet zone were required to provide necessary labor for state enterprises. Another edict, Order #153, of November 29, 1945, permitted the mandatory assignment of work for unemployed persons, without the right of appeal. This practice of compulsory work recruitment was confirmed by Allied Control Council Directive #3, of January 17, 1946, which allowed labor to be considered a form of reparations payment; (See chapter 4 for details of the Yalta Agreement on conscripting German labor for work for the Soviet Union.) The Soviet uranium industry recruited most of its workers in its early years on that basis. (It is interesting to note that the Western Allies tried this system to recruit miners for the coal industry in the early days of their occupation of Germany, , but failed, basing future recruitment only on incentives.) [17]

In April 1946, forced labor recruitment began in Sachsen province by the Soviet occupation authorities, when the labor exchanges sent 800 workers to the Aue Mines. Despite the assistance of the Red Army in supervising the transport of workers from other enterprises to the mines, the demand was not met. The NKVD then began to look for workers in refugee camps, including the use of German middle men, who received a bonus for each worker recruited. The following was reported about these transports to the mines: *"The people were not medically examined, nor were they miners by profession...the transport consisted of amputees, sick people, and old men and women."* [18]

A new order, issued on October 23, 1946, stated that interference by the NKVD in recruitment by the labor exchanges was to stop immediately. Nevertheless, recruitment of forced labor for the uranium industry increased in the last quarter of 1946. Over the objection of the German civilian authorities, workers were withdrawn from the coal industry in East Germany and together with refugee miners from Silesia (Silesia became Polish and the Germans were expelled) formed the core of the skilled work force in the Wismut Mines. [19]

Due to labor-intensive production methods in the mines, labor exchanges were required to meet Soviet demands and were judged on the basis of reaching these quotas. The German official responsible for labor affairs in the province of Brandenburg wrote to the labor exchanges on September 4, 1947: *"The recruitment of voluntary labor is preferred, but if the numbers are insufficient, they have to be supplemented by compulsory labor. Labor exchanges must inform the state labor office by telephone straightaway, daily, how many workers were provided, for the ore mining industry."* [20]

In order to meet the mandatory targets, labor exchanges often had to resort to force to send many thousands of workers to the uranium mines, many of whom proved unsuitable for mining. One method that a prospective miner had available to avoid labor in the mines was to obtain a medical certificate, indicating that he could not do this work. Doctors at the mines, upon examining new arrivals, divided them into three groups: workers suitable for underground mining, recruits suitable to work only above ground, and people totally unfit for mining. The physicians who were in charge of examining the newly arrived workers were urged by Wismut management to declare them fit for work, although many were not. If doctors deemed too many men as unfit for mining and released them, they themselves were in danger of being arrested by the NKVD. In urgent cases, CC Directive #3 could also be used to force unemployed office workers to the mines.[21]

The demand for labor continued to increase significantly. On August 1, 1947, in a secret order, the Soviet military administration demanded 20,000 additional men for the uranium mines, even though there were no living accommodations for them. Forced labor was channeled through the town of Aue, which was then known to the conscripted workers as the "gateway of tears." Fresh recruits arrived at Aue in large groups under military guard. From there, they went to the various Wismut Mines, reporting to the personnel department and accounts offices. They received medical examinations and registered for Wismut rations (which were higher than the normal rations in the SBZ) and in the process, lost their home ration cards. If they could not find private accommodations, they were sent to transit camps.[22]

Compulsory recruitment led to flights from forced labor in the uranium mines. Tens of thousands of workers ordered to work there fled to the Western zones of occupation. Bad working conditions in the mines as well as fear of the Soviet security forces added to their reasons for fleeing. Rumors had it that the uranium mines were just a way station to the GULAG camps in Siberia. Living accommodations were terribly inadequate and reached their lowest state in 1947–1948. Despite favorable comments in the Communist press about conditions in the uranium mines and improved food supplies in later years, flights continued. The Soviets then decided to tighten control on the miners. On their arrival at the mines, workers had to release all their personal documents to the Wismut administration, including ration cards, receiving their Wismut documentation in return. In a further attempt to prevent the flight of miners, rail transport of recruited workers from Northeast Germany avoided Berlin, to prevent their flight to the Western Allied sectors of the city. It is difficult to ascertain the exact numbers that fled, but information gathered after the collapse of the GDR, from the personnel department files of Wismut AG, indicated that every other recruited man either fled or was incapable of working in the mines. [23]

In 1948, as prisoners were beginning to be released from the special camps, some MVD officials thought to send them to the mines; however, this decision was not approved by higher MVD authorities. Moreover, some war prisoners released at this time were sent to the Wismut Mines, although most were in poor physical shape. On the other hand, civilian ethnic Germans who were held in GULAG camps in the Soviet Union, numbering 24,481, of whom 14,948 women, were transferred to the Wismut uranium mines in Saxony at Beria's order of March 20,1948. Their terms of service for forced labor in the mines was set at three years.[24] Also, every effort was made to recruit skilled German volunteer miners who had been expelled from Poland and Czechoslovakia. This effort did have limited success because workers were promised higher food rations, more consumer goods, cigarettes, and alcohol. Their number amounted to about 5% of the work fore. [25]

As other supplies of labor dried up in 1948, Wismut and the labor exchanges increasingly turned to female recruits, for work both above and below ground. In the fourth quarter of 1948, some 10,000 female recruits joined the approximately 15,000 women already there. In many cases, the labor exchanges recruited indigent or homeless women by promising high wages and good living conditions. Local doctors reported that more than half of the new female recruits carried some form of sexually transmitted disease when they arrived for work at the mines. The women were kept in terrible accommodations; conveniences were lacking, and those that existed were in poor condition. Overcrowding was typical, and they had to take turns sleeping. The women were completely demoralized by the working and living conditions. Russian guards also frequently exploited them sexually. In 1948, the proportion of working females, in the total work force, was 30%. By Order #239, in October 1947, women were banned from working underground, but this was not enforced by management at the time.[26]

Werner Knopp, in his 1948 book, *Prowling Russia's Forbidden Zone* (Alfred A Knopf, Inc.) relates meeting two young women from Weimar (Thüringen) who told him the following history of their experience in the uranium mines. They had been arrested for minor political offenses, and were sent by a Russian major to a penal battalion at a uranium mine in Johanngeorgenstadt, in the Erzgebirge.

"We were in good physical shape on our arrival," they said. *"A German doctor, supervised by a Russian woman, declared us fit for work as loaders on the ore face. The Frisch Glück shaft was close to a large factory near the station. Half of it had served as an airplane factory during the war, and the other half as a concentration camp. The whole area was surrounded by a green wooden fence, three yards high and heavily guarded by Russian military police. We were quartered with 50 or 60 other women in the former*

concentration camp building, whose wooden pens still bore the carved names and messages of Hitler's victims. The old airplane factory housed Russian soldiers [now] serving short terms of hard labor. They were clad in rags and treated with a brutality that made us wonder how any of them could survive."

They were asked, *"Was it safe to be in the same compound with those prisoners?"* They replied, *"We couldn't have been safer anywhere. The penalty for talking to us was 40 strokes with the nagaika (whip); the penalty for touching us in any way was death."* Then they added that , in any case, the Russians started work at 7:30 in the morning, and by the time they returned at 8:30 at night, they had had 12 hours of hard work and were unfit for anything but sleep.

The two girls had to put pitchblende into aluminum containers and carry these vessels, weighing 60-80 pounds, over a distance of 100 yards through an unventilated passage. The old safety regulations had not permitted miners to be sent up to the face within less than an hour after each blasting operation. Yet the women employed in Frisch Glück were driven back after 10 minutes into passages filled with poisonous gases from the explosion and full of mineral dust.

"Every night on leaving the shaft, "they said, "we were tested for uranium ore, (probably with a Geiger counter). A rod with a small antenna and. connected to an instrument panel was moved over the body of every miner to detect any ore that might be hidden on us."

"Why should the Russians have done that?" They said, *"We couldn't understand that either. Since we lived in the compound and were kept as prisoners, there was no chance of our smuggling any ore out. But perhaps they wanted to make doubly sure. In any case, Ivan seemed determined not to let any pitchblende fall into unauthorized hands. The moment the ore had been tested by Soviet geologists, the containers were carefully sealed, stacked in railway wagons that also were sealed, and then moved under heavy military guard to an unknown destination."*

The two girls continued. *"We lost weight rapidly"* they said, *"and could no longer fulfill our daily 'norm.' As a punishment, our rations were cut; for every one per cent we fell behind our norm, 20 calories a day were deducted from our food issues. To have carried on like that would have meant the end. For if we could not stand up to our work while eating well, we certainly could not endure it on reduced rations."*

"Moreover, sleep was often made impossible by the swarms of vermin, bedbugs, and lice that came over from the Russian quarters, although every night the women spent half an hour delousing each other. If one of us had a fever, she was given the water cure---wrapped in a wet blanket and tied down on a pelisse filled with wet sawdust. No medicines were given, and the tortures of the helpless sick from the bites of the vermin were unbearable."

"There was only one way out," the girls went on. *"Every Sunday morning, we were addressed by a Mongolian officer who asked for volunteers for the brothels near Annaberg. (Erzgebirge).We decided to go, as the chances of escape seemed to be greater that way,' because in Schneeberg we were never allowed outside the compound. Three other women volunteered at the same time, and the Mongolian told us that we would be sent to the officers' quarters, as we were pretty and going of our own free will."*

"We were given no more work in the mines, and after a few days of good food and rest, and supplied with a set of new clothes, we left in a truck---five women guarded by two Mongolian soldiers with tommy guns. Near Schwarzenberg, about halfway to our destination, the truck stopped and picked up a load of common prostitutes and tommy gunners, all of whom had been drinking. The Ivans produced several bottles of vodka and schnapps, and by the time we came close to Annaberg, they and the women lay in a heap of intoxication."

The two girls managed to escape, a fact that did not seem to bother the Russians very much. After the soldiers had fired a few wild rounds, they went and grabbed two women coming from a field. [27]

In 1949, Wismut failed to meet its production plan which Soviet managers blamed on the wrecking activities of class enemies, with the real reason probably being the high turnover of workers. In 1949, 109,000 new workers joined the labor force, and 48,000 left Wismut that year— including 17,000 who were presumed to have fled. In the first three years of operations, about 50,000 fled and 15,000 left for health reasons. The uranium industry received a terrible reputation in the Soviet Occupation Zone, which severely discredited the SED and the GDR government. The high level of public distrust of this industry and of the Communist government induced many to flee to the West. This greatly concerned the Soviet military administration and they complained to Serov that even workers with left-wing sympathies and SED membership preferred to flee to the West than be forced to work in the mines.[28]

WORKING AND LIVING CONDITIONS IN THE MINES

The miners' day began with a long journey by foot or bicycle to the mine shaft. There was no public transportation. At the beginning and end of each shift, the miners' papers were examined by Soviet guards. Every miner had to be checked by a Geiger counter on leaving the mines to make certain their clothes or shoes were not contaminated. After going through the gate, they had to pick up their work tools. In the early years, miners used ladders to go into the pits. Their work was then assigned: clearing the rubble from the previous days' blasting, loading trolleys, and taking them away. The hardest work was in the shafts. Holes were drilled, then they were filled with explosives, and the fuses were lit. When everything went well, the shift ended after the blasting. There was no electricity, compressed air, or boring rods. When the miners struck a seam of uranium, special regulations came into force. The seam could not be blasted and had to be taken out with pick and axe and placed into boxes and stored in a strictly guarded warehouse. High premiums were paid for each box.[29] The miners worked up to 12 hours a day, guarded by Soviet convict soldiers. If the daily norms were not met, there was punishment for the miners. The mines were not mechanized and there was no ventilation. The most elementary safety devices and health precautions were not present. Syphilis was raging due to the brothels established by the Soviets.[30] Additionally, the FDGB (East German government sponsored labor union), under pressure from Wismut management, introduced "voluntary" Sunday work in August 1948. It was strongly opposed and resisted by the miners, but nevertheless in 1950, it was enforced by management, and many miners reported in sick on Monday mornings.[31]

Due to the primitive mining conditions, health and safety conditions in the mines were terrible, thereby reducing the number of workers laboring in the mines at any one time. The East German government reported that the number of accidents was growing and "that in the first quarter of 1948 there were 574 accidents reported, in which on the average, 10 or more people died."[32] Severe health damage also resulted from uranium mining. Because ventilation in the mines was poor, miners breathed radioactive dust. In the early mining days, "dry mining" was employed, meaning that the ore was not kept wet to reduce the amount of dust. It was not until the end of the 1950s that the practice of wetting the ore in order to reduce the amount of dust was introduced. The miners also suffered severe exposure from radiation as they worked knee deep in radioactive slime.[33]

Resulting lung cancer led to the death of 7,163 Wismut uranium miners between 1946 and 1990. Until recently, former miners continued to die from the disease.[34] Studies showed that Wismut uranium miners also had a high risk of contracting other cancers, such as oral, bone, leukemia, and liver cancer.[35] Tuberculosis infections also appeared frequently, the result of the miners breathing the silicates present in the radioactive dust.[36]

Living conditions and wages in the mines were poor. Wage scales, originally set September 1, 1946, were disregarded by management and there was no minimum wage. Workers suffered irregular payment of wages, tough penalties for insignificant misdeeds, insufficient supplies of work clothes and no washing and changing rooms.. Wismut management relied on a mixture of production premiums and penalties. If workers did not fulfill their norm, they did not receive a hot meal, for example. More severe penalties included a shorter leave period, reduction of wages and premiums or detention in the special camps. Miners were also punished by being placed in pits where working conditions were difficult: no ventilation, insufficient mechanical tools, and a higher radiation risk. The miners called these special punishment pits *Strafschachten.*[37]

In the years after the war in East Germany, food supplies were more valued than wages. As an incentive for voluntary labor in the mines, daily rations in the uranium industry amounted to about twice the rations offered to industrial workers in 1949 and, at that time, uranium miners stood at the top of the food availability hierarchy in the Soviet zone. The system of production incentives was later improved upon with coupons for consumer goods such as clothes and shoes, in addition to extra food coupons. Two other incentives were offered to the miners. One gave every Wismut employee who worked underground two to five liters of tax free alcohol. The other was "Stalin parcels," which were rewards for exceeding norms by 150%. They contained large jars of fruit preserves, meat, sausage, flour, cheese and tinned food. They were productivity parcels and could be had every month, This was a policy of "sausage socialism" and better rations were a very strong inducement to keep the miners as well as recruiting new ones.[38]

Lack of proper housing for all the miners was one of the greatest problems in the mining areas. Wismut AG and the East German government at that time did not respond to these needs until after the Saalfeld miners' riots in the summer of 1951, (See note below on the Saalfeld riots), at which time the East German government began a crash program of building 5,000 housing units in the mining areas. After the nation-wide revolt of June 1953, the building program was again increased.[39] Conditions in the mining towns were also a deterrent for keeping miners in Wismut, as well as for recruiting volunteers. Living accommodations were mostly in dormitories and were comparable to POW camps. Weak and sick people who were dismissed from the mines were forced to find other work. Towns around the camps did not want to accept them and the people were shifted from one place to another, often becoming homeless.[40]

The FDGB (the East German government trade union) pressed management of the Wismut AG to improve working and living conditions. These included the following benefits: enforcing the wage scale, setting a minimum wage, and granting appropriate leave (the guarantee that those workers, residing elsewhere, would be able to visit their families) Additional ones were: use of only financial penalties to punish offenses by the miners, a supply of sufficient work clothes and boots, support for the works safety commissions by management so that accidents could be avoided, and full cooperation with the work councils according to the existing (East) German laws. These demands were passed on to Molotov, and then to Beria via the Soviet trade union organization and some changes were made in the middle of 1947. Warm meals began to be served in all Wismut mines, rest homes for the miners were created, and a minimum wage established.[41]

IMPROVEMENTS IN WORKING AND LIVING CONDITIONS

A leading SED member , an official in the Labor and Welfare Administration demanded that the SED executive deal with the problems of the uranium workers. In an August 12, 1947 letter to Grotewohl, he wrote that the conditions in the mines "were extremely bad," reporting the following:

"*Often, people are drafted into this work whose health and physical condition make them inappropriate for mining. Given the strenuous labor, their housing and upkeep is completely inadequate ... Protection of the workers is less than insufficient, the effects of which are even worse, given the fact that the greatest portion of the workforce are novices. The physicians, who are in charge of health supervision, are urged, against their convictions, to declare workers fit for work, although they are not."*[42]

These complaints finally resulted in Grotewohl meeting with Major General M.M. Maltsev, the NKVD head of the Wismut mines. Maltsev agreed to improve the salaries and increase the allocations of food to the miners as well as to institute regular vacations. By the end of 1947, conditions did indeed improve for miners, in part, because of the intercession of the SED.

The Soviets were also able to attract more volunteers through higher salaries and better rations. Nevertheless, the continuation of old methods of drafting labor and the new tactic of making promises that were often not kept continued to give the uranium mines a terrible reputation throughout the SBZ.[43] As late as August 1949, Wilhelm Pieck, future President of the GDR, reported:

"As a result of this practice [deceptive recruiting] and the methods that were used in the past to recruit workers for Aue (a uranium mine) by forced labor, the people-- including a broad segment of members of our own party-- look at being conscripted to Aue as the worst punishment that an inhabitant of the Eastern zone can face." [44]

As the NKVD head of the Wismut mines, Maltsev was under strong pressure to succeed in meeting output levels; he agreed to work with the FDGB to ensure that minimum welfare standards would be met. His program to apply GULAG production methods to the uranium industry was stopped. The FDGB pressed for a reduction in compulsory labor on the basis of SVAG Order #234, of June 2, 1948, regulating protection of employees' rights. Compulsory recruitment was to be used only in exceptional cases and required the approval of the FDGB. Contracts were now limited to six months. Despite these improvements, however, illegal procedures did not cease and Wismut's Soviet management tried to circumvent the new rules, particularly the six months contract limit. Many workers were not released after their contracts had expired because management refused to return the miners' papers or pay their premiums at the end of the contract period.[45] State employees and workers in nationalized industry were also told how many workers had to be provided to the Wismut mines, even on an involuntary basis; moreover, heads of personnel still sent workers who were politically suspect to the mines.[46]

In 1948, however, the number of voluntary workers began to grow, (even though sometimes volunteer labor became forced labor). Labor exchanges now reported that voluntary workers in 1948 were 60% of the total, and in 1949, it was 90%. In 1950, all workers sent to the mines went on a voluntary basis, although these figures were considered exaggerated at the time.[47] Better food rations were a major reason for the strong recruitment. While tens of thousands of Wismut workers fled in the period up to 1948 and went to the Western zones of occupation, after that, with the new policy of ample food, better working conditions and incentives, labor quotas were presumably filled by volunteers.[48]

Nevertheless, there was still a great deal of deceptive reporting by Communist organs on favorable conditions, in order to attract volunteers for the uranium mines. East German newspapers reported the mines' excellent working and living conditions, particularly the abundance of food rations, not available elsewhere in the GDR. Workers were alleged to be living in their own houses, some even with gardens. The SED also recruited volunteers on the basis of their patriotic duty to build the GDR, which was said to have had some positive results.[49]

Finally, Wismut wages became so attractive that this was the main reason for the increase in voluntary labor. In the middle of 1948, a broadly based recruitment effort was made throughout the SBZ. With the founding of the GDR, in October 1949, this effort increased, with a strong propaganda drive, showing the benefits of working in the Wismut mines. The Soviets finally discovered the advantages of inducements for voluntary labor, as compared to compulsory conscription.[50]

Despite the improvement in pay and food supplies, in the 1950s, living conditions in the mines still remained poor, especially in the lack of lodgings. The SED itself wrote, "the housing situation was very bad," and was only alleviated, in part, after the workers' revolt in 1953. People continued to be frightened of being sent to the mines. Certainly thousands of skilled workers left for the West to escape such a fate. The low health standards and primitive working conditions in the mines continued, so that Wismut's demand for labor was always great, as a large numbers of miners always had to be hospitalized or released, or died on the job.[51]

CONCLUSION

The uranium industry grew in the early years after the war at an extra-ordinary rate, reaching its highest number of employees in autumn 1950 with over 200,000 workers . Wismut AG became the largest enterprise in the SBZ. The initial program of compulsory labor was eventually supplanted by volunteer labor, responding to higher wages and better working and living conditions. Wismut health records indicate that at least 20,000 miners died of or suffered from lung disease "induced by exposure to radiation and dust." Germans today are still living with the by-products of Wismut. Mounds of radioactive waste are scattered near abandoned shafts all across the Erzgebirge. Fear was fundamental to the Wismut mining enterprise. Only flight to the West could guarantee that workers would escape the fate of being forced to work in the mines. The Soviet desire for uranium helped bring the Communist system to East Germany by exposing the people to repressive Stalinist terror. For most forced labor, their Wismut service was a terrible experience, hated by everyone.[52]

(Refer to http://www.thegulagineastgermany.com for Illustration # 17: Mine waste hills in Ronneburg , Thüringen. Source: Bundesarchiv – Wikimedia Commons)

When the founder and head of the *Bergpolizei,* Gotthard Schudy, fled to the West, he stated that arrests of miners had been carried out on the grounds of mere suspicion. Confessions were forcibly extracted from the suspects and many were sentenced to long term imprisonment. In addition to crimes of sabotage and other offenses against the security of the mines, there were accusations resulting from miners' errors, which were not politically motivated. Human mistakes were criminalized, and managers often attributed inability to meet production plans to the wrecking activities of the class enemy.[53]

The Wismut uranium mines continued to be worked until the collapse of the GDR in 1990. A total of 220,000 tons of uranium were produced. In the early years, it all went exclusively to the Soviet uranium weapons program, and thereafter to Soviet nuclear power plants. More than 400,000 people had worked in the mines at one time or another. With German reunification, the Federal Government undertook an immense clean-up operation of many years duration.[54]

NOTE: THE SAALFELD RIOTS

In the late afternoon of August 16, 1951, two drunk Wismut miners were arrested in Saalfeld's market square by the *Volkspolizei,* for disorderly behavior. Saalfeld is a uranium mining town in the Erzgebirge, in South Eastern Thüringen. (See Map #8). The police promptly threw them into jail in the local police station. This news traveled rapidly throughout the town and soon a small crowd gathered in front of the station, demanding the prisoners' release. The protestors forced their way into the station several times, but were repeatedly thrown out. In this melee, two more miners were arrested, but, meanwhile, the crowd in front of the police station had grown.

Shortly thereafter, the crowd left for the center of town to seek more supporters. Meanwhile, the *Volkspolizei* met with local state and Soviet authorities. The Soviet representative of the Wismut Mines stated the Soviets would ensure the safety of the uranium mine, but that it was the responsibility of the GDR authorities to maintain public order. In the early evening of August 16, 1951, a larger crowd arrived and forced its way into the police station, insulting and threatening police officers.

The police and Soviet official were unable to convince them to leave. The *Volkspoizei* then called for reinforcements from neighboring towns. After their arrival, the officer in charge told the police officers that under no circumstances were weapons to be used. This order came directly from Erich Mielke, Minister of State Security and SED general secretary, Walter Ulbricht.

The standoff continued well into the late evening, when the *Volkspolizei*—with the concurrence of the Ministry of State Security—decided to release the prisoners.[55] Instead of putting an end to the confrontation, the demonstrators considered it a sign of government weakness and now increased their demand for the release of all prisoners in the police station, as well as the arrest of the two policemen who had been the cause of this confrontation. More miners arrived, and, with them, came violence. They took over the police building, threatening officers with their pickaxes. They destroyed telephones, typewriters, and office equipment, also breaking windows. Police documents were gathered and burned in the market square.

The head of local State Security then spoke to the crowd, promising that the guilty police officers would be punished and, in the future, the *Volkspolizei* would be a true peoples' police force that would defend the interests of the working class. With that, the miners finally left the police station at about 2:00 AM. Also on that day, there were demonstrations at the courthouse where prisoners were kept. The miners released two jailed Wismut miners and threatened to lynch the police officer on duty. As a further indication of the hatred for the *Volkspolizei*, miners drove around town that night shouting for an end to this police force.

To confront the next day's possible riots, additional police troops were sent to Saalfeld, so that by the 17th, there were approximately 800 police officers present. Additionally, the SED sent in about 2,000 Communist "agitprop" (agitation and propaganda) workers to mix with the crowds, diffuse the tension, and isolate the leaders for possible arrest. The police forces were again instructed not to shoot at the workers These strong measures indicated how seriously the leadership of the SED and Soviets viewed this workers' confrontation..

In the late afternoon of August 17[th,] unruly protesting broke out again. This time, it was the court prisons where the demonstrators demanded the release of all Wismut workers. Now, the crowd was reinforced by many Saalfeld merchants, craftsman, and other workers. The Thüringen Minister of the Interior attempted to calm the crowd, but they were not interested in hearing him. He then permitted it to select a delegation of three Wismut workers to go into the prison to see if there were any Wismut miners. They determined that there were none, and the crowd then disbursed without violence. The riots were over, ending as quickly as they had begun.[56]

The reasons for the riots were clearly evident, as explained in these paragraphs; it was the Soviet system of forced labor coupled with the abuse of the miners. The riots were spontaneous explosions, arising from pent-up frustrations and severe, long-term maltreatment. There are several themes in these riots, which should be noted.

The first was that the rioters did not press for improved working conditions, (although conceivably this was their primary unspoken demand,) or for any political changes, such as the institution of a new democratic society, as the June 1953 workers' uprising demanded. They just wanted their fellow miners released from prison and the *Volkspolizei* officers who arrested them jailed.

The second was that the miners were joined by townspeople, due to their opposition to the Soviet/SED repressive system.

A third significant and relevant factor was the universal hostility, almost hatred, of the *Volkspolizei* and its overbearing, arbitrary security state in the mining district. As for the Soviets, they blamed the riots on the usual foreign agents assisted by local anti-state elements. They were astute enough, however, to make certain changes in Wismut, especially in the building of more housing for the miners.

(Refer to http://www.thegulagineastgermany.com for Map # 8: Wismut Uranium Mining Areas of South-Eastern Germany.Source: Wikimedia Commons)

Notes

1. Werner Knop, *Prowling Russia's Forbidden Zone*, (New York, 1949) 138–139.
2. John Tagliabue, "A Legacy of Ashes: The Uranium Mines of Eastern Germany," *The New York Times,* March 19, 1991.
3. Zbynek Zeman and Rainer Kartsch, *Uranium Matters; Central European Uranium in International Politics 1900–1960,* (Budapest, Hungary, 2008), 161–163.
4. Ibid., 166.
5. Ibid., 174.
6. Ibid., 177.
7. Ibid.
8. Ibid., 194.
9. Ibid., 196.
10. Ibid., 195.
11. Ibid., 186–187, 198.
12. Ronny Kabus, *In der Gewalt Stalins und der SED,*(Norderstedt, Germany, 2011), 138.
13. Zeman, and Kartsch, *Uranium Matters; Central European Uranium in International Politics 1900-1960,* 222.
14. Ibid., 168.
15. Ibid., 169.
16. Ibid., 170–171.
17. Ibid., 183.
18. Ibid., 184.
19. Ibid.
20. Ibid., 185.
21. Ibid.
22. Ibid., 186.
23. Ibid., 187.
24. Polian, *Against their Will: the History and Geography of Forced Migrations in the USSR,* (Budapest, Hungary, 2004), 291.
25. Zeman and Kartsch, *Uranium Matters; Central European Uranium in International Politics 1900–1960,* 190.
26. Ibid., 192–193.
27. Knop, *Prowling Russia's Forbidden Zone,*(New York, 1948), 159–163.

28. Zeman and Kartsch, *Uranium Matters; Central European Uranium in International Politics 1900–1960*, 188.
29. Ibid., 211.
30. Knop, *Prowling Russia's Forbidden Zone*, 138.
31. Ibid., 212.
32. Norman M.Naimark, *The Russians in Germany, A History of the Soviet Zone of Occupation, 1945–1949*, (Cambridge, Massachusetts, 1995), 246.
33. Sourced from, Peter Diehl, *Uranium Mining in Eastern Germany: The Wismut Legacy*, http://wise-uranium.org/uwis.html
34. Ibid.
35. Ibid.
36. Ibid.
37. Zeman and Kartsch, *Uranium Matters; Central European Uranium in International Politics 1900-1960*, 223.
38. Ibid., 211.
39. Ibid., 218.
40. Ibid., 190.
41. Ibid., 201.
42. Naimark, *The Russians in Germany, A History of the Soviet Zone of Occupation, 1945–1949*, 241.
43. Ibid., 243
44. Ibid., 244
45. Zeman and Kartsch, *Uranium Matters; Central European Uranium in International Politics 1900–1960*, 204.
46. Ibid.
47. Ibid., 205.
48. Ibid., 212.
49. Naimark, *The Russians in Germany, A History of the Soviet Zone of Occupation, 1945–1949*, 245.
50. Zeman and Kartsch, *Uranium Matters; Central European Uranium in International Politics 1900–1960*, 205.
51. Naimark, *The Russians in Germany, A History of the Soviet Zone of Occupation, 1945–1949*, 247.
52. Zeman, and Kartsch, *Uranium Matters; Central European Uranium in International Politics 1900–1960*, 208.
53. Ibid., 225.
54. Peter Diehl, *Uranium Mining in Eastern Germany: The Wismut Legacy*, http://wise-uranium.org/uwis.html

55. Andrew Port, *When workers rumbled: The Wismut upheaval of August 1951 in East Germany, Social History*, Vol.22. No.2 (London, 1997), 152.
56. Zeman and Kartsch, *Uranium Matters; Central European Uranium in International Politics 1900–1960*, 237–238.

About the Author

Ulrich Merten was born in Berlin, Germany, and came to the United States as a small child before the Second World War. His family were political refugees because his father was a lawyer in the Prussian Ministry of the Interior, active in prosecuting the Nazi Party.

Mr. Merten grew up in New York City and, after the war, returned to Europe, studying at the University of Zürich, Switzerland, and the University of Zaragoza in Spain. He subsequently earned his BA degree at Columbia College, Columbia University, and his MA at Columbia University. He also undertook postgraduate studies at the Securities Industry Institute at The Wharton School, University of Pennsylvania.

In his professional life Mr. Merten was an international banker, a senior executive of the Bank of America, working almost exclusively in Latin America and the Caribbean, over a period of thirty-eight years. Subsequently, he was a managing director of an NGO involved in democracy building in Cuba.

Mr. Merten's book *Forgotten Voices: The Expulsion of the Germans from Eastern Europe after World War II* was published in 2012 by Transaction Publishers, New Brunswick, New Jersey. In 2015 a companion history volume *Voices from the Gulag: The Oppression of the German Minority in the Soviet Union* was published by the American Historical Society of Germans from Russia (Lincoln, Nebraska). Mr. Merten lives in Miami with his wife of many years.

Bibliography

Agde, Gunter. *Sachsenhausen bei Berlin,Speziallager Nr. 7,1945–1950.* Berlin: Aufbau Taschenburg Verlag, 1994.

Applebaum, Anne. *Iron Curtain, 1944–1956.* New York, Doubleday: 2012.

———. *Gulag, A History,* New York: Anchor Books, 2003.

Barwald, Helmut. "Terror als System." In *Verfolgt-Verhaftet-Verurteilt; Demokraten im Widerstand gegen die rote Diktatur-Fakten und Beispiele.* Edited by Günther Scholz. Berlin:Westkreuz Verlag, 1990.

Beschloss, Michael. *The Conquerors; Roosevelt, Truman and the Destruction of Hitler's Germany, 1941–1945.* New York: Simon & Schuster, 2002.

Biddiscombe, Perry. *The Denazification of Germany, A History 1945–1950.* Stroud, Gloucestershire: Tempus Publishing Ltd., 2007.

Bringmann, Fritz, and Hartmut Roder. *Neuengamme –Verdrängt-Vergessen- Bewältigt? Die Zweite Geschichte des Konzentrationslagers Neuengamme 1945-1985.* Hamburg: VSA-Verlag, 1987.

Bruce, Gary. *Resistance with the People, Repression and Resistance in Eastern Germany, 1945–1955.* Lanham, Maryland: Rowman & Littlefield Publishers, Inc., 2003.

Buschfort, Wolfgang. "Die Ära Adenauer." In *Die Sowjetischen Speziallager in der gesellschaftlichen Wahrnehmung, 1945 bis heute.* Edited by Petra Haustein, Annette Kaminsky, Volkhard Knigge, and Bodo Rischer. Göttingen, Wallstein:Verlag, 2006.

Buschfort, Wolfgang. "Gefoltert und geschlagen." In *Verfolgt-Verhaftet-Verurteilt; Demokraten im Widerstand gegen die rote Diktatur-Fakten und Beispiele.* Edited by Günther Scholz. Berlin:Westkreuz Verlag, 1990.

Buschfort, Wolfgang. *Die Ostbüros der Parteien in den 50er Jahren.* Berlin: Schriftenreihe der Berliner Landesbeauftragten für die Unterlagen der Staatssicherheitsdientstes der ehemaligen DDR, 2006.

Buschfort, Wolfgang. *Das Ostbüro der SPD.* BWV Bayerne.V., 2008.

Dallin, David J., and Boris I. Nicolaevsky. *Forced Labor in Soviet Russia.* New Haven, Connecticut: Yale University Press, 1947.

Danyel, Jürgen. "Zwischen Repression und Toleranz: Die Politik der SED zur politischen Integration der ehemaligen NSDAP-Mitglieder in der SBZ/DDR." In *Speziallager in der SBZ.* Edited Reif-Spirek, Peter, and Bodo Ritscher. Berlin: Ch.Links Verlag, 1999.

Davidson, Eugene. *The Death and Life of Germany: An Account of the American Occupation.* New York: Alfred A. Knopf, 1959.

Diehl, Peter, *Uranium Mining in Eastern Germany: The Wismut Legacy.* Retrieved from http://wise-uranium.org/uwis.html, 2011.

Erler, Peter. "Zur Tätigkeit der Sowjetischen Militärtribunale (SMT) in der SBZ/DDR." In *Sowjetische Speziallager in Deutschland 1945 bis 1950 Band I,* Edited by Sergej Mironenko, Lutz Niethammer, and Alexander von Plato. Berlin: Akademie Verlag, 1998.

Finn, Gerhard. *Die Politischen Häftlinge der Sovjetzone.* Pfaffenhofen, Germany: Ilmgauverlag, 1960.

——. "Über den unechten Antifaschismus." In *Verfolgt-Verhaftet-Verurteilt; Demokraten im Widerstand gegen die rote Diktatur-Fakten und Beispiele.* Edited by Günther, Scholz. Berlin:Westkreuz Verlag, 1990.

Fischer, Ursula. *Zum Schweigen verurteilt: denunziert-verhaftet-interniert: (1946-1948).* Berlin: Dietz Verlag, 2002.

FitzGibbon, Constantine. *Denazification.* New York: W.W.Norton & Company, 1969.

Foitzik, Jan. "Organisationseinheiten und Kompetenzstruktur des Sicherheitsapparates der Sowjetischen Militäradministration in Deutschland (SMAD)." In *Sowjetische Speziallager in Deutschland 1945 bis 1950 Band I.* Edited by Sergej Mironenko, Lutz Niethammer, and Alexander von Plato. Berlin: Akademie Verlag, 1998.

Greiner, Bettina. *Verdrängter Terror*. Hamburg: Hamburger Edition HIS Verlag, 2010.

Greve, Uwe. *Lager des Grauens: Sowjetische KZs in der DDR nach 1945*. Kiel, Germany: ARNDT-Verlag, 1990.

Haustein, Petra, Annette Kaminsky, Volkhard Knigge, and Bodo Ritscher. *Die Sowjetischen Speziallager in der gesellschaftlichen Wahrnehmung, 1945 bis heute*. Göttingen: Wallstein Verlag, 2006.

Jahn, Ralf G. Christlich-Demokratische Union Deutschlands, (CDU) (Ost). Retrieved from http://www.adel-genealogie.de/CDU-Ost.html.

Jeske, Natalja. "Zur medizinischen Sterblichkeitsstatistik von 1945-1950." In *Sowjetische Speziallager in Deutschland 1945 bis 1950 Band I*. Edited by Sergej Mironenko, Lutz Niethammer, and Alexander von Plato. Berlin: Akademie Verlag, 1998.

Jeske, Naalja. "Speziallagerstatistik." In *Sowjetische Speziallager in Deutschland 1945 bis 1950 Band I*. Edited by Sergej Mironenko, Lutz Niethammer, and Alexander von Plato. Berlin: Akademie Verlag, 1998.

Kabus, Ronny. *In der Gewalt Stalins und der SED*. Norderstedt, Germany: Books on Demand, 2011.

Kilian, Achim. *Einzuweisen zur volligen Isolierung, NKWD Speziallager Mühlberg/ Elbe*. Leipzig: Forum Verlag, 1992.

Knop, Werner. *Prowling Russia's Forbidden Zone*. New York: Alfred A. Knopf, 1949.

Kozlov, Vladimir A. "Die Operationen des NKVD in Deutschland wâhrend des Vormarsches der Roten Armee (Januar bis April 1945)." In *Sowjetische Speziallager in Deutschland 1945 bis 1950 Band I*. Edited by Sergej Mironenko, Lutz Niethammer, and Alexander von Plato. Berlin: Akademie Verlag, 1998.

Leonhard, Wolfgang. *Child of the Revolution*. Chicago, Illinois: Henry Regnery Company, 1958.

Lipinsky, Jan. "Mobilität zwischen den Lagern." In *Sowjetische Speziallager in Deutschland 1945 bis 1950 Band I*. Edited by Sergej Mironenko,

Lutz Niethammer, and Alexander von Plato. Berlin: Akademie Verlag, 1998.

Lipinsky, Jan. *Die Strasse die in den Tod führte*, Initiativgruppe Internierungslager Ketschendorf e.v.Speziallager Nr. 5. Leverkusen, Germany Kremer Verlag, 1998.

Macdonogh, Giles. *After the Reich: The Brutal History of the Allied Occupation*. New York: Basic Books, 2007.

Marcuse, Harold. *Legacies of Dachau*. Cambridge: Cambridge University Press, 2001.

Mironenko, Sergej, Lutz Niethammer,and Alexander von Plato. *Sowjetische Speziallager in Deutschland 1945 bis 1950 Band I*. Berlin: Akademie Verlag, 1998.

Morsch, Gunter, *Totenbuch sowjetisches Sp[eziallager Nr. 7/1 in Weesow und Sachsenhausen 1945-1950*, Berlin: Metropol Verlag, 2010.

Muller, Hanno, Editor. *Recht oder Rache? Buchenwald 1945-1950*, Frankfurt/Main: Dipa-Verlag, 1991.

Naimark, Norman M. *The Russians in Germany, A History of the Soviet Zone of Occupation, 1945–1949*. Cambridge, Massachusetts: Belknap Press of Harvard University, 1995.

Naumann, Gert. *Besiegt und Befreit: Ein Tagebuch hinter Stacheldraht in Deutschland 1945–1947*. Starnbergersee, Bavaria, Germany: Drufell Verlag,1984.

Niethammer, Lutz. "Alleierte Internierungslager in Deutschland nach 1945, Ein Vergleich und Offene Fragen." In *Sowjetische Speziallager in Deutschland 1945 bis 1950 Band I*. Edited by Sergej Mironenko, Lutz Niethammer, and Alexander von Plato. Berlin: Akademie Verlag, 1998.

Ochs, Eva. "Erfahrungsgeschichtliche Aspekte des Lagerlebens." In *Sowjetische Speziallager in Deutschland 1945 bis 1950 Band I*, Edited by Sergej Mironenko, Lutz Niethammer, and Alexander von Plato. Berlin: Akademie Verlag, 1998.

Ostbüro der SPD, from *"Jugendopposition der DDR"* Bundeszentrale für politische Bildung und der Robert-Havemann-Gesellschaft e.V. Berlin. Retrieved from http://www.jugendopposition.de.

Otto, Wilfriede. "Die Waldheimer Prozesse." In *Sowjetische Speziallager in Deutschland 1945 bis 1950 Band I.* Edited by Sergej Mironenko, Lutz Niethammer, and Alexander von Plato. Berlin: Akademie Verlag, 1998.

Peterson, Edward N. The *American Occupation of Germany: Retreat to Victory.* Detroit, Michigan: Wayne University Press, 1978.

Petrov, Nikita. "Die Apparate des NKVD/MVD und der MGB in Deutschland (1945-1953), Eine Historische Skizze." In *Sowjetische Speziallager in Deutschland 1945 bis 1950 Band I.* Edited by Sergej Mironenko, Lutz Niethammer, and Alexander von Plato. Berlin: Akademie Verlag, 1998.

Polian, P.M. *Against their Will: the History and Geography of Forced Migrations in the USSR.* Budapest: Central European University Press, 2004.

Port, Andrew. "When Workers Rumbled: The Wismut Upheaval of August 1951 in East Germany." *Social History*, 22, 2 (May 1997).

Possekel, Ralf, Editor. "Band 2: Sowjetische Dokumente zur Lagerpolitik." In *Sowjetische Speziallager in Deutschland 1945 bis 1950 Band I.* Edited by Sergej Mironenko, Lutz Niethammer, and Alexander von Plato. Berlin: Akademie Verlag, 1998.

Preissinger, Adrian. *Death Camps of the Soviets,1945–1950.* Ocean City, Maryland: Landpost Press, 1994.

Prittie, Richard. *Germany Divided: The Legacy of the Nazi Era.* Boston: Little, Brown and Company, 1960.

Richter, Michael. "Vom Widerstand der christlichen Demokraten in der DDR." In *Verfolgt-Verhaftet-Verurteilt; Demokraten im Widerstand gegen die rote Diktatur-Fakten und Beispiele.* Edited by Günther Scholz. Berlin:Westkreuz Verlag, 1990.

Reif-Spirek, Peter, and Bodo Ritscher, eds. *Speziallager in der SBZ: Gedenkstätte Buchenwald und der Landeszentale für politische Blildung.*Thüringen, Berlin: Ch. Links Verlag, 1999.

Schieder,Theodor. *The Expulsion of the German Population from the Territories East of the Oder-Neisse Line, Vol 1.1 & 1.2.* Bonn, Germany: Federal Ministry for Expellees, Refugees and War Victims, l956.

Scholz, Günther, ed. *Verfolgt-Verhaftet-Verurteilt; Demokraten im Widerstand gegen die rote Diktatur-Fakten und Beispiele.* Berlin:Westkreuz Verlag, 1990.

"SPD-Ostbüro Kartoffelnerfroren." Der Spiegel, July 11, 1996. Retrieved from http://www. spiegel.de/Spiegel/print.html.

Tagliabue, John. "A Legacy of Ashes: The Uranium Mines of Eastern Germany." *The New York Times,* March 19,1991.

Taylor, Frederick. *Exorcising Hitler, The Occupation and Denazification of Germany.* New York: Bloomsbury Press, 2011.

Turner, Ian D. *Reconstruction in Post-war Germany; British Occupation Policy in the Western Zones, 1945–55.* Oxford: St. Martin's Press,1989.

Vonau, Jean-Laurant. *L'Epuration en Alsace.* Strasbourg: Editions La Nuee Bleue, 2005.

Von Flocken, Jan, and Michael Klonovsky. *Stalin's Lager in Deutschland 1945-1950.* Berlin: Ullstein Verlag, 1994.

Weigelt, Andreas. *Berichte über sowjetische Speziallager in Deutschland.* Berlin: Metropol Verlag, 2008.

Wember, Heiner. *Umerziehung im Lager, Internierung und Bestrafung von Nationalsozialisten in der britischen Besatungzone Deutschlands.* Essen, Germany: Klartext Verlag, 1991.

Zeman, Zbynek, and Rainer Kartsch. *Uranium Matters; Central European Uranium in International Politics 1900-1960.* Budapest, Hungary: Central European University Press, 2008.

INDEX

www.ingramcontent.com/pod-product-compliance
Lightning Source LLC
Chambersburg PA
CBHW020526270326
41927CB00006B/467